Peter Holmes à Court had a twenty-year career as an executive and company director, running companies in the US, UK and Australia. As the founder of Back Row Productions, he produced artists in thirty countries. As CEO of the Australian Agricultural Company he ran what is today the largest cattle company in the world. As Executive Chairman of the South Sydney Rabbitohs he and partner Russell Crowe turned around one of the most loved football clubs in Australia, taking it from bottom of the league to winning the premiership in 2014. And as Chairman of Brand Sydney he got to market a city that, frankly, sells itself.

As a writer he has been a media leader at the World Economic Forum's annual meeting in Davos since 2012, and his articles and images have appeared in numerous publications, including *The Guardian, The WorldPost, The Australian, Huffington Post, Financial Review* and *The Sydney Morning Herald*.

Peter is married to photographer Alissa Everett, and they live in Nairobi, Kenya, with a couple of dogs and a couple of Land Rovers. Together they write and photograph on humanitarian and climate issues and safari as often as they can. They are building a library in Kakuma Refugee Settlement in Kenya.

RIDING WITH GIANTS

My struggles with modern capitalism,
the lessons from children and
the joys of cycling fast

PETER HOLMES à COURT

VIKING
an imprint of
PENGUIN BOOKS

VIKING

UK | USA | Canada | Ireland | Australia
India | New Zealand | South Africa | China

Viking is part of the Penguin Random House group of companies whose addresses can be
found at global.penguinrandomhouse.com.

Penguin
Random House
Australia

First published by Viking in 2020

Cricketing at Timbertop, photograph by Christopher O'Callaghan; the author presenting
for Brand Sydney and the Greater Sydney Partnership, 2010, Fairfax Syndication;
Robert Holmes à Court and Sammy Davis Jr, Westpix. All other images by the author
(Canon Mark III, 24-70mm f 2.8 and 105mm f 1.4.).

Cover design by Alex Ross © Penguin Random House Australia Pty Ltd
Cover image by Grandfailure/Getty Images
Typeset in Goudy Old Style by Midland Typesetters, Australia

Printed and bound in Australia by Griffin Press, part of Ovato, an accredited
ISO AS/NZS 14001 Environmental Management Systems printer

A catalogue record for this
book is available from the
National Library of Australia

NATIONAL
LIBRARY
OF AUSTRALIA

ISBN 978 0 67007 794 6

penguin.com.au

MIX
Paper from
responsible sources
FSC® C009448

For Elsa and Madison, George and Robert,
for whom I started this, and Alissa,
without whom I would never have finished.

'The first thing to understand is that capitalism doesn't exist. Talking about "free-market capitalism" is like talking about "the weather" or "music". It leaves out all the important details: hot or cold, pouring or drought, string quartet or garage band or drum circle?'

– Jedediah Purdy, 'The (Im)morality of Capitalism', 2012

INTRODUCTION

Sometime in my early teens. Wicketkeeper was
where they put me, out of the way.

When I was eleven I was sent 2000 miles from home to a
boarding school on the other side of the continent, because,
apparently, it was the best in the land. The school's extensive
campus spread across a piece of southern Australian coastline.
It occupied a low promontory next to Corio Bay, an uninspiring
mouthful of Bass Strait, the turgid slice of ocean that separates
mainland Australia from its island cousin, Tasmania. Its
boarding houses, dining halls, classrooms, chapel and deco-
ratively fortified clock tower were red-bricked monuments
to the way things have been, and the way things were sure to
stay, settled – or so was hoped – forever. More English than
the English, it was an antipodean facsimile of a British private
school, a transplanted piece of Victorian certainty, full of dark
corners and sharp edges, with strict rules for uniforms and uniformity. With nearly a century of operations, there was ample
evidence of its authority and little room to argue. Its location

had been chosen to fortify its students with daily exposure to the sea breezes of the Southern Ocean. Instead, the easterly winds brought the mildewy funk of the bay's decomposing seaweed, while the westerlies added the gaseous discharges of the enterprise at the other end of the peninsula: the Shell Petroleum Refinery, proudly Australia's largest distiller of auto fuel.

To those expected to be the country's future leaders, and one who stands to be the next King of England, the venerable institution provided all the requisite markers of the correct education. In reality, it was a morally bankrupt sportocracy with militaristic underpinnings and unenthusiastic religious instruction. We were buttoned tightly, under well-pressed sky-blue uniforms, but the thin facade of unquestioned propriety only barely concealed a deeply embedded system of institutionalised bullying with more than a hint of sexual abuse.

It was all made possible thanks to commercially distracted parents and an unholy alliance of teachers and student prefects. I was not well prepared for my introduction to the curious habits of the Establishment. I was a year younger than most of my classmates, and immature for even that. I was stick thin and bullied regularly. I didn't understand why – why me, and why they, the luckiest of the Lucky Country, made the subjugation of the already weak such a serious pursuit. It hurt: hurt my thin arms, dented my exposed ribs, dented my heart and shaped my soft soul. Most of all, it was just confusing.

No matter how bad it might have been for me, though, there was a type of comfort that came with knowing that worse befell others. Today, when the school's administration does write to me, it is either to solicit a donation or reiterate the offers of the free psychological counselling that they provide for students who were abused in deeper ways than I was. To be fair, the school did produce plenty of the type of leaders it was set up to manufacture: independent, articulate and good looking in a blazer, well-rounded in the modern disciplines of commerce and sport, merciless soldiers of industry.

Beginning at around age fourteen, we were required to attend meetings with the school's Careers Guidance Officer. Standing outside his small office at the base of the imposing clock tower, I joined a line of self-assured, well-bred boys who all seemed able to recite a well-reasoned career track for themselves. Often it sounded suspiciously like the one their father had taken. It was a rigid pathway, built on the disciplines of finance and law, a railroad that led with divine inevitability to a corner office in some urban centre of commerce; into a role that would fund at least one house, and the production of at least two children, each of whom were suitably primed to follow their father's (or in rare cases, their mother's) footsteps back to the school where my consultation was about to take place.

When I began this career tracking, what I really wanted to be was a jockey. As I was approaching six feet tall, I knew I had to find another profession to discuss with the humourless mentor in charge of charting the path of my life's labour. So, when he asked me what I wanted to be when I grew up, I said that I wanted to be a photographer – *I mean, if there is really no way I can be a jockey.*

As far as the Careers Officer was concerned, I was making the mistake of speaking the wrong language. I was told I was talking about a hobby, by a man I seriously doubted had any. He sat on the side of the sensible, with the moral force of the Establishment, and as sure as the world spins to the right, I was going to track in the approved direction. Study Maths and English, he said, followed by legal or financial training – that would be the sensible path for me. I knew I had as much chance of reversing this force as I did of swimming to Tasmania, so I did as advised, and placed all creative dreams into a small bag labelled 'Distractions'.

For a while, I tried my best to keep my passions alive. I joined the school camera club and filled rolls of 35mm film with my photos. I carefully developed the film and printed the images in the school's darkroom, spending countless hours in the cramped red-lit dark space. To a teenage boy, it was one of the most erotic places I had ever spent time. Paper coated in silver oxide, exposed to light for just the right number of clicks of the timer, darkened in trays of delicious chemicals, gradually revealing my photos on the white rectangles, a few of which were actually in focus.

During our holidays we were required to take on at least a week of what was called 'work experience'. I was lucky enough to be accepted as a cub photographer on a city newspaper. 'Lucky' in the sense that my father owned the paper. Quite understandably, nobody on staff took me seriously, and it didn't go so well. With this 'out of my system' I went back to doing what was expected of me: I finished school, left with A's in Maths and English, got two good degrees, one in Economics in the US, and the other, as if to play the counsellor at his own game, in Law from Oxford. Starting from cubicles of New York skyscrapers, through various entrepreneurial and executive paths, I worked my way to the office location that would have delighted the Careers Officer. If my dad had lived to see all this, I think he, too, would have been proud.

For twenty years I ran companies in the US, UK and Australia, in the industries of live entertainment, beef production, professional sport and city development. As a director, I sat on boards that ranged from city redevelopment projects to charities focused on Indigenous issues to giant rail companies. Along the way I got married to a very smart lady, had a set of beautiful twins, and then another beautiful set of twins. I filled a large house with stuff, and then a weekender with stuff. There was no great logic to my path; many steps I took were opportunities that simply opened before me. I had successes – some bigger than others – and sharp falls. I had picked up the necessary skills, wore well the suit jacket of success, talked with ease, and was aware that thanks to a distinctive last name, and the 'right' schooling, I had started my business life with an embossed invitation to the inner circles of commerce.

Not that I was ever comfortable there, as I could never forget the fist that the offspring of the Establishment had extended towards me on our first meeting at a young age. That pain was never far from the surface; indeed, it was a low fire inside me that I kept stoking. The drive that it gave me surely served me, even if I didn't entirely appreciate the cost of this internal combustion.

While the businesses I led appear to have been entirely unconnected, the role of the boss can look pretty similar regardless of the industry. Isolation being the most constant theme, a seat I was happy to sit in. Holding any top office is notoriously lonely; but it's positively crowded compared to the segregation that visits those who fall from any great height. I had been in business long enough to have watched or ridden through the volatility that comes before and after the different versions of global financial storms – the 1987 Stock Market Crash, Asian contagion, the first Tech Bust and the second Tech Bust, amongst other shocks to the system. At the start of the most recent crash, the Global Financial Crisis of 2008, or GFC to its friends, I was already riding an unseasonably large wave. One of those monsters that is so large that onlookers gather to watch the brave who attempt to ride it, cheer when they do, cringe when it consumes the foolhardy. For most of the ride I had been conspicuously successful, enjoying all the joys of public and commercial success, but when the dumping came, it hit me particularly hard.

It took me a few years to pick myself up, clean up some messes, reorganise my activities, straighten my suit. Shortly after righting myself, I was appointed to a great new role. I was to lead a new branding and advisory body for the sprawling, disorganised, brutal but beautiful metropolis that is Sydney. I had a great office, a tremendous team, and powerful board of directors. I had accepted the position from a leftie Mayor and a conservative premier. It had given me an opportunity to have an impact on a city I had grown to love and put me on a stage with other global city leaders. It was a big challenge and a social vision I believed was important. It also paid well. It felt like the best job of a life already full of great jobs.

Through my various roles, the ups and the downs, I had documented plenty of the stories from my adventures in business. I was asked to talk publicly about it, was paid well for the privilege, and audiences seemed to like it. All of this convinced me that I would one day be able to bash out an easy-to-read business book, full of nifty insights and helpful lessons, beneath a bright cover that would stand out in airport bookshops.

This is not that book.

This is the story of what happened when I went to write that book, and the writing of the book rewrote me.

I

Only One Attempt to Turn Around

If you see these, you've gone too far.

Our destination was four kilometres from the village of Hommes, 210 kilometres south-west of Paris, and half a planet away from Sydney, Australia. La Petite Briche is a tiny village in a remote part of rural France, where – for reasons I didn't understand – my mother had purchased one of only three buildings that made up the micro-town. She was proud to tell me it had once been part of something quite grand, part of a brave social experiment, where a man she described as France's Henry Ford had attempted to build his agro-utopian dream. That was in the nineteenth century, and it had failed, so by the time she bought it, it was just in time to save it from crumbling. With her partner, Frits, they had worked with a team of local artisans to restore the house to better than its former glory. I am one of four children, and as two of my siblings had visited and not reported very positively, until that time I had never even vaguely considered coming here.

My mother and Frits had come from Australia to help us settle in and were waiting for us. Ever safety conscious, she had made me promise I would arrive during daylight hours, as the roads get icy after dark. That evening's unspectacular sunset was now about four hours ago.

I was moving to La Briche in an aluminium Land Rover with nine large bags and two cold seven-year old girls. I had left late that morning and stopped too often. We'd stayed the night before with my sister in her holiday house, in a snow-coated village in the Alps. I blame my sister for the slow start; she decided to tell me exactly what she thought of my predicament just as I was saying goodbye. I was, she made it clear, 'in deep shit': my life must be pretty bad if I had to move half my children to 'nowhereville France in the dead of winter'. I rarely agree with my sister, even when I know she is right. I just listened, waved confidently, and then started driving, turning up the radio in the hope different words would fill my head.

En route, I shared with Elsa and Madison everything I had learned from Mum and Frits about our destination. It wasn't much. I taught them that *petite* means small, and distinguishes our little house from the area, called La Briche, and the larger *Le Château de* la Briche in which we wouldn't be living.

I told them what I knew about the man who built it all, making it sound as romantic as I could. He was a man from the age of steam trains, born in a house with dirt floors. His name was Jean-François Cail, which I mispronounced, calling him Kale, as I hadn't learned yet that the French use plenty of letters just for their looks, and it was properly pronounced 'ky' as in 'Kyle', but without the 'l'.

What few years of schooling he got were enough to put his parents in debt. As was the custom of the time, to pay off the obligations he was sold off as an apprentice. A tireless worker, he completed his training as a boiler-maker, progressed through the ranks up to foreman, and became an inventor, factory owner and international industrialist. He became possibly the richest self-made man in France in his time, living in one of the biggest houses in all of Paris. When he reached the top of society, La Briche was his attempt to extend the benefits of the Industrial Revolution to France's poor rural communities. Feeling that the girls weren't much interested in early Industrial Revolution history, or the origins of social mobility, I told them that our house was built 150 years ago, pretty sure that in all their lives they'd never been in a house that old. Few buildings in Australia of that age have survived either the termites' determination or the developer's bulldozer. I added enthusiastically that our house had once been a school for the youngest workers. In retrospect, living in a ghost-filled schoolhouse isn't a selling point for most children. I tried my best to hype Cail's experiment, but in my rear-view mirror I could see the girls were finding the description of 'child labourers' unnerving, and 'industrial farming' correspondingly boring.

What the girls did like was that I told them Cail had been a friend of Eiffel's and his name was printed on the side of the famous tower in Paris (which was true) and that Cail had supplied the steel with which it was built (which turned out not to be true). I'd later learn that Eiffel's tower was made of iron, and it wasn't Cail's. The girls made me promise that we'd visit what was possibly the only place they knew about in France. A father under pressure will agree to anything his daughters ask for, and I made a firm commitment on the spot to plan a trip to *la tour* as soon as we were settled in.

The girls' main passion in life was playing with other children, so none of this mattered as much as finding out who lived nearby. The buildings of the former school had been divided between three owners, my mother being the most recent arrival. One house was owned by an intellectual French couple, and the other owners were a family of musicians: orchestral (parents) and electronic (their adult child). When the households weren't fighting among themselves, each group was doing its bit to reinvent La Petite Briche as a sanctuary for artists and musicians. The girls listened to all of this and only asked a couple of questions which I did my best to answer.

No, sorry, there are no other children, although some of the adults do speak a bit of English.

What also helped was telling the girls that 'grandmother Janet' would have a warm meal prepared for our arrival. It was now hours since the first time they'd asked if we could stop for dinner. Their grandmother lives in Perth, and all of Western Australia is significantly hotter and drier than where we were heading. The state is almost five times the size of France and is the least densely populated state on the planet. Why my mother – a former high-school science teacher, Veuve Clicquot Business Woman of the Year, and left-leaning social campaigner – and her new life partner Frits Steenhauer – a retired accountant, steel-bike rider and even further left-leaner – had chosen this isolated part of rural France for their holiday home was a question of the girls that I couldn't answer.

My map showed La Petite Briche as an H-shaped marking in the middle of some woods, off an unnamed dirt road, almost equidistant from three small villages: Continvoir, Rillé and Hommes. My task that day had been to find this triangular needle among the hayfields, in the dark, after driving the width of the Republic. The *autoroute* had a top speed of 130 kilometres an hour, my car not much over 100. The French drive on the right, but my car was English and left-hand drive. It did have rudimentary heating, which we had to augment by all wearing our ski jackets and wool hats. It had no GPS device, which I had made up for by getting my brother-in-law to print a few pages off Google Maps.

The sheets had blown around on the passenger seat but appeared to have done their job and I found what I believed was the correct juncture off the D749. I couldn't be sure as the intersection was completely free of any signposting. I drove down what I hoped was the correct road, a narrow dirt track that headed right and promptly disappeared into a thick forest.

Mum's email had said I must stay on the road for a kilometre and that if I saw the end of a giant old barn, I'd gone too far. At a speed not much more than walking pace, I carefully navigated the smartest route through the ankle-deep potholes.

After a brief section inside the belly of the forest, the canopy of branches opened and we were surrounded by fields, well-lit by the moonlight. The left was mostly obscured by thorn bushes as tall as the car's roof. To our right, stood a partially harvested and now blackened crop of sunflowers, their heads all drooping down at the same angle. They resembled a vanquished army of thin, sad soldiers that I imagined were frozen in the act of retreating from La Briche.

After a full day of motorway driving the suspense was high and there was silence in the car. As much as a two-tonne Land Rover can creep, we were moving stealthily. As we approached the only house on the road we were suddenly greeted by two large and loud dogs. They were the size of small horses, looked prehistoric, bred to a genetic recipe that had been perfected when they hunted mammoths in these parts. Unkempt, wire-brush scruffy, they each had a set of wraparound teeth that looked like they'd been borrowed from a much larger creature. The hounds were barking apoplectically and hurling themselves against a fence so flimsy it looked temporary. We drove on slowly, the silence inside the car now more awkward than anticipatory, none of us sure of what to make of what we'd just seen.

After the farm house, the road got even worse, the potholes now large enough to swallow not only my shoe but also half my calf. By this stage I was convinced that artists and musicians could never live down a road like this. I'm sure the girls thought nothing good could live down this road at all.

I turned around, drove back to the intersection with the main road, and tried to dial the house on my mobile. Unable to get any coverage, I continued to retreat for a few minutes and pulled over to call again. Still unable to get any mobile coverage I raced another few kilometres, this time dialling while I steered with my knees. I was finally able to get a scratchy connection and, from what little I could decipher, I understood that Frits had kindly volunteered to drive down to the correct intersection off the D749, wait for us and guide us in.

I drove back and found him parked at the same turn-off I had just tried. He waved hello and gestured for us to follow him. I proceeded to accompany Frits up a full kilometre, past the dead sunflowers, the still-barking predators, the hungry potholes and to the gates of La Petite Briche.

As our cars turned in the gate, our lights cut through the surrounding forest, across the winter-cruelled grasses and provided glimpses of a grouping of pale stone buildings for my vehicle's eager audience of three. Then as the road curved left, our lights swept cinematographically across the buildings until they settled on Mum's house. La Petite Briche had made its slightly-less-than-grand entrance.

Before arriving, I'd only seen an artist's impression of our destination. The previous tenants of the schoolhouse, artists Ian Chapman and Vicki Parish, had spent an enjoyable year living in the house when their son Bryn was six years old. Ian's pencil drawing had clearly been an idealised rendering: like a portrait where the subject has the right bone structure but none of the wrinkles. His drawing was black and white, which certainly matched the monochrome of what we were seeing, except that now the windows of Mum's house emitted a golden glow. In one, I could see the edges of warm red curtains and guessed that would be the kitchen where I knew she would be hard at work.

My father had been a great man, but around the house he was never a great help. My mother had raised four kids while simultaneously looking after his every need. After a long day of work by his side, she'd often been left to feed (clean up after, wash and so on) countless large groups.

Despite arriving after 9 pm, we were greeted by a three-course meal of leek soup, stew of rabbit, roast chicken (prepared in case the girls didn't like *lapin*), two types of green vegetables and a brown loaf fresh from her bread machine. Within moments of stepping in the door, two bewildered girls – hair tightly smushed to their heads after a day under warm hats and with eyes wide with hope – and their dad – hands still ringing from eleven hours of driving and eyes bloodshot from the same – sat happily, semi-conscious, and began to silently absorb one of Janet's famous warming feasts.

Frits had participated in dinner's preparation only as a spectator, and he was therefore the only one of us with a full store of energy. He is rarely short of something to say, always something helpful, even when you wish he wouldn't be. He started by asking about our drive, how my sister and her family were, and was clearly heading in a direction that was off limits: where was the rest of our family and what were their plans? I share my mother's deep commitment to avoiding difficult subjects, so I flashed my eyes at her so that she'd change the subject. An expert in the art of keeping that which is not said unsaid, she directed Frits to a conversation line that she knew would keep him going: the house's renovation and the surrounding villages.

Starting with the story of the table we were at – hardwood rescued from somewhere in the project, legs made by a local steel worker, a design based on something found amongst the rubble when digging out the basement – Frits carefully worked his way through the renovation of the house. Mum added the helpful side comments of who had done the work ('an incredible young woodworker from Nantes'), whether the thing could hurt us ('be very careful on the slippery stairs') or if we could hurt it ('which means you must switch it off if you go away for the weekend'). If I'd been taking notes, I could have built a safety manual for living here. If I'd been sketching, I would have had almost enough to draw construction plans. But what I think they wanted us to hear was a love story, a relationship between two people and an old house.

When Mum or Frits talked about this place it was impossible to separate the work done from those who did the work and from the context of the work. Through the stories of friends, and the settings of various movies, I imagined European renovations to be torrid affairs, always enthusiastically commenced, pursued out of love, physical attempts to rebuild oneself or a relationship, but never without the project tearing down all those around it before it's completed. The work here had been done no less passionately, but perhaps more pragmatically. Between the two of them they had a clear vision for the purpose of the project, a focus on the quality of the work, and an appreciation for the integrity in the process.

In the renovation, the cost of a job or a part was always a product of that thing's function and its quality. Frits was born in the Netherlands, and frugality was just one of the stereotypes of the Dutch that Frits wore effortlessly. Here, he shopped almost exclusively in the *brocantes*, the local second-hand markets. The colours in his sweaters dated them from at least two decades ago. He could tailor any old part to another use, recycle kitchen tins into useful metal strips, cannibalise one bicycle to rebuild other ones.

His modest collection was kept under the house, and he was already kindly encouraging me towards a time when I could ride them as often as I wanted. Not that he was beyond a little polite competition: he knew that in any triathlon of thrifty purchasing, bicycle repair and road racing, he had me completely outclassed.

Frits had taken over the introduction, and wound us outwards in concentric circles of explanation. Next came his overview of the surrounding buildings of La Petite Briche: who lived here, who visited, their names, all information thrown out quickly, punctuated by his pointing in a direction that was useless for us as it was deep into the night's dark. There seemed to be the usual type of neighbourly tension in most directions in which he pointed, all of which I offered to stay well away from.

The next ring out was the larger La Briche, its ruined industrial-sized barns, the grand château under its own renovation, the pathways that were once the farm's private network of railway lines, all of which was the vision of the one industrialist. Frits had his own take on the man he also pronounced as Kale. His rail locomotives were the fastest on the continent, but their first use was to supercharge the first wave of consumerism. He won the respect of Napoleon III, and when the self-proclaimed Emperor needed help to defeat the Paris Commune of 1870, the first such populist uprising of its type, Cail turned over his cannon-making factory free of charge to the Emperor. Further away, his patented method for processing sugar was responsible for extending the colonialisation and slave trade of the Caribbean.

I knew enough to be careful accepting all of what Frits offered – a politically distorted lens has a great impact on how we see distant objects. Some things were more objective, like the elevators that I'd take the girls up at the Eiffel Tower; others pure fiction, such as when Jules Verne wrote that the *Nautilus* was also built by 'Cail and Co'. As grand as his life became – and it must have been pretty grand as his Parisian residence is now an office building that fits a couple of hundred employees – he never forgot his roots. He chose this part of France to apply the best technology of the time – steam, steel and rail – combined with a vision of allowing the rural poor to participate in the great acceleration of the Industrial Revolution. At a time when more than half of the population was engaged in agriculture, La Ferme de la Briche, 'The Farm at la Briche', was the Silicon Valley of Ag.

Where we were sitting, La *Petite* Briche was his accompanying social experiment, something that we would now call CSR – corporate social responsibility – that was equally ahead of its time. It was a radical program to reform wayward young men through the application of family support, work training and education. If more detail was needed, Frits pointed out that classes were once held in the very room in which we were now eating.

'What happened to him?' one of the girls asked.

'Died,' Frits answered.

'Young too,' added Mum. Neither comment seemed particularly helpful to my goal of softening the girls' arrival.

In the next ring out, in the mini-universe according to Frits, were the surrounding towns: the three villages of about a hundred people each, one with the school, one with a pharmacy and one with a restaurant. In the middle, somewhere, was a bicycle factory. Dotted through the geography, like human landmarks, were the key people we needed to know. Bubbly Corrine the pharmacist, retired Air France stewardess and French teacher Marie-Françoise, beautiful Aimée the school teacher, and hard-working Colette and brunette Lorent – both to be found from 9 am at the one local restaurant. Mum just rolled her eyes at most of this but did agree about the school teacher.

Frits painted a picture of a tight community, of people who would help each other, and, now, us. It was a story full of history, of colourful characters, of materials of stone and wood, water and earth, of cheese and old bicycles. A world that seemed to have the economic structures left behind by the steam age. For anything else, such as discount retail, to buy anything made from synthetic fabrics, or to fix an iPhone, we'd have to leave this galaxy and go about an hour south to the towns on the Loire river.

I was happy not to have to say anything, but knew I was missing important details. It was the type of introduction where wisdom is dropped by those before you, but you walk over it as you try to keep up with them. Where you know what you're being given is important, but not what to do with it. There were important names I knew I wouldn't remember ('Corrine will solve anything medical that comes up'), information that is essential but you don't know it yet ('open six days a week but closed every lunchtime'), and valuable advice that wouldn't become clear until I'd already learned it myself ('the lunch menu is exactly the same as dinner, but half the price').

The geography of the region continued to be given with fingers prodding in the direction of the thick darkness, and the information flowed as quickly as the wine. I accepted another glass of the red ('cabernet franc is the only wine they are allowed to grow here'), ate the rabbit with thanks ('it was market day today in Continvoir'), and let the information slip past me.

Nobody from our side of the table was in much of a mood to talk, so we agreed to discuss everything important in the morning. As soon as dinner was inhaled, we said goodnight and I took the girls upstairs to find their room. I was reassured that the house's heating was on, and warned again about the slippery stairs. I didn't feel I needed a fourth warning about walking upstairs from my mother, but as we began our ascent I understood her insistence.

Thanks to 150 years of use, the steps now slope down and away from the wall to which they seem only tenuously attached. In the house's recent renovation someone had thought it a good idea to polish them to ice-rink smooth. Mum made me promise that the girls would always wear rubber-soled slippers when in the house. I had them in our bags and committed to retrieving them first thing in the morning, thinking that, frankly, crampons would be more useful. I could have done with a few additional warmth providers for the girls and a toothbrush or three, but I was sure Madison and Elsa could finger-brush their teeth and sleep in their long underwear that night.

Mum and Frits had arrived from Australia two days earlier to open the house and turn on the heat. Frits' Dutchness means his definition of 'the house is warm' is not the same as mine – and certainly nothing like that of my girls. They'd grown up with an American mother whose version of a warm house has heated floors that give the underside of your feet a tan.

I found their room and, knowing that it was going to be a cold night, pushed the two single beds together, making a queen-sized pad for the girls to snuggle in together. One peed while the other brushed her teeth, then they swapped. They were fading fast, wobbling as I helped them undress, unable to keep their balance. I tucked them in to bed, encouraging them against the cold of the sheets. The long day and large dinner weighed heavily on their eyelids and they quickly fell asleep, passing out like two little drunks.

I left the door ajar, as promised, and got myself warmly dressed for bed in my room across the corridor. I found a tooth-brush in an airline amenities kit in the bathroom, the type of thing that sensible travellers take from business-class flights for the benefit of their house guests. Thanks, Mum, I thought. I adjusted the mirror above the basin so I could see my face. I brushed vigorously and for too long, more for the warmth than the dental hygiene. It was a chance for one last meditation on the events of the day. Lost in my thoughts, I stood observing, but not understanding, the man looking back at me.

Without warning, Madison appeared in the doorway behind me.

She was crying, and muttering something in her unique combination of sense and non-sense. Madison is a sleep-talking sleepwalker, and she wasn't abiding by Janet's rules on appropriate footwear on the third floor. She continued to talk incoherently, but mostly she was just crying. I carried her back to her room, and decided to stay with her, hunkering down between her and her sister. For reinforcements, I pulled in the support-pillow Madi had brought from Australia. For a few years now she'd been virtually inseparable from a cream and brown soft toy that looked like someone had gently flattened a cow. Despite having udders, and going by the name Cowie, he was absolutely a boy.

One of my tricks to get her to sleep calmly had always been to sing made-up songs to her. We both know it will be tone deaf, melodically inconsistent and repetitive. But she loves them, and I think that part of the point is just how lame they are. While painful to others, they usually elicit a little smile, which seems to calm her. They always start with the same rhyme.

My name is Mad-i, and I love my Dadd-y,

The rest is improvised for the setting.

I'm in France now, and I am sleep-y . . .

Elsa glued herself tightly to my right, Madison lay on top of me, and my thin feet protruded from the bottom of the covers. Madison wet my chest with her tears, and, in her moments of coherence, kept asking why we were here. And why her mummy was not.

I still didn't have any good answers to give her. I promised, promised, promised, to give her an answer at breakfast the next day. We'd have a 'Janet omelet', I added, knowing the promise of melted cheese and eggs would distract her. I didn't know how to explain why her mother had taken off with her brothers to drive across Europe. Because I didn't really understand it myself. Or what I had done to cause it. Nor how to explain why her dad had transplanted her and her sister from the warm comforts of a Sydney summer to a frozen French farmhouse in a European January.

Why are we here?

The logistics of turning around and heading back to Australia occupied my sleep-muddled brain. I had quit my job, against all the principles of persistence and responsibility I espoused. I imagined how foolish I would feel returning prematurely, just weeks into my widely publicised 'year-long sabbatical'. I ran through all the excuses I could use – too cold, too French, bad school, bad food – and decided that any listener would soon reach the conclusion that I'd made a last-minute decision, too quickly and without enough planning.

They would be right, of course.

That first night was an epic battle. Elsa and I were woken countless times by Madison and her muttering. We fought con-stantly to get the covers right: pawing the down-comforter from one side of the bed to the other, and then throwing it off when one of us woke in a sweat.

We cuddled tight for warmth and security but kept rolling on top of the one next to us. The child at the bottom would shriek in claustrophobic confusion and blame the innocent sister.

Maaaa-di! Or *El-sar!* they would cry, the words stretched by the Australian accent – a lilt that is at its most pronounced when used in a whiny complaint.

The accused, feeling falsely so and woken once again, would scream her innocence. I'd accept the blame, rearrange the bodies, pillows and covers, and plead that we try to fall asleep again.

Our night was both a physical tussle for comfort and a mental struggle for an answer to Madi's question. Our three bodies had tossed and turned, wriggled and twisted, interrogating a query that arrived with the accuracy of an angel's arrow, the force of a child's innocence. If only a four-word ask could be answered as succinctly.

11

Expo-ing Oneself (Six Months Earlier)

The author presenting. That, or demonstrating
slow-motion karate.

The route from Sydney to Shanghai took us over the top of
seven nations – organised into three democracies, two mon-
archies and two communist republics – a planeload of mainly
Australians, wrapped up in papers, movies and sleep, skimming
over the top of roughly 2.1 billion people. I was as guilty as
most on board for having limited my interactions with the
countries below to time spent flying over, or transiting through,
them. With the exception of one adventure as a late teen – a
ham-fisted attempt to explore the annexed territories of Tibet –
when I'd ventured beyond their airports my time had been
spent under the sun of their beach resorts or inside their city's
conference centres.

The flight is eight hours, and while the earth was spinning
away a day's light, we'd be flying half-a-planet north. Amongst
the business class, the flight feels like just another day in the
office, where the paper shuffling and digital vacillation is done

in a semi-recumbent position. I was being sustained by a bottomless glass of chardonnay, perked up by concurrent coffee service, and distracted by a steady stream of recently released, light-fare movies.

My laptop was open to a presentation that I'd been told was urgently needed for translation, something I'd been urged to deliver since the middle of the previous week. It was a speech I was due to give the next day, and it still ran over one hundred pages. It needed to be half that. I moved back and forth through the slides. The presentation opened well but lacked a conclusion and got murky in the middle. The jokes worked in English; how well they would in Mandarin I couldn't tell. Most importantly, it needed the author to know what he believed in, and sadly for me there is no drop-down menu for that, no spellcheck to correct one's values, no helpful hints the software could provide.

I peered in the direction of my screen, more through it than at it, and tapped away, while trying not to get too drawn to the small movie screen protruding from my seat's arm rest. With the middle finger of my right hand I sent the presentation steadily forward. With my index finger, I sent it flying backward. Images and ideas flew up, and then away. Then up again. None lingering long enough for a conclusion to congeal by itself. I was making progress: a ten-slides-forward, seven-slides-back type of progress.

> I need to link the history of urban development with the
>   growth of human capital . . .
> Find a way to suggest investment returns even with strict
>   environmental controls . . .
> How to hint at diversity while staying inside the approved
>   government guidelines . . .
> Wow, Meg Ryan does look good with dark hair.

The flight attendant interrupted with just the right mix of familiarity and helpfulness, carrying a bottle in each hand, labels out.

'Thanks. I'll stay with the chardonnay.'

Through the window, the clouds parted to reveal a rich tapestry of greens below us, indicating we were back over land. Then they closed again. It's easy to dream up here, a little tipsy, breathing a little less oxygen than is needed. It's a cabin of the comfortably successful, all sitting comfortably, loosely strapped into padded chairs.

I didn't get close to finishing the presentation before our descent began and we were asked to bring our seats to the upright position, put away our screens, fold down our laptops. Our landing was noticeably gentle, our deceleration a smooth glide. With a slight left off the runway and a short taxi to our gate we slipped in between a litter of other new arrivals. Simultaneously a walkway extended towards the plane, a steel-umbilical that served the dual purpose of connecting us to the terminal and advertising a global financial institution.

The forward door of the plane opened outwards, and there was a pause while a clutch of blue-suited officials boarded the aircraft. They had arrived to usher our party off before anyone else could deplane. Just after the second HSBC logo, another official directed us out a side door and into the airport air; warm, moist and full of its sweet mix of pollutants. I took a full breath of China, and liked what I smelled. If I ever develop a solvent-sniffing habit, I think my fume of choice is going to be this Avgas blend.

Our party of diplomats and business ambassadors, in sharp heels and leather soles, carefully made their way down the metal stairs onto the tarmac where awaited a small convoy of black limousines. One member of the blue-suited army directed me toward the largest of the dark fleet, the one flying two small red flags above its lights and, saying 'you tall', offered me the front seat. I said it was unnecessary – I was not the leader of our delegation, after all – but I soon took the seat as he'd suggested. Any car looks small when tucked under the wing of a 747, but our full-sized Mercedes had plenty of leg room, even for those in the back. Which was a good thing, as I was sharing a ride with the Premier of our state – the leader of our delegation – and it was already clear that the fact that she was a woman meant she wasn't being immediately recognised as such.

I was part of a trade mission from Australia, here to attend *L'Exposition Universelle de Shanghaï*. This was the forty-sixth version of the events – Expositions, Exhibitions, World Fairs – that are most frequently simply called Expos. They're held every five years, a type of Olympics for development, where the disciplines are invention and growth, pride and nationalism and, more recently, country marketing and city branding. It's a 200-year-old format that mixes full-blown trade show with elaborate circus-like entertainment.

Before the self-proclaimed 'Great Nations' began settling their quarrels on the battlefields, they fought for bragging rights by staging larger and more expensive Expos. France (who started it in 1844), England (who perfected it in their Great Exhibition of 1851), Germany, the US and even Australia (well, Melbourne, which at the time acted as if it was part of England) hosted huge, six-month-long carnivals-to-progress. Each country touted its nation's technological achievements, built impressive structures (matched only by their impracticality) and showcased its agricultural prowess, all while loudly promoting its particular world view. Above all else, the Expos were designed to be great; less in the sense of very good, but great as in expansive, such as *Great Britain* and the *Great War*. Science was progress, and progress accelerated everything, and each Expo reinforced an unrestrained mania, the collective pursuit of bigger is better, as is faster, longer, higher.

Shanghai's version was a $60 billion, one-thousand-acre theme park for city planners. It would be the largest, most-expensive, longest-running, most-visited, most expo of all Expos. There would be four million t-shirts sold, 100 million other items of official merchandise vended, and seven million litres of caffeinated drinks drunk. Given the stifling heat of a Shanghai summer, almost all of it would take place within the purpose-built pavilions of the one hundred exhibiting nations, including the Australian pavilion, in which I'd be doing my work.

On this trip my obligations were relatively modest: I had to host a breakfast, witness a number of signing ceremonies, including one with a company I hadn't heard of before, a diversified tech company called Huawei that seemed to have its fingers in everything. Most importantly, I had to give a speech that hopefully would whip a group of Chinese businessmen into an investment frenzy. To the Premier sitting in the back seat, I confirmed I was ready to do this over lunch tomorrow, knowing I still had that night to finish the presentation.

As we drove across the vast tarmac, our driver told me that the main terminal of Shanghai's Pudong International Airport was the world's largest steel-suspension building. To help me comprehend its scale, he described it in terms of its multiple of football fields. 'Six,' he said, with noticeable pride. I'm attracted to the idea of someone seeking to prove this fact by staging half-a-dozen simultaneous games of soccer, balls flying across baggage counters, wreaking havoc in the duty-free stores, tickets and tourists flying through the air. But, alas, we wouldn't be seeing this metaphorical spectacle as we were heading to the VIP terminal.

As our convoy sliced through the airport traffic it was clear that the hierarchy was well understood by all: size mattered when it came to planes, but style when it came to those without wings. We'd all yield to aircraft, but the trucks, service vans and baggage trains would halt for us. Standing above us, boldly painted commercial planes rolled by, while to our side stood row after row of the sleek white thoroughbreds that we know as private jets. I've been travelling all my life, in pretty much every class. I was lucky to catch the tail end of the romantic age of flight, which is perhaps why I loved the ozone-destroying habit of air travel.

It began for me in the mid-1970s, when my sister and I would sit in economy for the long hauls from Perth to London. When we asked, the stewardesses would bring us up to the front cabin of the plane to be shown to our parents. If I was lucky, Dad would take me up the spiral staircase to the upper deck, a child's peek into the confines of adulthood.

The entire top deck of those early 747s was turned into the grey-leathered smokers lounge reserved for First Class passengers. My dad had already gained a reputation in business and the pilot would often pop out to meet him and share a smoke. He'd leave the door to the flight deck open, allowing me to wander in to try on the hat of the co-pilot or chat to the side-seated navigator.

Changing economics, technological progress and the events of 9/11 have all combined to create what is today an almost unrecognisable system of air travel. Cockpit doors are now securely locked, the side-seated navigators have been made redundant, and the internet has delivered a downgrade in both prices and comfort for the majority of passengers. At the same time, we've seen the arrival of private suites, private entrances and the normalisation of private jet travel. It is one thing for society to walk in different circles, to sit in different classes, it's another for it to be moving in different orbits. Real separation occurs when you can no longer see it.

In the context of all the enormous machines and buildings around us, the VIP terminal was a slight disappointment. It was a relatively modest single-storey building, right-sized for about four games of ping-pong. The overly-lit greeting room sparkled, its tiled floor shined past the point of reflection, its wood-veneered walls as free from character as it's possible for wood to be. In the centre of the room stood a Chinese and an Australian flag next to each other. Flowing down from their stanchions, the bottom tip of each flag was touching the other, giving them the posture that businessmen make when they're left awkwardly holding hands.

We were met by another small battalion of the blue-suited army, including one who, wearing white gloves, took our passports. He promised only a short delay while Immigration and Customs tended to our documents. As the formal greetings of the delegation began, I moved back to observe.

The reciprocal introductions of this type are well choreographed, full of eye contact, appropriate head angles, set to the sounds of polite but controlled laughter. Each side had its own group of minders, providing direction and translation. It was all conducted without anyone knowing exactly how much of what was being said was being understood by the other side. It resembled a type of martial art, where the goal was to establish the power structures without anyone noticing your exertion. Such was the intensity of the protocolic dances that I knew nobody would notice if I slipped away in search of a bathroom.

I pushed open a door sliced into the wood panelling and found myself in a deserted open-plan office. I crossed its carpeted floor, past the neat cubicles, and turned down a corridor. Around another corner I found, to my right, the door to the unisex facility. To my left was the front door of the mini-terminal, unguarded steps falling to the street outside. I had slipped, entirely unintentionally, past Chinese immigration. I entered the bathroom and pulled the door closed, more deliberately than usual, tingling with an impish desire to do something clandestine. The bathroom was large enough to comfortably park a medium-sized car, and was comprehensively clad in white marble, every inch covered in high-polish whiteness.

No-one had seen me enter, and I paused for a moment to consider my options. I had, after all, just snuck into China. By now, Tintin would be straightening his fake moustache; James Bond would have changed into his dinner jacket. I was still fumbling for my zipper.

On the plane, I'd prepared answers to give Passport Control:

Six days.
Business.
No, this is not my first time. I've been here on business before.
Oh, and I went to Tibet too, a long time ago. So, you might
    count this as my third.

I had readied a pithy geopolitical point, about nation expansion and the creeping hegemony of a dominant economic force, about change and loss of different cultures, but equally the finger could have pointed back at me. The changes on the map, of growth and urbanisation, coincided with changes in me that were just as pronounced. The adventurous teenager who'd made his first trip here was all but lost to the man standing in the fine suit now.

I had waited only four days after finishing high school to fly out of Australia. With two other conspicuously tall teens as travelling companions, I joined a low-cost tour (because it was subsidised by the Chinese Government) to the recently reopened annexed territories of Tibet. It was the middle of the 1980s, and the Chinese were keen for the trade opportunities that come with international acceptance. One of the barriers to that was the political issue of their invasion of Tibet. Since the Dalai Lama had escaped the invading Chinese forces, he had created something of a human-rights embarrassment for China. The Chinese hoped that by bringing tourists to see the Tibetan people living happily under their Red Army rulers, any bleating by their exiled spiritual leader could eventually be drowned out by the clamour of international commerce.

Entering from the Nepalese side, we mini-vanned it up the dizzying road to a military checkpoint above 16,000 feet. Squeezed shoulder to shoulder, we twisted towards the border, each switchback bringing us closer to the highest road pass in the world. We studied every village as it changed from the Nepalese to the Chinese environs: slightly taller people, slightly rounder faces, less stone, more concrete, fewer of the small colourful flags, more of the large red ones. And many more guns.

The Tibetan plateau was treeless desert – the visibility seemed endless, the army everywhere. It was sparsely populated by what appeared to be a primitive but happy people, well guarded by what appeared to be an abundant but bored military. Frozen, beige-coloured earth extended in every direction, rising to a crescendo of snow-capped summits, one of which was the legendary Mount Everest. Only our guide wasn't sure which one it was. We had decided in advance to slip away from the official tour, and this provided the perfect excuse, despite the complaints of the guide and his warnings of Chinese military and Tibetan bandits.

In our bags we'd snuck a contraband copy of *Seven Years in Tibet*, the story of the Dalai Lama's escape – but we lasted just two days. Out of food and overwhelmed by altitude sickness, we surrendered to a Chinese army barracks only to discover they weren't the least bit concerned about anything but our health. We were treated to fresh oxygen and chalky pills pulled from amber bottles, and released, free of charge. Our only option was to hitchhike out, and we found a smuggler of plastic shoes who agreed to get us down to a safer altitude. We brokered a deal without language, a bargain sealed with our remaining rupees, dollars and yuan. Our smuggler stuck to his handshake and bundled us and his contraband across the border into Nepal, where we savoured the thick air and ate noodle soup, our heads clearer, our wallets lighter.

Despite the adventurous trail I thought I'd been on, I had really been a prop for the Chinese Government. At the time, China was viewed with a combination of deep suspicion and dismissive scepticism, a conclusion that the Western intelligentsia reserves for anything it hasn't spent time bothering to understand. The slow-motion collapse of the Soviet Union meant that few people were betting that rapid growth would come from its less-developed, also communist, Asian comrade. China was reorienting itself towards the West, a plan that involved a manufacturing revolution and global trade initiative that has shaped the world more profoundly than any other theme of my lifetime. It was important for China that young impressionable men like me visit their country. Our 'job', in effect, as ambassadors with backpacks, was to report back that China was not such a scary place, that it was open for business.

On this return trip, a decade into the twenty-first century, while I'd only made it to the bathroom I was part of a trade mission going in a different direction. The books in my bag were full of business opportunities, and what I was trafficking was the legal stuff of cross-border investment. I was representing a city, Sydney, and its new flagship development, a $10 billion precinct called Barangaroo. I was seeking outbound investment, hoping for a slice of the capital that the recently rich China was allocating overseas. I had arrived in official company, but in my search for the bathroom I had happened on my first look at the new China, and it looked worlds away from the old Tibet. Everything on display here was clean and organised, in accordance with the image the nation was now projecting, except that on the bathroom floor, between the washbasin and the toilet, in a white plastic bucket someone had placed some sort of small freshwater lobster. He was scratching his way around the bottom with only a half-nibbled chicken thigh for company. He had just enough water to splash his disapproval when I looked down on him.

I had no idea why he was being farmed there, but he had nothing to fear from me. I stood above the toilet bowl, did my business carefully, and assured him I wasn't the least bit hungry for bathroom-raised lobster.

You're safe, I said to him, *I had the fish on the plane*.

To prove my intentions were merely touristic, I used my free hand to take a photo with my phone. I left the bathroom dressed exactly as when I had entered. As I was closing the door

I ran into my group who were being ushered out the exit doors. We'd been processed, and nobody had missed me. It was now smiles all round. At the bottom of the stairs waited our fleet, their curb-facing doors held open. Our family of vehicles had grown slightly with the addition of some motorcycled police to help convoy us to our hotel.

It was near midnight when we reached our accommodation, a tall, glass-sided envoy of an American hotel chain. We all had an early start the next morning. So, true to our well-earned reputation, the Australian delegation agreed to reconvene in the hotel bar after quickly dumping our bags in our rooms.

In less than ten minutes I had checked in, hung tomorrow's suit, and was seated on a leather settee in the triplex bar that began on the fortieth floor. Floor-to-ceiling windows framed an entirely man-made panorama, a low ceiling of highly polluted fog, punctured intermittently by other skyscrapers that eerily disappeared into the sooty skyline. In my hand, a glass of red that had taken the same trip I had flown, albeit in a lower grade of travel. We'd flown half a globe only to drink wine made down the road from where we lived.

The sky on the Tibetan plateau had been the lightest shade of blue I'd ever seen – but over Shanghai it was not to be seen. 'Ever,' the barman informed me. Far from being dull, though, thanks to the primary-coloured neon lights wrapped around buildings and bridges, the low clouds pulsated with a constantly-changing light-scape. It was an oddly peaceful show; however, I knew the spectacle was only possible because a layer of suffocating pollution had turned the sky into a perfect projection surface. For the last few years I had been a director of the largest rail company in Australia. With four thousand kilometres of rail line, hundreds of locomotives and thousands of wagons at our disposal, each year we'd transport a couple of hundred million tonnes of coal to the ports of Queensland. From there it would be loaded onto giant ships that fed the steel mills and power plants of China.

By particles of coal dust per million, or perhaps by CO2 as a percentage of all gases, what is my personal responsibility for the choking cloud over this city? Should I worry that it might be possible to calculate that one day?

I sip my wine instead. Or rather, anyway.

The human response to screwing up nature seems to be to screw it up even further. The lights I'm watching are powered by burning our coal, the smoke from which will result in a thicker blanket of smog. In turn, this will require more lights to brighten it, and more coal to be burned to power those lights. It's a spiral that goes in only one direction, increasingly unsustainably. It all made this China appear as unstable as the one I'd observed as a teenager. Back then, my job had been to tell folks that China was a good place to do business. I was returning, in the twenty-first century, to tell deep-pocketed Chinese investors that the same was true about Australia. That is, if I could ever finish my presentation. So, after we found someone willing to expense the drinks to their room, we headed towards our respective chambers.

My room's desk was small but adequate, the type of hotel hardware that is inoffensively stylish, production-line quality. The bed was large, room for three. A corner had been turned down, the sheets parted with a neat fold, obligatory chocolate wrapped in the hotel's logo sitting on the pillow. I opened the curtains for another take on the neon-washed sky and allowed myself to enjoy the dirty spectacle once again. I woke my computer and double-clicked on the latest draft of my presentation. On the desk sat a card from the hotel. 'Enjoy your night,' the printed side said. I opened the card, unwrapped the chocolate, considered the note, ate the chocolate. It was a handwritten, personalised welcome that purported to be from the hotel manager, which, in neat blue cursive, once again encouraged me to enjoy my stay.

Perhaps they knew something about me that I didn't, or perhaps because it is our only real job, to enjoy wherever we are, whatever we are doing. To be a happy tourist through life. But I had other things on the back, and at the front, of my mind. There were the emails that were still arriving asking for my final speech, now mixed with my questioning of what I was selling and to whom I was selling it. And questions about me. Or at least, the me that had arrived here today.

I typed, copied and pasted, resized images and edited words. Then cut, cut, cut. I added an all-caps addendum of 'FINAL' to the file name, saved it to a USB stick, closed the document, closed the curtains, and into the triangular aperture of crisp white sheets I slid.

I I I

Sharing in Shanghai

Barangaroo: in reality it is much bigger and not
made of foam.

My speech was to be given over lunch, deep inside the
Australian pavilion. Our nation's contribution to this Expo was
a giant metallic amoeba, two acres of exhibition space housed
in a curvy, window-free, six-storey building. The exterior was
made of sheets of pre-rusted Australian-made steel, treated
with a type of acid that gave it a uniform patina of rich red rust.
It cost $80 million to fabricate and lay over the surrounding
asphalt, as if you'd melted the Eiffel Tower, then left a puddle
of iron to corrode. To its credit, the design of the Australian
pavilion was brave and had been accepted warmly by the architectural community. Amongst the Expo visitors, it was also
wildly popular. In Expo parlance, popularity was described by
the number of hours the public spent queuing to get in.

I arrived later than I'd promised, thankful that the VIP
entrance was queue free. A discreet set of revolving doors led
to a private elevator that lifted me into a sophisticated network

of meeting rooms and function halls. In one of the many emails requesting my presentation I'd found the email addresses of the Chinese translation team and had made contact with them directly. I'd arranged to bring my USB stick to them personally. I found the three-person team, two men and one woman, huddled in a room a bit bigger than a telephone booth. They were young and confident, professional and hip, with more than a hint of American to their English. Chinese university students, I learned. We talked through some of my jokes, I took their suggestions, and they set about the translation and reformatting the entire presentation and all images for the correct screen proportions.

The presentation was set to follow lunch, which gave me enough time to take a tour of the Australian pavilion and then find a quiet space to practise.

From the outside the Australian pavilion might have been the architectural representation of industrial brutalism, but inside it was culturally sensitive, well past the point of a committee's concessions to political correctness. It was full of creative montages of images, beautiful large landscape photographs, historical dioramas, powerful quotes (including one from my mother), stuffed marsupials attached by chains to the wall, and well-chosen Aboriginal artifacts.

An image of the women's world surfing champion, also part of our delegation, dominated one room. She looked down from a wall above the entrance, printed twenty times larger than reality. Hovering next to her was an aerial shot of a boat steaming a cargo of iron ore towards China, represented at one-hundredth its real size. The proportions of the two were pleasing, but misleading: manipulation of scale makes things easier to comprehend, but harder to understand; easier to swallow, but harder to digest.

The pavilion was a display of how Australia likes to see itself, or at least likes to promote itself: a country full of modern medical advances, a land of abundant sporting achievements, high-end chefs and solid mining prowess, all of which was tastefully mixed with indigenous art and respect for the hard workers who built our country. On the pavilion's top floor was the main attraction, a 360-degree cinema where a series of rotating and spinning videos screened an animated film featuring three cartoonish children – one white, one black, one Asian – discovering everyday life in Australia, a multicultural paradise with lots of sun.

There was no mention of the darker periods of our history. Left out was the precipitous fraying of the country's social fabric, the decline in mateship, the less than friendly welcome given to those that arrive by boat today. Also left out of the history was any mention of the incarceration of the first men to attempt to organise English workers who were sent as convicts to the colony of New South Wales. Nor was there any allusion to the resulting slow-motion genocide of the continent's traditional residents. There was plenty about agricultural origins, including a diorama that featured a former Prime Minister squeezing the testicles of a startled ram. To an extent that would be lost on 99.9 per cent of the visitors to the pavilion, Australia really is all of this.

I found a quiet place to sit before lunch, knowing confidence in delivery was a good proxy for being sure of yourself. Three hundred people arrived punctually and were suitably primed with a multi-course degustation of nouvelle Australian cuisine, featuring grain-fed beef and line-caught fish. For some reason, people don't mind their beef being highly-farmed, but for our fish we apparently appreciate their wildness. The cows must go quietly, but fish, for some reason, are best if they put up a fight. Wines of both the red and white variety were served, cards on the table helping us understand that they were courtesy of pavilion sponsors. Over lunch I continued to concentrate on running through the presentation in my head, letting the official speeches wash over me, a series of long introductions and formal statements that were as necessary as they were meaningless; protocol that was present only because its absence would offend.

The well-choreographed introduction to my speech was given by the Chinese hostess, in both English and Mandarin, which was to be followed by a video projected onto a giant screen behind the podium, and onto the monitors dotted around the room. The video was set to describe the Barangaroo project in the context of Sydney Harbour and its place in the Australian economy. Due to strict protocol issues, I had not been allowed to edit the video back in Sydney, only allowed to see a draft. I understood what the producers were trying to do. They'd combined sweeping helicopter footage of a sunset-washed Sydney Harbour with computer-simulated images of the development and stock video of happy people of different ethnicities happily working together. It did a great job of showing what a beautiful, multicultural, hard-working, coffee-drinking nation Australia was. What it didn't do was play on the venue's equipment.

After much fussing, multiple apologies and delays caused by several reboots of the system, the hostess was told just to continue, which she did as if the video had just played.

As you have seen . . . she said first in Chinese then in English.

From these images you can appreciate . . . she continued unwaveringly, her determination almost effective in distracting from the surreal nature of what she was doing. There was some quiet mirth, soft chuckles alternating from the Chinese members of our team and the English speakers. Most of the room just nodded through the presentation of nothing. Blank screens encircled the gathering, ceviched fish and rare fillet continued to be consumed, while the official narrated an invisible vision of the future that, had they been able to see it, was itself computer-generated. We were being told in two languages what we had just seen and how it made us feel. Like the food that was presented, most seemed to just eat it up.

With that as my introduction, and disregarding the strict orders from the Head of Corporate Affairs not to deviate from the just-translated speech, I began to do my work. In my role as Head of Brand Sydney, I had the nebulous charge of helping position Sydney as a global city. What *exactly* is a global city is yet to be defined, and the breadth is wide. It included ensuring Sydney was mentioned in the same breath as New York, London, Paris, Tokyo, was printed on the sides of the shopping bags of luxury brands, slipped into the lyrics of rap songs. Sydney is the smallest in this club by at least fifty per cent, the youngest by a couple of hundred years, but the one with the best natural advantages, and the only one with beaches. It was a still-congealing vision that was designed to ensure Sydney competes for the type of enormous conventions that you're not aware of but are worth millions of dollars to a city, land the next Olympic-like thing, win the regional headquarters for large corporations.

Today's specific task, however, was to seek investment for the real estate project Barangaroo. The project takes its name from that of the wife of Bennelong, an Aboriginal man who was kidnapped by the settlement's first Governor to educate the first white occupiers of Sydney Harbour. For their services to the new English colony, he and his wife were given a small house on what is now called Bennelong Point. A hundred and eighty years later, Bennelong's plot was redeveloped and became the foundation for Australian's most celebrated building, the Sydney Opera House. Australians don't like to think of ourselves as having been slave owners, but we were. Nor do Australians think of themselves much as users of opera houses either, but we have the most famous one of those in the world.

When completed, the Barangaroo development will feature over three million square feet of offices and apartments, a casino, and a water's edge that, at a cost of over $100 million, was being returned to the same curves it had at the time of discovery by white explorers. The man who gave Paris its most controversial steel structure of the 1970s (the Pompidou centre) and London its most controversial steel building of the 1980s (the Lloyd's of London building) had been chosen to design the three steel office towers at the core of the project. Lord Rogers' shining metal structure, the most environmentally advanced building of its time, complete with full water recycling and passive solar systems, would become the western gateway to the city of Sydney. I was there today to sell something the world desperately needed – compact, environmentally sustainable, 'green' cities – to investors who were looking for sustained, above-market rates of returns.

Caught between these two conflicting ideals, and aware of the responsibility and restrictions on what I was expected to say, I gave it my all. It helped that I truly believed in what I was selling. I just didn't believe in me.

I have no idea whether anything I then said had any impact at all. I put the development in the context of the Opera House, both beautiful structures built on a beautiful harbour. I left out that both were built on the land of Australia's most celebrated husband-and-wife slave team. I talked about steel structures, and compared our project to Eiffel's tower, a stretch at best.

When the Parisian landmark was completed, it was four times the height of neighbouring buildings, the only thing to surpass the spire of Notre Dame. Moreover it was built out of a material few people had seen used for this purpose and designed unlike anything ever built. Around its first tier, Eiffel carved the names of the greatest scientists, inventors and industrialists of the time. The seventy-two names, including CAIL, embossed in two-foot-high gold all-caps, were Eiffel's gods from the age of progress, a tribute to those most responsible for the new freedoms that mankind enjoyed thanks to a century of remark-able advances. With the giant towers of Sydney, I might have been selling the new cathedrals of commerce, one of the largest 'green' developments in the world, but in the end they were still shiny office buildings.

Ten years before he proposed his tower as the western gateway for the 1889 Paris Expo, Eiffel had designed the internal structure for the Statue of Liberty, which was discreetly hidden behind a curtain of draped copper sheeting. But with his tower, there was nothing but function on display. It was unapologetically an object of raw utilitarian beauty, needling though the surrounding femininity of the Haussmann-designed Paris. Here, in the magical intersection of quality, function and integrity, the disciplines of science and art don't just overlap, they are the same thing. Not that I had time to get too philosophical – I had a few billion dollars to attract.

I was confident that I knew what I was doing. I was going to show that while Sydney might not be the best place in the world to work, nor necessarily the best place in the world to live, it *was* the best place in the world to live *and* work. The video, had anyone been able to see it, was the best evidence of our intentions, and showed a smooth vision of the future where the light was always perfect, and from a perspective only possible if one was able to helicopter through life. The fantasy we'd intended to present was to see life as if you were some sort of drone – not in the impotent type of worker bee, nor in the silent sky-high military hardware, but in the remote-control camera way, moving in and out, up and down, occupying a space that was a safe distance from others.

Perhaps one day, without having spinning blades on all four corners, we'll be able to fly with VR goggles through our entire life. I doubt it will ever be compelling enough for people to resist the temptation to look at reality, as there's nothing more consistently imperfect, and therefore fascinating, than humans themselves. So, to tell the story of the best place to live and work, I used images of the many human faces of Sydney. Colourful, beautiful and diverse; a couple of drag queens, no opera singers, but lots of Aboriginal football players. If we couldn't give Bennelong back his land, I'd try to celebrate some of the achievements of his descendents. If we couldn't talk about human rights issues, at least we could highlight the beautiful person in a pink dress who happened to be a man. As the environmental challenges of our hosts weren't to be discussed either, I'd been provided with images of clear skies over Bondi

Beach. When projected thirty-foot-wide behind me, they stood in contrast to the dense grey that could be seen through the windows outside.

Back at my table, and after letting the thank yous from the stage fly over my head, I was led by minders into a frenetic session of business-card-exchanging and hand-shaking. I accepted the solid back slaps from associates and understood the polite ribbing from friends who detected that I'd gone a bit off script at the start. The Premier said I'd done a good job and our champion surfer told me I should have slowed down and breathed more. The handlers of both sides began to set up a private space for a conversation between me and a man they said was eager to meet me.

Just as we were about to meet, it was whispered in my ear that he was responsible for investing the pension funds for the Chinese Army. 'It's the largest fund in the world,' the minder added, guessing (correctly) that I didn't know that. The unassuming financial titan passed me his business card and, in an unnecessarily deferential tone, asked for mine. I smiled and expressed my honour to meet him, but just before I could get out my business card, another minder stepped in, and away he was whisked. Apparently, this fish would be landed by someone closer to the investment decisions. I'd done my job; I guess I was the bait in this case.

I then did the minimum-acceptable level of grinning, which I mixed with an appropriate level of serious-faced nodding, but soon I headed towards the elevator, aware I was the first one of the official party to leave the luncheon. I had the lift to myself as I dropped back to ground level. However, before I could escape the building, my path was blocked by the Head of Corporate Affairs. A short-haired, rugby forward of a woman, she was there to strongly and publicly reprimand me for my behaviour. Yes, I had gone off script, but my greatest sin apparently had been to make direct contact with the translators, against express instructions.

I apologised, honestly. The wheels of government-greased commerce turned mysteriously to me. I might have been coming in and out the VIP doorway, and in terms of commerce I was working at the very top end of the system, but I had lots to learn about this world. I was just as thrown by the military-like protocol of the organisers from the supposedly surf-loving nation of Australia, as I was by the eager greeting of the Red Army's pension-fund manager asking for my business card.

IV

A Carnival of Certainty

Eiffel, below his tower: initially built as the western
entrance for the Paris Expo 1889.

I accelerated through the arc of the revolving doors and spun
out onto the paved expanse of the Expo, leaving the pavilion
with as much speed as I could disguise within a walking gait.
On regathering my composure, I realised I was standing in front
of the line of people waiting to enter the pavilion through the
public entrance. It may have been the biggest queue I'd ever
seen. They stood six to eight wide, in a rectangular corral that
went for about 100 metres, before turning back upon itself,
eight times. A few faces turned towards the sight of me, but
mostly they were focused on the line in front of them, and the
attendant who was releasing small clumps of them towards
the public entrance.

'About four,' the attendant informed me, were the hours that
would be spent today by those trying to get to 'Australia'. Just
then, our national surfing treasure arrived, the second to leave
the official delegation. She joined me to marvel at the crowd.

Hundreds, no thousands, waiting patiently to get into what we had just escaped. Just after entering, the visitors would be greeted by a 20-foot-high version of the woman standing next to me who, in real life, was just a bit over five foot four. From all across China they had come to see a presentation of the island continent and its people, wrought in plastic, projected onto walls, glowing out from video displays, yet, in front of them, stood the real thing. Not that either of us was of any interest to them. They looked straight through us and shunted towards the presentation of the fake-surfer, pushing past the real one.

For the next three long days, I expo-ed like the best of them. For my work, it was like a masterclass in understanding city branding and it put the development of Barangaroo into the context of similar ones around the world. I was keen to help Sydney compete against other cities, and at times it felt like someone had put the event on just for me. Except that I'd be joining close to one million other visitors each day. On my neck dangled a lanyard of official accreditation which gave me powerful queue-slicing abilities. I visited as many of the national pavilions as I could, looking for a country with a vision of the future that made more sense than the ones I'd been working with so far.

Through my travels, Expos had haphazardly entered my consciousness, mostly because of the architectural detritus they'd left behind. Between Manhattan and its JFK Airport stands a dome and orbit structure ('Space World'), outside Montreal there's a precinct of odd-shaped buildings, in Munich a partially operational velodrome, in Melbourne the sprawling Exhibition Building. While the pyramids, Stonehenge and the heads of Easter Island mark ancient cultures in stone, the relics of Expos are built from iron and steel. The most famous is still Eiffel's tower, and the best kept of the lot. Commerce is no static theology; its icons and disciples are quickly replaced. Unlike religions where the followers go back to the ancient places of worship, commerce worships the new, and then sells the even newer. The great structures of Expos past all served their purpose, to showcase the things from the future, and, while they rust, the things they introduced continue to live with us today.

The belief that happiness was more likely to be found in science and progress than in things of a spiritual nature started to find acceptance during the Reformation. It began as a German idea, but it was the English who supercharged its spread thanks to their experience in world trade and the machines of the Industrial Revolution. It was this version of hyper-capitalism that I knew had its roots in England, before jumping the channel to France and western Europe, and then taking hold in the New World, of the Americas and far south to Australia. As the centre of global trade shifts towards China, set to be the largest economy in the world in a few decades, it's understandable that this carnival has landed here in Shanghai.

The pavilions represented an astonishingly diverse range of structures. The pavilions lay across a 1000 acre 'park' of bitumen that had been recently levelled across reclaimed flood plains. So modern was the collection of buildings that it all looked like a parking lot for spaceships. On their roofs spun their air-conditioning fans, which provided the constant white-noise buzz over all public space. The spinning blades may as well have been their propulsion method, ready and waiting to lift them off and fly them all to another city when this Expo ended, a squadron that spread a vision of our future to us. In this sense, Eiffel's tower was a rocket that never took off, riveted to the side of the Seine, where it remains as a tourist attraction. A bold pantheon for the giants of science and progress, now relegated to a bucket-list attraction.

Each of the nearly 100 exhibiting nations appeared to have given their architect the brief to build a structure that didn't look like anything ever built before. There were buildings shaped as coils, asymmetrical domes, creations of Lego, deflated kidneys, and tea cups, united in their futuristic exteriors and a tenuous – at best – link to the nation they represented. There were also the 'theme' pavilions that presented an overarching vision of future living, of mobile technology and urbanisation. There was a space set aside to consider the environment, which was produced by WWF, the World Wide Fund for Nature, and it won the award for the best pavilion. However, the most expensive and largest was the Saudi pavilion – an almost life-sized oil supertanker. The most popular, as demonstrated by the queues of up to eight hours, was the Oil and Gas Pavilion, where visitors waited patiently to see its 4D projections of the benefits of a life full of oil and gas, petroleum and plastic.

For most visitors, their trips to the country pavilions would be the closest they would get to these lands. Better still, the visions presented were not the messy current version of these countries, but a stylised future you could visit today. Understandably this is a popular fantasy, and there were people everywhere. For the first time in my life, when I said, 'It feels like there are a million people here,' I would have been out by only a few thousand. At times I may as well have been swimming in a people sea. Fortunately, as I was taller than most, it was easy to keep my head above the flow of humans that carried me along.

As different as each pavilion appeared on the exterior, inside each nation was telling a story of heading in the same direction. The developed countries were selling the benefits of development (beyond just better teeth on the children) and the less developed countries were showing where they were making progress on the standards set by those who had developed earlier. Nobody was offering up famine, or rising sea levels, or totalitarian leaders, or a widening gap between the rich and the not rich. The ten countries that account for 80 per cent of the oceans' plastic waste were here to exhibit, but none were showcasing the sea-choking contribution they make to our planet. The concentration of power in fewer and fewer corporations was shown, but only out of sight of the tourists. No countries had anything that others didn't have, just different versions of it. Globalisation is the game, and everyone is all in.

Technology is good, screens are god. Trade is to be free, progress not questioned. The assumption of the planners and the exhibitors appears to be that nobody wants anything different.

The first pavilion that visitors reached was New Zealand, ironically the last place on the earth we inhabited. A group of Maori dancers, naked from the waist up, danced a form of non-violent Haka. The tiny twin-island nation had been awarded the Expo's prime location because it had been the first country to sign a free trade agreement with China. Global trade is a big thing, but it also comes with some nice side benefits. These were nods to the past – the French rolled out the same Rodin bronze that had wowed people in 1889 – but what was really on display were innovations that were just better ways to use the same stuff we already had – such as faster computers, smaller phones, sleeker trains, more automated factories.

When Paris got its chance in 1889, the future that was on display was very different from the world of those attending. In one place, the Great Hall of Industry, visitors marvelled at the arrival of electric lights, the first automobile, the telephone and Thomas Edison's moving-picture system. Visitors saw perfectly clear ice, partly an invention of Rudolf Diesel's; perfectly white sugar, partly an invention of Jean-François Cail's; and thanks to Madame Clicquot, always bubbly champagne. The founder of Mercedes-Benz displayed his first car-like thing, while nearby Rudolf Diesel exhibited some of his engines that ran on plant-based fuels and discarded household waste. Nikola Tesla also attended, although there is no record of what he thought when Benz adapted his car's engine so that it powered the electric lights used to highlight its own display.

The role of the corporation was entirely different in that era, with only a handful of major entities existing at the time, almost all of which were family owned. While Benz could simply name his car after his daughter, Mercedes, Elon Musk would need board approval to name one Kai. Today the degree of corporatisation was shown in the different degrees of corporate sponsorship, an indication of the eagerness of the world's top corporates to be doing business in China. The US pavilion was, for example, proudly 100 per cent sponsored by a dozen large corporations. As the corporate sponsorship increased, the displays slid from the cultural to commercial. On one display, visitors could hold up a small grey tablet in front of their chests and then, with a push of a button, a different corporate logo would appear, and a photo was automatically taken of them. A form of selfie where they were now replete with a multinational's logo, filling a void that perhaps they didn't know they were missing in that day's outfit.

The Paris Expo had promoted an entirely new way to live, introducing countless things that the visitors had never seen before. The physical manifestation of progress were the products that were now on sale, and the way to participate was to buy things. As consumerism reshaped society, a giant machinery was built to meet the demand, to supply more products at lower prices, with ever more variety and increasingly rapid delivery. Paris introduced the promise of consumerism; Shanghai was offering a continuation of this globalisation.

Because nobody was promoting a different version of the same future, today's pavilions were exercises in country branding – every nation putting different stickers on the same thing. I had both my Brand Sydney and Barangaroo development hats on, and could imagine there was someone like me, for every city, doing the same things.

> *Mumbai may not be the best place to live . . . but it is the best place to live and work.*
> *Accra may not be . . .*
> *Nairobi may not be . . .*

All countries had large real-estate developments similar to the one I was representing. Based on their displays they were certain to be completed on time thanks to the cooperation of the international community. From the lifestyle images shown, I got the impression that everyone in every country shared an aspiration to drink hot beverages in white cups while seated around small tables at the side of the street. Somehow, a French roadside ritual, Parisian café culture, had become the de facto symbol of progress. The future, if the consensus is correct, will be spent drinking coffee while watching small cars drive themselves past us.

I became one with the crowd, my head above it, but otherwise very much of, and in, it. Walking and spinning, gazing at displays until I was pushed forward by the crowd. The closest I'd come to this was as a young man in Amsterdam, carried by a thick wave of voyeuristic tourists flowing through the city's famous red-light district. I was on a date. We were probably tipsy and certainly wide-eyed, spectators of the street variety, marvelling at how unusual the sights were to us, yet how unspectacular the scenes appeared to be for the locals. So natural, it seemed, that Dutch families were to be seen living amongst it, going about their daily life.

Downstairs from one establishment, marked only by a subtle sign, a young girl and boy were playing in the street; the boy sitting on a stool doing some colouring-in, the girl fussing with the hair of her doll. I was that tourist, the tourist who lets it all wash over them, appreciating it all. Until I took a closer look. In the boy's hand he held a fat crayon, and the book he was 'colouring' was actually a printed cartoon book, with no white space. He was just pretending to be colouring. The young girl wore her hair in ponytails, in a way that matched her doll, and as she looped her fingers through one tassel, which she was doing non-stop, her tongue fell slightly over her bottom lip. The boy's shorts looked too tight to be comfortable, and both the girl and the doll wore matching skirts that were just a little too short; their socks pulled just a little too high.

With the veneer cracked, my belly filled with shame. The crowds I had naïvely joined were the necessary cover for other nefarious activities, abuses that were on clear display if anyone were to stop moving long enough to pay attention.

It is one thing to go to an Expo for the first time and discover that your future is on display, showcased and sponsored alongside carbonated sodas. It's another to know that inside each pavilion, hidden from public view, is a frenzy of corporate activity, buying and selling our collective future. It is yet another thing to realise that you are personally a member of the elite team doing the transacting.

Had it ever been any different? I asked myself, willing the answer to be yes. Yet, in the 1889 version of the Expo, right next to the Great Hall of Industry, with all its exciting inventions set to make life much better, stood the Hall of War which showcased ways to end it quicker. Machines now allowed man to make even larger cannons, and the first 'machine' guns offered the convenience that comes when 'everything is done automatically . . . simply [by] keeping the button pressed down!'

That Expo was meant to celebrate a new golden age brought by science and industry, proof of the benefits of 100 years of democracy on the continent. However, the greatest use of much of the exhibited science was to develop innovative ways to wage the wars that preoccupied Europe for the next fifty years. The same factories where Cail & Company made the elevators to go up the Eiffel Tower also made the cannons that took down other structures. Diesel's dream was to see his engine give power to the independent tradesmen and farmers to allow them to compete with the larger owners of steam power. However, at the time he jumped to his death, the only two buyers for his invention were the British Navy and a German engine maker, who put his engines into the tanks that worked hard to flatten Europe. Even Eiffel's tower had its wartime role, serving as a transmission mast for the radio broadcasts of the Nazi invaders.

The closer I got to the end of my visit to Expo land, the more desperate I was to find any vision of the future that would allow me to put this one in context. I knew that if I'd walked here for a month I wouldn't have found what I was looking for: the Hall of Uncertainty, any displays titled 'Your guess is as good as ours', or the Pavilion of the Alternative. Perhaps motion always appears at first to be progress, innovation always as improvement, and it seems better still if we're all going in the one direction. While there was a universal nod to the opportunities for renewable energy, missing was anyone selling a system based on anything other than oil, global trade and economic growth. Everyone had as the goal to increase Gross Domestic Product. The tiny nation of Bhutan had been a late withdrawal, so there was no-one to present their alternative measuring system that measures increases to Gross National Happiness. And there were no dissenting voices, no-one taking a different direction – or if they were, they were hiding it well so as not to miss out on the deals that were to be done.

It was a lot to take in, even if it was light fare. I felt like I'd been trapped in a convention for carbonated soda manufacturers: thousands of different varieties, from colas to juice-based drinks, from the 'healthier' options to the caffeinated ones in thin tubes, but it was all still sugary water in a can. I finished bloated, but empty, as I crawled into my taxi to head back to my hotel for the last time. My only remaining tasks before heading home were to attend an official dinner and to catch the train to the airport the next morning.

I do dinners well, but I have a habit of making even the simplest of travel tasks look difficult.

V

Making a Plane

Selling the cities of the future to citizens of today.

I was responsible for leaving the hotel late, but Shanghai was responsible for the traffic. My assistant knew me well enough to point me towards the 7 am train, knowing the 7.30 could just get me to my flight. Now I was at risk of missing the fall-back departure. I'd stayed up too late, woke and swum more laps than I had time for, and hadn't factored in the standstill traffic – despite being able to see it clearly from my room.

My driver did a remarkable job, somehow weaving his small sky-blue taxi through the traffic with a fluidity that usually came from riding a two-wheeled vehicle. We arrived when the digital clock on his dash and my iPhone agreed it was 7.29. All I had to do was get to the elevated platform that hung about three storeys above us. I paid the driver cash and ran. The day was already heavy with a mix of heat and humidity, and when I reached the entrance to the station I found the escalator was not escalating, presenting me with the longest flight of stationary metal stairs I had ever seen. I ran, clumsily swinging my bags above the hand rails, knowing my shirt was doomed. I reached the platform and paused momentarily to work out which carriage was for me. Sweat dripping, already.

The train from downtown Shanghai to its airport is a shining double-ended phallus of Chinese confidence. In trainspotting terms, it's a 'mag-lev', short for the propulsion system of magnetic levitation. This one train spends its life going out and back to the airport, so has neither a front nor a back. Thanks to the technology, it doesn't have an engine either, nor rails. Nor a driver. It is put in motion by the reverse polarity of powerful magnets that lift the train above a central concrete strip. Once suspended, the entire floating train is sucked forward by magnets in front of the train that are turned on to tease it forward, and then switched off just as the train reaches them. The result is the world's fastest passenger train, but also a machine in which it's impossible to figure out which seats will be facing forward, and which seats will guarantee motion sickness.

I played the game of chance and sat down in a seat. Exactly as my phone showed 7.30, the doors silently closed and the train effortlessly glided out of the station. My stomach let me know I had chosen a backwards-facing seat.

I pointed my forehead towards the thin breeze of air-conditioning and celebrated that morning's small victory: making my train. My success had been over a challenge entirely of my own creation. All I'd done was caught a train, after all, a stationary object that was to be at a precise location at a known time. It was me who had done the gyrating. But I could now frame my trip here as a success. I had made my talk, I had made my train, and it looked like I would make my flight. But any celebration was cut short as now I had to accept that, for other reasons, also of my own making, I was accelerating towards uncertainty.

A few months earlier my wife, Divonne, had announced that she was leaving me. It wasn't quite said like that, but it felt like it. It involved an elaborate plan to take our eleven-year-old twin boys, George and Robert, out of school on a year-long road trip. She was American born, but her formative years had been spent in Europe, and she wanted to recreate some of that experience for our boys. We'd been in Australia for nearly a decade, and she'd found success in Sydney, but said it was feeling like a long way from anywhere. The very thing I was enjoying retreating to had become one of her main reasons for leaving.

I was not invited on her road trip, nor was our other set of twins, Elsa and Madison. I faced the Sophie's Choice of either staying in Sydney with them or moving to somewhere uncertain in Europe. Digging in my heels would divide the family, which didn't seem right for anyone, least of all the young girls. I feared that if I quit this job my career trajectory would take an indelible hit, and besides, I liked it. Both seemed pretty shitty options, which had led me to the strategy of not deciding anything. Once again, I was demonstrating my capacity to make dramas out of my own procrastination. I guess that was another reason why my wife was leaving.

The train continued to accelerate on its elevated path, sliding past, and also through, buildings. We dissected the built-up city of Shanghai before easing onto our own corridor, the train's personal green sheath that safely separated it from other activity. A digital display at the front of the carriage showed that we were climbing smoothly, ticking over 100 kilometres per hour. When the display showed we'd gone above 200 kilometres per hour, it began to feel fast, but only because of the small shake that was vibrating the carriage. Humans can't feel speed, as we have no bones that let us know whether we're standing still or moving above the speed of sound. The only thing we really feel, thanks to a tiny bit of the inner ear, is acceleration, and its inverse, deceleration.

The train continued to accelerate, the digital numbers climbing with metronomic consistency. As we ticked over 300 kilometres per hour, the leaves and bamboo to the side of the train became a blur. Behind them the blanket of small houses and the sporadic tall apartment buildings began to melt. Of course, the world itself doesn't liquefy at this speed – the bamboo remains just as upright, the houses just as stable. It was me doing the muddling. Not only were my eyes incapable of processing the images, I was on a shaky foundation. I was heading home, flying in fact, and shaking inside as much as the train was now rattling.

I stood up to video the display with my iPhone. The digits climbed smoothly to 341 and then paused. I'd joined the human movement that no longer feels it is enough to just experience something, I had to capture it in some way. Perhaps we record so much because the things around us are moving too fast for us to get a good understanding with just our eyes.

Most days of our species' existence were spent in the same village, hunting the same beast, gathering the same berries, toiling in the same field, walking behind the same herd. It's not hard to work out your speed from those images. But now? My day had started by throwing open the curtains for a fortieth-floor view across the financial capital of China, then laps in the hotel's overheated underground pool, pressing a cab though the relentlessly chaotic Shanghai morning traffic, to just make a ride on the world's fastest train. If all went to plan, I would next pass through a steel and polished concrete monolith of an airport, fly over most of Asia, find out if Meg Ryan did escape the kidnappers in a South American forest, drink the same chardonnay as the flight up, and wonder how the fish could possibly be 'sustainably harvested'. I'd land in the Pacific-air blessed city of Sydney, where a Pakistani-Australian taxi driver would speed me to my house. I would run in, go upstairs and kiss my daughters as they slept, telling myself they'd notice. The day would end when I pressed the button on the automated curtain system, sending both the decorative outer layer and the blackout backing gliding to a close.

I am not sure we evolved to be able to comprehend days like this, or days vaguely as complex.

Our train's cruising speed remained at 341 kilometres per hour, our altitude just two inches, and if the deceleration was any indication, our journey was disappointingly short. The airport loomed up quickly and as the power seeped out of the magnets the train was lowered onto cushioned rollers and we came to a stop like nothing had ever happened. There was no panting horse at the front of the dray, no steaming locomotive or jet engine winding down as testimony to the drive that had got us here. It was as if we'd been beamed to this spot, which in a way I guess we had been. In total, the ride had been just seven minutes long.

I stepped off the gleaming train onto the spotless platform. If this was the future, it sure was clean. Mighty warm, though. My assistant in Sydney was sending me increasingly urgent text messages urging me to hurry as I could still theoretically make my plane. I pulled my bags down the platform and broke into a fast shuffle mixed with short runs. Besides, my earlier dash had already ruined this shirt.

I stopped to scan the departures board, a series of vertically aligned monitors listing flight times and their gates. I searched up and down for my flight, not helped by its alternating between Latin and Chinese characters. Flights were shown in escalating colours of stay-calm green, hurry-up orange and start-sprinting red. My flight flashed blue. Blue? Blue is not even an emotion I understand in travel terms. It turned out, as detailed in yet another column, that blue meant delayed; and our flight was flashing-blue delayed, which meant an indefinite wait, but in any case no shorter than five hours. I'd travelled on the world's fastest train and yet I could have leisurely ridden a bike, perhaps stopped for breakfast, certainly saved my shirt, and still made my departure.

The delay extended to eight hours, a life pause that gave me time to think about my future. Also to change into a t-shirt.

Where to next?

Dividing the family didn't seem a great option and perhaps it would be better to go to Europe and hide than face my private failure in the public glare. But quitting wasn't my style either. There wasn't a path here that I could have anticipated when I took on this fantastic job six months earlier. Where was that high school Careers Advisor now? Nothing in my past prepared me for this decision.

When finally on the plane, I took my seat without talking to the person next to me. After meal service and all announcements, the other passengers either placed the domed headphones over their ears or eyeshades over their eyes. The cabin staff disappeared, slipping away through the curtains that covered the brightly lit galley and indiscreetly divided the classes.

I'd been moving fast all my life, lots of it through the sky. Flying always has an undercarriage of sadness for me. Everyone, it seems, is either leaving ones they love or heading towards them. We are sitting close together in the awareness of the distance between us. Travel is the separation and joining of people who love each other, where the act is performed in the company of strangers. Maybe that's why I've moved so much: because it includes a lot of sad, an emotion in which I sit comfortably.

Silence enveloped the cabin and I opened my laptop. For good measure, I also turned on the inflight entertainment system, found the correct Meg Ryan romantic adventure I'd started on the way up, and skipped past the bit I could remember. My computer is the last version of the Macs to be made without a solid-state drive, which means it has a whizzing memory disk and a small fan to cool it. Somewhere in my travels, I'd given the fan a knock, so mine spins slightly louder than Steve Jobs had intended. In the quiet confines of the cabin, the fan's soft whir was the loudest noise.

Eclipsed only by my tapping when I began to compose my resignation letter.

V I

Why Are We Here?

La petite, petite, Briche.

When I woke it was 8 am, and still pitch black; the air was somehow colder and definitely French.

In truth, I didn't as much wake as become aware my stomach was trying to go downstairs. Breakfast smells had wound their way up two flights of stairs, proof that Mum's time off from kitchen duty had been brief. Madi's question still floated in the thick darkness, mixing now with the odour of melting butter and congealing in the cold air. I lay still to see if any clarity would magically emerge.

Perhaps she'd asked it without knowing its full power, as the issues it raised begged answers for the division of our family, queried the choice of this isolated location, and stretched to the essence of existential doubt. Any one of these was currently enough to bring me to my knees. Not that all of these were mine to address now, but I knew, sooner rather than later, I had to help the girls understand why half our family was sleeping in one bed in their grandmother's barely-heated attic bedroom. I reckoned I had until the end of breakfast to come up with something.

I slid out of bed, careful not to let the warm air escape and, on account of the roof beams, kept my head low. The girls lay motionless inside the goose-feather dome we had warmed all night. Figuring that they'd be most comfortable if they got dressed within the cocoon, I picked up the girls' clothes, turned them right side out, and tucked them under the covers to defrost.

I left the room to wake up in the shower and to search for some sort of a response to give Madi. Two skylights had been cut into the house's angled roof during its renovation. One of the benefits of being my height in a converted roof space is that the skylights are low enough for me to see outside. Last night's description of this tiny village had been provided without visual aids – a mix of lefty politics, steam-punk economics and layman's French history. This morning we'd be able to match the built environment with the hopes I'd held for it before I arrived, the description provided by Frits, and the concoction I made of it all in the dreams of our tumultuous night.

Sunrise was still half an hour away, yet there was enough light in the grey for me to see into the leafless forest behind the house, in which I could make out the top-heavy shape of the water tower. It had a base of carved stone and a top clad in wood palings that were detailed to make it resemble a fort. Behind it stood the three triangles of a barn end, the resolution of a giant farm building that was now missing. In the further distance, the outline of a large château. Figuring that a faux-militaristic water source, a fallen-down barn and a fancy house we wouldn't be living in weren't going to give me any answers, I walked next door to get dressed.

I pulled on yesterday's clothes in the room that would become mine – as soon as my child-warming services were no longer required. From this window, I could see across most of

La Petite Briche. From this height it was clear Google had done a good job, and it was indeed laid out in the shape of a capital H. Our house sat at the bottom left side. The rooftops of the rest of the left-hand side were a single-storey section that had been the main halls of the former school.

These were owned by the Australian concert cellist, Daniel Sachs. I'd been told by Frits – and I think it was meant as a subtle warning – that Daniel's house was inhabited by his twenty-something son, Ian, who was renovating the crossbar of the H into a recording studio. For emphasis Mum had added that the music was not at all orchestral.

The work was being done with the help of Vince Neoplan, a physically imposing stonemason with blond dreadlocks, an itinerant group of friends, and an even larger collection of dogs. Last night I had learned Vince had just finished a job rebuilding part of Notre Dame in Paris. At the top of the right-hand upright of the H, a pointed cap on a building indicated a small chapel, also in need of renovations, which suggested Vince and his fellow stonemasons wouldn't be out of a job for a while.

I went back to rouse the girls. I opened the curtains with a flourish, more for the noise than any light they let in. Still no movement. From their window I could see more forest, distant fields and the faintest outline of a town, its church spire providing a tiny blip on an otherwise flat horizon. I turned around and my forehead was reminded of the disadvantages of being my height in a converted roof space: rustic beams that were no less painful just because they were authentic.

FUCK!

I swore at the beams, and then apologised. They were hardly to blame: at the time this house was built, a man of my size would have been chest, head and shoulders taller than the average European man. I regretted that these were the first words my daughters had heard on waking in their new home of France, and to cover it up I apologised again, and said there was no rush. Soon their clothes would be nicely warmed, so I told them that when they were ready, just dig around under the covers to find them.

My last interruption to their attempt to fall back to sleep was to reiterate the need to be careful when coming down the stairs; advice I immediately forgot to heed. As soon as I took my first step, my socked-feet started to ski me downwards, and I lunged for the delicate handrail, grabbing it with imprudent force for its size. Thanks to the detail of last night's introduction, I knew it to be the original curved wooden barrier from one and a half centuries ago. Fortunately they made things well back then.

Standing firmly again on the first landing, I took a moment. From here I had a view out the front of Janet's house and could now see the rest of the buildings of La Petite Briche: the small stone house adjacent, a better view of the chapel, various out-buildings and the rusted remains of fences and cages. The ropey arms of vines, stripped of their leaves by winter, looked like they were holding things together well.

With the exception of the church, the buildings on the right had been converted into the home of the politically radical French couple somewhere in their forties. Roger, who goes exclusively by the name of 'Merit'oh' in reference to a joke I would never understand, is a retired electrician for racing cars, and now builds handmade vacuum-tube amplifiers for audiophiles. Of course. His wife, Catherine, is a professional archivist, who organises the records of local councils; a profession I didn't even know existed until Mum had informed me of it.

La Petite Briche was all in a state of disrepair, but by no means disgraced. We'd landed amongst the most intriguing of ruins – it just wasn't clear in what direction they were going. Was man's work being resumed by the land, its trees, vines and moss, or, out of the remnants of Cail's collapsed utopia, was an idyllic retreat being reassembled?

Now with the full picture, I knew that Madison was not going to get any visual clues to address the quandary of our combined dream. Worse, she was now going to be unsure what century we had woken in. Forgetting the advancements we take for granted – electric light from the flick of a switch, hot water without first lighting the boiler, nylon in our socks – looking around our new home, it would be easy to think we'd lost 150 years in the last twelve hours. La Briche had shrunk to the point where it had been possible to double the number of permanent residents with the arrival of an unemployed businessman and his two girls. Cail's name may have been imprinted on the tower that is – second only to EuroDisney – the most visited destination in Europe, but from what I could see, the remnants of the once world-class La Ferme de la Briche may well have been the least visited.

Madison's question arrived on the ground floor with me. I would have to get very precise for her, as she has the type of child-mind that instantly produces a string of questions if an adult tries to brush off a question with a partial answer. Did she care about the *here* in the question? I'd filled her head with stories of Cail, of science and inventions, of steel and rail. Or was it why are *we* – Madi, Daddy and Elsa – here? Or more precisely, why their mum was not. Nor their brothers. That was partly a story of a marriage coming unstuck, and partly a result of my wife's unconventional European childhood. We'd tried to manage the disintegration of our relationship sensitively, like two parents losing control of the family station wagon, careening off the highway, kids asleep in the back. 'Be quiet,' one says, 'we don't want to wake the kids.' As to the *why* of the breakdown, I could have told Madi a lot of my stories, but she probably knew the truth more than I did. Children have the benefit of perspective, even if it is from a child's eyes, while what I observed was rarely my own mistakes; my eyesight particularly poor when it came to seeing my actions.

To answer the *why Europe* part of the question, I'd have to get into another story of spinning wheels, which also had its beginnings in the Industrial Revolution. It's a story about a system to beat the house in the casino game of roulette. The system was first discovered by Joseph Jagger, a machine operator from a cotton mill in the north of England. In his day job, he operated and repaired giant weaving machines, each the size of a small truck. Jagger had access to what was the best new technology of the age, and in the late 1800s he and his small team of 'calculators' terrorised the casinos of Europe, famously breaking the bank of Monte Carlo.

In the early 1970s, the world's top exponent of Jagger's system was a professor of forensic medicine, Dr Richard Jarecki, who worked over the casinos of Europe, always with his wife, Carol, and young daughter in tow. That daughter was the girls' mother, about the age they were now.

Both Jagger and the Jareckis exploited what is known as the biased wheel strategy. It's based on the theory – one that Jagger knew well in practice – that no machine made by man could run flawlessly. Even a tiny imperfection in some part was enough to throw it off. In roulette, this meant that the balls' path would not be completely random, delivering certain numbers slightly more often than others and thereby negating the casino's advantage. All you had to do was work out which numbers they were. For this, Jagger used a team of six assistants to collect the data, while Richard worked alone with Carol. Together, starting in the late sixties, they wreaked havoc across the roulette tables of Europe. The bespectacled professor, and his glamorous American wife, reached their pinnacle with an Italian job, breaking the bank of San Remo in 1971.

For nearly ten years, Richard and Carol moved their operations in search of casinos in which they were not yet banned, shuffling between the impossibly elegant resort towns of Europe. To win, Richard would have to spend mind-numbingly long hours watching at the tables, memorising long strings of numbers and taking them to his hotel room at night. At times, Richard would work multiple wheels in the one casino for long stretches. Losses could be distressingly large, losing runs could last for weeks. While Richard had to stay to watch a particular wheel in a casino, Carol made sure her daughter was exposed to more than the lobbies of five-star hotels, flying her across Europe in a four-seater Cessna that she would pilot herself.

With that as my wife's early childhood, her plan to drive across Europe for a year in a rented car with two eleven-year-old boys didn't sound so crazy. She'd had an extraordinary experience that she was attempting to recreate for our sons. Her unorthodox curriculum was going to give them exposure to Europe at its best and most interesting. I had no experience with which to counter her proposal, given that she knew that when I was the boys' age all I'd been learning was how to dodge the punches from a schoolyard bully.

There were challenges to her plan, and we, the three left behind, were the ones living it. The girls and I would be spending our year in a place that felt a long way from the ritzy European resort towns of the early seventies. Unlike the girls' grandfather, the girls' father wouldn't be spinning any glamorous wheels. Instead, I planned to learn to ride a racing bike, and write a book, a much less remunerative activity than professional casino gambling.

I entered the kitchen, accepted a cup of hot something from Mum, and exaggerated the amount of sleep I'd managed. I was hoping for something stronger than tea, and added a request for coffee to the tasks Mum was juggling: the bread baking, omelet mixing, butter melting.

I'd learned how to faithfully reproduce 'a Janet omelet', and I'd always given her full credit whenever I cooked one for the kids. As a result, the recipe held a special place in my young family. She whips eggs until they are fluffy – augmented by a half shell of water per egg – pours the mixture into a well-buttered pan and adds a handful of grated cheddar cheese. She has the patience to leave it on a low heat (something I struggle to do) and when it's sufficiently firm, she folds one side over the other, pocketing the melted cheese within. Countless mornings of my childhood were fuelled by these golden semicircles, a high-cholesterol tradition I'd done my best to pass on to my children.

I was sipping my first coffee when Elsa and Madison entered the room together. They silently made a beeline for the table, seating themselves eagerly in the same seats as last night, wearing all the same clothes as last night, giving the impression that they'd never left the table. Their eyes were still half closed, and today's hair was wildly tousled. Some rest had smoothed their faces, and their tan was more apparent, an imprint from the Australian summer we'd just left.

Mum worked two pans simultaneously and served the omelets with the instructions to eat them while they were hot. Elsa and Madison accepted them silently, eyes widening with every bite. For now, Madi's question was going to be satisfied by a grandmother's omelet, a warm, cheese-filled manifestation of family love. Perhaps that was all that had been needed.

VII

Our Introduction to European Bureaucracy

Cheer up, men, it's not that bad.

While my boys were going to be with their mother on an educationally-unorthodox, admittedly eye-opening, but sadly family-dividing drive around Europe, I knew I had to recreate something for the girls that felt like home at La Petite Briche. Young girls, in my limited experience, thrive on a type of stability that can't be provided inside a rented Renault Scénic. Elsa and Madison had just finished their first year of school when they were plucked from Australia. They loved it and were besotted with their teacher. While they enjoyed the learning bit, I suspect what they enjoyed most was the time it provided to play with friends. For this reason – and the French legal requirement to educate all children – my highest priority was to get them into school.

Before agreeing to come here I'd relied on the assurances of Vicki Parish, who'd promised me that the local elementary school in Continvoir would 'absolutely' take the girls. With the assistance of an online translation tool, I composed a polite email explaining that I was Australian but that I'd be living in my mother's house in the district and detailed my desire to have my two girls attend Class One. In retrospect it wasn't my finest writing. What I'd actually written was that I had 'two mothers' who I wanted to school. When Google had done the translating it had let me down with the particularly unhelpful line:

> My mother Janet Holmes for the court to life 'The Little Briche' a man.

I emailed two addresses at the local Mayor's office – the *mairie* – and one for the school I found on its official website. For good measure, Vicki sent it to a former teacher who had retired to a house next to the school. I attached the girls' first-term reports (in English) and their complete immunisation forms that showed they represented no risk of reintroducing diphtheria to France.

When I didn't receive a response, I re-sent the information to all the addresses and added a few photographs as if for proof. One had the girls in neatly pressed school dresses. As their expressions were slightly pensive, and fearing that this might be interpreted as a lack of enthusiasm for the education system, I added another photo of them with broad smiles – this one showing the three of us in bathing suits, knee deep in the surf of a Sydney beach.

After three weeks the only response to my emails was one from the over-the-school-fence neighbour who relayed that it would probably be okay. 'Probably' and 'be okay' didn't do the job. I had nothing from the school nor anything more formal to rely on. Vicki tried to reassure me, telling me that complete silence was quite normal rural French email pattern. I should, she advised, interpret it as meaning: 'We are working on it, and we'll get back to you if there is a need.' It didn't comfort me. If the little school in Continvoir didn't work out, I figured the next closest alternative was back in Sydney. Our urgent task that first morning was to visit the town's *Maire* – the Mayor – to see if my request had been received favourably.

The rule in Anglo-Saxon countries appears to be that all administrative buildings must be dour lifeless structures, some form of punishment for the people working for the government. France seems to have it the other way around. Here, the town hall, the *mairie*, is nearly always the grandest building in sight. The origins of the convention lie in pre-Revolution France, which was run by a holy alliance between the church and aristocracy, meaning power was housed in the château, castles and churches. When the revolutionaries changed who did the administration, they were wise enough to make sure people saw that their nation was still run from impressive structures.

The *mairie* system is the sixth and lowest level of French government. It copied the division of the country made centuries earlier by church parishes, which were effectively the town councils for village life, the keepers of the records of births, deaths and marriages. France remains divided into smaller units than any other country in the world: there are more districts – *communes* – with self-administration in France than there are incorporated towns (the closest equivalent) in the US, even though the population of the latter is five times larger. Through Anglo-Saxon glasses, this appears to be the height of inefficiency. The village of Hommes gets one *Maire* for 789 people, Continvoir one for 476, Rillé one for 314, while the cities of Sydney, New York and London each do with only one Mayor for millions of residents. After the Revolution, a key part of its early success was the simultaneous devolution of much of the administration to the regions. Every town got its own elected *Maire* and its own *mairie*. In this way, the French people got to have their nation, but kept their villages too.

I drove to the *mairie* with Mum for support, the girls as evidence, and wishing I had Frits for translation services.

He'd said he had a few things to do that morning at home; so obviously an excuse that neither Mum nor I commented on it. The *Maire* we were anxious to visit was named Monsieur Grandemange, which Frits didn't need to help me translate as 'Mr Big Eats'. He worked three half-days a week managing town records, changing parking rules and garbage-collection times and planning the general beautification of the flower beds and parks. When not doing this, he ran an electrical sub-contracting firm. In Continvoir the *mairie* was the town's only three-storey building. Like all of them across France, it had the motto of the revolution, *Liberté, Fraternité* and *Égalité,* chiselled into its stone face. In one nod to more recent evolution, it flew the European flag next to the Tricolore.

I parked in the empty lot that served both the *mairie* and the school and I held the girls' hands as we followed the signs for the *bureau.* The receptionist directed us straight in to see her boss, who sat in a tidy wood-panelled office and showed no signs of living up to the English translation of his name. As soon as we entered, he looked up from his desk, and pointed his finger and clicked his tongue as if the combination would assist his recall. As he looked towards the two fragile girls, a smile spread across his face.

Ah, les filles Australiennes!

It was a phrase that was well within the limited comprehension of all of us and I squeezed the girls' hands firmly, partially to celebrate with them, partially to help me push back tears.

The *Maire* let us know the extent of his understanding of our language.

Je ne parle pas Eng-gul-ish.

It was clear to all that there was no point trying to make small talk, so he stood up and gestured for us to follow him out of his office to show us the school. He let us know that English would be spoken where we were going.

Aimée parle Eng-gul-ish.

The three rooms of the school occupied a single-storey building adjacent to the *mairie* and had a staff of two. We were introduced to the headmistress/primary-class teacher, Annette, and the girl's future teacher, Aimée. Vicki had assured me that they both spoke passable English and were kind and enthusiastic. Frits had added that they were also tall and distractingly attractive. All descriptors appeared to be accurate, and I quickly understood why Frits had gone on about Aimée in front of my mother.

Annette passed me some paperwork and Aimée offered me an infant-sized chair to sit in while I filled it out. I sat down, knees almost above my shoulders, and entered what information I had at hand. The rest could be filled in later, Annette suggested, including deciding on an option to insure the girls for the year. Ten euros seemed a good deal for full coverage for two priceless daughters. Before I had time to get uncomfortable, the documents were complete, and we were asked to return in two days to start school. I pulled myself up to their height and asked if that was all there was to do.

Oui. See you Thursday.

As we all said goodbye, Aimée mentioned that the girls needed to bring a bag to school to carry homework and any notes from her. They'd be going swimming in a few weeks, she added, and we laughed – me awkwardly – that she knew the girls already had swimsuits from the photos I had sent.

The radical idea that education should be free for all was another key tenet of the French revolutionaries. Like many of their ideals, it got trapped at the implementation stage by the inefficiency of democracy, and was only implemented thirty years later by the thoroughly undemocratic, self-appointed Emperor, Napoleon I. A further fifty years later, the third Napoleon extended the definition of 'all' to include females. Another 140 later, the Republic's offer of free education was being further stretched. It would now extend to include seven-year-old Australian twins who, with their father, happily accepted the magnanimity of the revolutionaries, the generosity of two Napoleons, and the hospitality of two unexpectedly attractive French women.

Bemused by the lack of bureaucracy, confused by the simplicity, and too quickly released from a month of anxiety to feel properly comfortable, I stumbled out of the school. I may also have been blushing a little knowing who Frits would be quizzing me about that night.

VIII

A Good Deal More

What happens when the village is of use to retailers
only as a place to advertise somewhere else.

The rest of today's lesson would be on French retail. The girls
were enthused with the idea of shopping – I'm sure it sounded
more fun than school registration – but Mum made it clear she
was no fan of the places we were heading towards.

I needed to buy the girls additional warm clothes, some food
they'd recognise, and materials for arts-and-crafts projects. We'd
arrived with no toys, electronic or otherwise, just two bulging
pencil cases of assorted tools of girl play. I was aware that
I looked like a well-grounded new-age father, cutting our digital
tethers and encouraging handicrafts in my daughters. The truth
is I hadn't thought through what they'd play with. Besides, they
seemed to love drawing and colouring, cutting and pasting.
They were going through paper, coloured pencils and crayons so
rapidly that at times I suspected they were secretly eating what
they played with.

The house did have a TV in Frits' unheated 'projects room', a small flat screen device that Frits boasted he'd got for 'virtually nothing' when it was on special at the Super U supermarket. Better still, in the eyes of the always frugal Frits, you didn't need an internet connection or a dish, as it gave access to countless free-to-air stations. The girls had quickly discovered that what you got for free here was all in French, and mostly regional news, which seemed to be exclusively stories about too little (or too much) rain in some region, residents of urban areas complaining about something small that had changed to their immense dissatisfaction, and lots of things about cars.

Before we'd left that morning, Madison had delayed us slightly while she furiously made a TV out of an old egg carton. 'I need a TV,' she had said matter-of-factly, as she cut the carton into a screen and used some scrap paper to make a colourful nine-button remote. She taped her TV to the wall, propped up Cowie, and put the remote within his reach. She said nothing and left the room.

The one DVD I'd found in a bag was part of the Toy Story franchise, in which the animated characters only talk when humans are out of sight. From repeated views of the one scratched disc, she'd developed the idea that her toys did the same. Her constant cushioned companion had been made with the disability of not having a mouth and she was concerned that Cowie wouldn't be able to play with the other toys. Hence the *need* for a TV. *How else would he pass the day?* she told me.

My mother had talked fondly about the weekly markets in each of the surrounding villages; describing each of their different characters, their own arrangement of stalls offering local produce alongside rubber boots and cheap socks, freshly cooked chickens and cut flowers. The markets operated on a coordinated roster, ensuring you could always find one nearby, as long as you knew in which direction to head. Some were held outside, while others were under cover, beneath a *halle*, a roof structure under which merchants set up their tables, usually located at the centre of town. By her description, they sounded like the things I knew as farmers' markets, but I guessed that as they weren't ever completely killed off here, they didn't need to be reintroduced with new branding. Mum enjoyed mingling with the locals, shopping side by side, filling their hand-pulled shopping trolleys and exchanging important gossip. Not that she could understand a word of it, as my Mum's French was, at ten words, about half mine.

Mum's stories of France were full of outdoor gatherings and invariably included these market visits. The colours were vibrant, the laughter crackling behind her descriptions. Her adventures all included humans, of whom I was seeing no evidence. In the winter months, all life had retreated indoors – as would ours, I imagined. I began to realise that the stories I'd been told of here might as well have come from time spent on a nearby planet. In winter, the towns were deserted, the squares empty, the grey omnipresent. My guide, in whom I'd placed my complete trust, hadn't actually been to this frosty version of rural France. So today's tour would involve driving through these little self-governed villages in search of some super-markets in the larger towns along the Loire river.

On the thirty-kilometre drive, we'd pass through four or five towns depending on the route chosen. Each village was made up of a continuous row of one and two-storey houses, all built with the same light cream shade of stone. During the colder months, neutral-coloured shutters were firmly closed over every window. The buildings were placed so tightly on either side of the road that it felt as if hundreds of years of passing traffic had cut each town out of the bedrock. Pressing my Land Rover through each village felt like I was navigating a series of narrow limestone gorges, steering a barge designed for a slightly wider river.

A few faded signs above shuttered doorways read BOUCHERIE, BOULANGERIE and COIFFEUR and were the last shadows of the butchers, bakers and hairdressers that had long since closed their doors. A few small stores did remain, but I couldn't work out how we'd ever shop there as they seemed to have nailed the *Fermé* sign to their doors. My mother, trying to cheer me up, promised that flowers would brighten these towns in the spring. In January, the flowerboxes were barren, and many had been removed, leaving only the empty brackets used to hold them in place. My mother – who I knew would be flying back to a southern hemisphere summer in a week – was making it worse. Her promises of warmth ahead served only to remind me of the cold of today. Looking out my driver's side window, the flowerbox brackets readily transformed into middle fingers, welcoming me with an impolite gesture.

Directly abutting the towns were small farms, meaning that a cow barn, parked farm machinery or a chicken coop could also be on the main street alongside the row houses. This proximity was once sensible town planning. The main roads acted as giant supermarket aisles stretching the length of France, allowing travelling merchants to facilitate a three-way trade between farmers, villagers and shopkeepers.

Before conscious consumers began to consider how far their food had to be transported to get to the shelf – looking at labels for the 'food miles' – much of the distance it travelled from producer to consumer could be measured in feet. Local farmers sold their produce directly to residents, as well as to local purveyors for further processing. Village bakers bought wheat directly from neighbouring farmers, and had it milled at the local mill. Residents bought table linen and other handicrafts from passing salespeople, many of whom walked the length of the country to sell different specialties. When travelling salesmen had sold out of their wares, they would simply buy a supply of whatever was that region's specialty and sell those products as they returned home to pick up fresh inventory.

One remnant of this system is the daily bread delivery. Each house pencils an order on a small piece of paper that's wedged into closed shutters. A few euros are put on the windowsill next to the order. The coins are exchanged for fresh bread by a *boulanger* driving a small white van with a brown paper sack full of baguettes as the passenger. Bread deliveries are the only remaining commercial use of the route trading system I could see, as the primary use of the roads now is for village residents to drive to the supermarkets of the larger towns.

The farms still contribute to village life by providing the perfume, sounds and vibrations of agricultural production. Windows that are closed to hold out the cold also keep out the smells of modern farming. I had our car's heating on, and the warm air was arriving with a mixture of man-made odours – mainly diesel fumes and the acidic releases from the plastic bales of silage – plus nature's staple, the potpourri of chicken, cow, horse and pig shit. While it may be a quality of life infringement for local residents, the large machinery that rattles village life allows the local farmers to participate in the sophisticated pan-European, and indeed global, food market. Almost all of the produce from this region – the milk, goat's cheese, corn – will make its way onto the shelves of French supermarkets, including our first destination, the Hyper U.

Mum pronounced its name as the 'ip-a-oo', and for once was pretty much correct. It is part of the Système U, one of the biggest supermarket chains in France, a 1000-plus store network that began its life as a farmers' cooperative called Le Pain Quotidien (the daily bread). It's still a cooperative, unusual among the publicly-owned multinationals which dominate the largest category of consumption.

The Système U is about a fifth of the size of France's largest supermarket retailer, Carrefour. Carrefour, itself, is only a fifth the size of the world's largest physical retailer, Walmart. (Walmart in turn is valued at only half that of Amazon, which now sells everything including groceries.) In this section of the country the Système U appears to have a monopolistic hold on the consumer's *bourse*. In every direction from La Petite Briche there is a version of the Système U: starting from a corner 'market' format, the Marché U, a true 'super' market, called the Super U, and peaking at the Hyper U, the very biggest in a family of big.

It is claimed – more by the French than the English – that the modern retail formats were their invention. Specifically, they point to Le Bon Marché, a Parisian department store that opened in the middle of the nineteenth century. The name is a neat double-entendre for 'a good market' and 'a good deal'.

Its founder, Aristide Boucicaut, is credited with inventing the *tout sous le même toit* (all under the same roof) multi-format retail store. The store introduced a wide variety of product lines arranged in 'departments' and featured radical innovations like fixed prices and similar versions of the same product displayed next to each other at different price points. Before this time, the consumers' options were either to buy at markets – true farmers' markets: loud, rough, outdoor affairs in which female shoppers might have to take a male chaperone to protect them from what was not yet called sexual harassment – or at the shops of tradesmen, which were universally small, single purpose in their offering, and highly regulated in what they could and couldn't sell.

While the original Le Bon Marché was small by current standards it was large and busy enough to disorientate the consumers who had no prior experience in choice. Rising from the option of one to three was a big leap. The modern incarnation we were heading to sold at least 200 times the number of different products or SKUs ('store keeping units') of the successful nineteenth-century experiment in bludgeoning the consumer with convenience.

Our local Hyper U, while far from the world's largest, was still a truly big shopping bazaar. Frits told me it was famous for its specials, which were announced over the in-store sound system. His favourite visit was when the 'special' was a cement mixer. If the perfect retail hell is designed to confuse and render defenceless the shopper, then a foreign language hypermarket has a headstart in the race to purgatory. As I entered I was immediately distracted by the array of entirely new brands and discombobulated by the products I'd never seen for sale in a supermarket before.

The juxtaposition of offerings was surely designed to disorient. The first wall was almost entirely flat-screen TVs – all showing the same Disney-animated clownfish. Next to them were positioned full-body brightly-printed synthetic pyjamas. I have no capacity to work out what is good value when the variation between proximate offerings is so large. Is a 900 euro TV desirable because it is next to 9 euro pyjamas? Or are the pyjamas cheap because they are just one hundredth the price of the screens to their left? And what about the wall of orange fish peering out of the TVs? The distinctive bulging eyes were Nemo's, a talkative fish named after the surly captain of Jules Verne's *Nautilus*, who, despite hailing from a reef off the coast of Queensland, was today in a French supermarket speaking to me in French. It was all working on some level: I was left wishing I could just curl up in the man-made fibres of the onesies and watch some television made for children.

If there were an aisle of self-pity, I would be rolling towards it. I began to feel as if I had it hardest of all the shoppers, given that what I needed was to find the ingredients to make a happy family. Of course that was absurd. I was really a very lucky shopper. I wasn't worried about my store credit, my hand wasn't shaking as I reached for the cheap whiskey, and my daughters weren't in my cart pleading for things I didn't want to buy them. Or worse, things I would buy for them but couldn't afford. That didn't stop me thinking others had it easier. I wasn't merely shopping for sustenance, a treat, or a replacement car battery. I was trying to make a house a home, to find items that would create an entire world of familiarity for the girls.

Into our lives had slipped countless products and food items that were signposts of normality – from the bread the girls preferred and the yogurt Elsa loved, to the yeast spread that both Madison and I couldn't go a day without. In many ways, the brands, the labels, the distinctive bottles were as important as what was in them. Yet here, not even the packaging was familiar, and many of the food items were entirely foreign to us.

The unwritten international standards for packaging were not being followed. Globally I knew that the cheapest items came inside the packages with the least writing, the most processed under the brightest colours (or even American flags), those that claimed some environmental consciousness used lots of green, and the most expensive stuff was packed in the darkest colours, often in black with sparse writing. The labelling here was also of no help. So many food items were wrapped in French pride, tied up in ribbons of equal parts red, white and blue, that it felt like there was an unofficial competition in Frenchness. What were the girls to make of so many products with a *château* on the label? I wasn't aware of anything being made inside the vaulted walls of such places.

The celebration of the hardworking peasant lady was another frequently used motif. What message does a label featuring a smiling woman in ancient peasant garb, breasts billowing, carrying a bucket, send my young girls about the yogurt inside? Will we as a society continue to romanticise the way things were made in the past, even when we've worked so hard to get rid of that way of life? Will the clothes of the future be sold with labels that show romanticised images of sweatshop workers?

I was challenged to comprehend many of the things the French sell in jars, and completely lost when translating the sizing system on the rubber-soled children's slippers.

Why was there no fresh milk but tonnes in long-life containers? Why so much yogurt? Seriously, how much yogurt can a nation eat?

Is it fair that one nation has this many varieties of cheese?

How can a baguette come in fourteen varieties? Isn't it all just French bread?

Why do they sell sliced bread with the crusts cut off? And – as my crust-hating girls would ask me later – why has nobody thought of that before?

The store lived up to Frits' hype and it really did have everything I could ever have imagined anyone using in their lifetime. The only exception was that I never found the cement-mixer aisle. This retail format is not exclusively French, of course, and I should have been better prepared. The system of 'stack them high, watch them fly' retailing seems to work on all humans, as evidenced by the domination of the system across the globe. And despite the collateral damage to the local area's vibrancy, there is little evidence anyone wishes that world's best practice retailing retreats from the Loire Valley.

Despite my confusion, what I could tell, thanks to the small digital displays below each product, was the price of everything I pulled from the shelves. One of the major advances of the first supermarket – besides not being groped while you shopped – was fixed prices. Now, these variable and centrally controlled electronic shelf labels had the impact of reversing this victory for the consumer. Digital price tags meant that certainty of the bargain had been replaced by ephemeral pricing. How could I know what the cost of a product would be if, by the time I got to the checkout, the price markers could have been changed by management without my knowledge or consent?

At one point Mum suggested I try to find some string beans. Apparently they were sold in little bundles, called *fagots*, in flat, easy-to-open tins. It would prove a good suggestion as *fagots* became a favourite of the girls. I hunted them down, scanning the wall of over half-a-kilometre of aisles, and found the crafty little containers hiding among the two thousand other things in cans.

I checked the display for the price and grabbed two. I was as proud as a child who'd caught their first fish, stopping just short of asking someone to take a photo of me with my catch. In fact, I *was* being photographed: as in most modern shopping, customers here are under constant surveillance. If the people behind the security cameras could have detected my delight upon capturing the tins, they'd be able to double the price while I walked to the checkout. Having done the work to find the beans, their value had increased accordingly; two cans in the hand were worth more than a couple of thousand on the shelf. I know that the retailer had intentionally created this environment where my finding the two tins was so hard, and they would know that when I found it, I would feel fantastic.

What chance do we have as consumers if retailers get to make the prices but have no feeling, while what we're prepared to pay is driven by our emotions?

When Le Bon Marché attempted to empower consumers with side-by-side choice for the first time, they were selling two or three of the same items, and only hundreds of items in the whole store. But what, now that I had to choose from among 150,000 options, is the benefit to the consumer of this level of choice? I was being put in fight or flight mode, constantly fearing the retailer was playing some sort of trick on me with the size of the product, the expiry date on the special offer items, the multipack combinations that are good value but more than I really need.

Even the surroundings had a degree of theatricality that I knew was fake but kept wanting to believe was authentic. Each section of the supermarket offered the promise of familiarity – the bread section was made out to look like a bakery, the meat section a butcher's shop, and so on. I was embracing this theatre, willingly giving in to a frequent suspension of disbelief, readily embracing it to add value to the product I was buying. Yet I couldn't relax. I was aware that all traps combine the lure of the familiar with a snare of some sort, and I was equally conscious that someone else was controlling this transaction.

It's never a fair competition, vendor on shopper. The different sections in a supermarket might be built like little shops, but they are missing the shopkeeper. The bakery may be decorated in faux wood, but there is no real baker. When employees are to be seen, they are mere shelf-stackers, with their backs to you. Their interaction is with the device that 'serves' you: the shelves.

Human contact has been replaced by the cold comfort of choice and an illusion that the pricing is in your favour. It's a selection process that starts at knee level, requiring you to bend over, and rises until the products hang over you like a Jenga tower, threatening to come down and humiliate you in front of your fellow shoppers. No wonder the shelf space at eye level is most highly sought by suppliers – it's the only ledge the shopper feels they can safely reach.

The modern supermarket shows all the signs of its heritage, displaying the traits of its forebears – a visual combination of the village market and the single-offering specialty shop. Even the announcements over the in-store speaker are like the hollering of travelling salesmen hawking specials. However, instead of paying after each purchase – which allows you to track your spending – you only get the bill at the very end, long after you've lost track of your budget. Worse, any queue behind you is pointed with impatience and judgement, and it's not designed to give any privacy to re-evaluate your purchases.

Like a market, people do walk around, but here we are pushing rather than pulling a trolley, greeting each other not with our fronts, but with our quarry on display in our glistening metal carts. Instead of standing with fellow consumers gathering and sharing helpful information, the modern shopping environment engenders no noticeable solidarity among shoppers against the retailer.

Perhaps the lack of interaction is because this ritual puts us at our most vulnerable. We are more than naked in front of each other: our insides (or at least what will soon be inside us) are out for others to see. We're pushing our trolleys towards each other, like giant bellies sliced open to display the undigested, still unwrapped, contents of our life.

It's an immensely personal livery one rolls around a supermarket, from our underpants to our choice of sanitary items to our preferred poisons. It's one level of intimacy to show that you've bought sleepwear here, but another to show that you've put four bottles of whiskey in your cart. Even more revealing might be that, from among the twelve varieties of goat cheese, you selected one that was neither local nor premium. With this degree of inner exposure, it's not surprising that we don't start organising a confederacy of shoppers.

There are, of course, benefits to shopping somewhere this size, beyond the fact that it is temperature controlled: the main one being price. With more purchasing power, retailers buy for lower prices, and the more stores they have the more efficient they are at getting the things on the shelves. The bigger the box in which you shop, the lower the cost of rent, overhead and salaries as a percentage of each product. Once the farmers were also the sellers; now even small supermarket chains are a thousand times the size of their largest farm suppliers. The invention of supermarkets has lowered the price of consumer goods, giving everyone the ability to buy more. We've given up community, given up human contact, given up shopping in a pack. In return we've gained the ability to buy more stuff that we don't seem to need.

Including me.

I had completely lost Mum; and had last seen the girls wandering in the direction of the TV department. I was alone, outnumbered, disempowered, and caught in the trap. I was exactly where the retailer wanted me. I was convinced that the only way to save myself was to consume: if I could just pack my trolley until it could hold no more, then I would have to leave. I filled the cart to overflowing, and as soon as I found the girls – safely being looked after by the French Nemo – made my escape.

Similar versions of this experience were repeated the next day until I was pretty sure we had the necessities: everything the girls needed to start school, stay warm and a variety of foods that they would be comforted by. In the process we'd driven through twenty small and visibly deserted villages. We'd visited three towns of great historical significance but bypassed their cathedrals, museums and château to park in the *centre du commerce* to visit their supermarkets.

We weren't completely heathen – we did try to shop in some of the remaining specialty shops. It was suggested we go there for some of the girls' clothing as they required items that were narrower and longer than those stocked in the supermarkets. But mostly we missed our target: we always seemed to arrive too late, too early, or right in the middle of the small shop's lunchtime.

Each time it was the same; I left the supermarkets at greater speed than I had entered, carrying or pushing everything I wanted, never sure I had what I really needed. I had covered the basics, layering over all sorts of gaps with things I now owned. I'd filled our life with piles of stuff that would cushion our moving to this new house. Now all I had to do was get the girls out of it and into school.

IX

A Better Space

Elsa with her tools.

I triple prepared to ensure I would get the girls to their first day of school on time. That's a level of preparedness about three times my usual readiness. I'd timed the drive to Continvoir and written out a detailed schedule for dressing and breakfast. I knew we had to leave La Petite Briche at 8.32 in order to arrive in the school parking lot on time. I wanted to warm up the car a bit for the girls' sake, so I planned to go outside before half past eight, start the engine, then go back inside and round up the girls and Mum.

There is no school at L'Ecole du Continvoir on Wednesdays. Like most primary schools in the French public system, *mercredi* is reserved for parents to organise sports and other activities for their children. Its critics say that busy parents simply resort to leaving their kids in front of the TV. But it was going to be great for me: I only had to get Elsa and Madison through two days of school and then I'd have a break to fortify them for their next two-day stretch. I can't imagine how it would be possible for families where both parents work but, as there wasn't anyone in our single-parent household who had to be somewhere on Wednesdays, I looked forward to this new schedule.

My strategy to keep the girls above the tear-line was pretty simple: break all our challenges into chunks, divide big obstacles into a series of small, highly detailed and quite achievable tasks, and then focus on the exact start and finish times of things. To help my girls, I'd act as if my emotions had been left Down Under. I would coil myself tightly and project boundless energy. When all this didn't work, I'd distract the girls with excited talk of the things we would do after school or on the weekends ahead, always with plenty of details and precise times. For the girls' benefit, I did my best to avoid any phrases that might include an emotional trigger. I avoided any mention of the word 'Mum' or 'mother'. To ensure the girls didn't think I was talking about *their* mother, I referred to mine formally as Janet. Definitely off limits were references to warmer climes, happier times.

Hey, that's Nemo, he's a long way from the Barrier Reef!

At times I was quick enough to stop myself mid-sentence.

Don't worry, girls, I promise it is going to be better when . . .

The girls could have finished the sentence themselves. I would be offering something that was clichéd and impossible to substantiate, the type of tepid assurances that parents say while searching for something smart to do. I knew that only my actions mattered, so I put my energy into getting the elements of domestic life absolutely right.

All would be okay, I believed, if I could only get the girls happily settled in school. Over the previous months I had narrowed my personal definition of success to this single objective. I believed that they would soon be consumed by new learnings, they'd fill their evenings with homework and, as natural sponges of the language, they'd help me with my French challenges. They'd make adorable little French friends who I would invite over for playdates. Their teacher would prove to be a gentle *maîtresse*, a warm support, and if the girls had any moments of weakness, she'd cuddle them to her breast. They would be content in their new school, and I'd be free of any guilt for having brought them to this cold place. With all this 'happy', any responsibility I might feel for our family disbanding would not have to be faced. I'd be released from the burden of being their only playmate in all of France and be free to write all day. Best of all, there would be no threat I'd have to return to Sydney, tail between my legs, unemployable and a bad, bad dad.

On that first Thursday, my alarm pierced the dark painfully early. On previous mornings I had helped the girls get dressed, but today they didn't need it. They applied layers of clothing – Madison setting a household record of seven layers on her upper body, four over her legs – and pulled up the matching socks they'd laid out the night before. The girls' descended the stairs safely, inhaled their breakfast, packed their bags, brushed their hair, cleaned their teeth, donned bright ski jackets and pulled on woolly hats: all thirty minutes before we were meant to depart. I knew arriving early might be as awkward as arriving late, so I invented some distractions to keep us inside for longer.

At 8.30 I went out to start the car, before returning inside to rally the troops. It wasn't needed: the girls were waiting inside by the door, toting their old pink-spotted backpacks that I hoped would provide a connection to their last school and their fond memories thereof. Janet sat shotgun, the girls climbed into the back, and everyone seemed steeled for what was ahead. For Janet, supervising my getting the girls into school was her last official task before returning to Australia. Sitting on the left where the steering wheel would be on a French car, she'd be on the side closest to the oncoming traffic, but without control of the vehicle. More than once in the previous days, as we wound our way to the Loire and back, she had attempted to steer with the handrail in front of her seat.

Next to the handle was a clock – true to Land Rover form, it was the type with two hands – but I could read it clearly nonetheless.

Perfect: 8.32. Girls, we're right on time.

It was still dark as we rolled out of La Petite Briche. As captain of our little unit, I was as proud as a tank commander, and driving a car that felt just as big. As we bounced down the potholed path to the main road, we were the only movement in sight, all of nature stiffened by a heavy frost. Passing again the dead sunflowers, this time in the same direction as their retreat. If the frozen sentries had been capable of turning their heads, they would have seen two brave troopers sitting silently in the back seat, protected by oversized jackets and knitted helmets that they'd pulled down to cover their ears and half their faces.

As we approached the junction with the D749, Janet warned me that the school bus flew past about this time, and that I should pay special attention for fast-moving traffic coming around the bend to our right. I turned left, overtly displaying my care, and drove the 3700 metres to Continvoir.

Despite my careful preparations, I pulled into the school's parking lot two dashes of my clock's dial after the nominated drop-off time. I came to a halt and looked for room to park amongst the neatly arranged cars of the more punctual parents. The rectangular parking area had room for about twenty cars, all of which were small and, as if by some local regulation, grey. In the summer I imagined it would be quite pleasant here, shaded by half-a-dozen mature trees. There was a rather formal-looking bandstand to my left and perhaps, when the weather was kinder, it would provide a stage for school performances and community events. But in early January, the murky water of the puddles was frozen, the trees were leafless and battle-ship grey, and the only light came from a cloud-obscured sun, a slither of which was just now suggested at the horizon.

I was still idling and considering my options when, suddenly, the school's impatient minibus rushed in behind us. It was faster moving than I had imagined, even given my mother's earlier warning.

I quickly put our car into gear and jerked forward. Finding a parking space assumed a new urgency. Fortunately, there was a perfect place right next to the entry door of the school. I pulled the car in, turned off the engine, and jumped down from my seat.

Nobody inside moved.

Come on, girls, if we get out right now, we'll be perfectly on time.

Pointing out the school bus that was behind us, I argued we were not late. The bus driver was gesturing to me with one hand and saying something from behind her closed window. As she continued to drive towards me, I worked out that I'd parked in the space she required to unload her cargo.

I smiled to show I understood her, waved politely, and leapt back into the car. I turned the key one click, and waited for the engine to warm. It's a requirement of all diesel engines that to start the engine you must wait until the cylinders are hot enough for the fuel inside to spontaneously combust. When the little orange coil light extinguishes on the dash, you can turn the key a second click and the engine will start.

Rudolf Diesel was a French-born German who started work in his father's book-binding business, and he'd watched as it struggled to compete with bigger enterprises that had access to the first steam-powered machines. He set out to invent an engine that was small and affordable to give artisans access to power. The initial machines ran on used cooking oil and the dust from the bottom of the coal bucket. The benefits of his system include burning the fuel more completely, making a more fuel-efficient engine. The disadvantages include throwing out a sooty discharge greater than its petrol-burning cousin. Another is that they require some patience each time you start the car. Perhaps this is one of the reasons less than 1 per cent of American car buyers choose diesel models, while more than 60 per cent of the French do.

It takes only four seconds to sufficiently warm the eight cylinders of my engine, but as I was gridlocking a school parking lot this delay was long enough for me to wish Rudolf had stayed working for his father, sewing paper sheets between leather covers with lengths of waxed twine.

As I lurched backwards, a dozen young faces pressed against the windows of the school bus. I imagined they were fascinated by the antics of the tall driver and his foreign car. More likely they were looking at the faces of the two new girls who, like brightly specked turtles, were slowly retreating into their ski jackets.

Finding a space close by, I reversed in, switched off the engine, then did my best this-is-all-going-okay leap out of the car. However, the bus driver was signalling again, now with increased animation. She turned the bus towards my new position and with her hands curving and darting in front of her, I was able to gather that I'd pulled into the space she uses to nose into before reversing into her drop-off position.

I waved acknowledgement once more, faked a smile, and returned to the car. The window-pressed children were getting a good long view of the colourful shelled creatures and their red-faced driver.

I made light of the confusion with my passengers, and again went through the two-step process of starting the car: one click to warm, wait four seconds, another to start the car. Finding a space was no longer difficult, because the prompt parents had already started to leave. I manoeuvred into one of the newly open spaces; our third in less than two minutes.

At this point, Janet stormed out of the vehicle. She said she was going to talk to the bus driver, but, as she spoke even less French than I did, I knew she was mainly distancing herself from the embarrassment I had caused.

The bus driver was clearly trying to tell us something. Even after I'd found a safe harbour, she was still calling out in our direction. She'd lowered the driver's side window so we could hear her, not aware yet that her sign language was more effective than her words.

Much to Mum's surprise, though, the bus driver was not actually complaining about my parking but trying to get us to buy a wad of red tickets she waved in her hand. Mum's ten words of French were enough to understand *les enfants, déjeuner*, or lunch, and *aujourd'hui*, today. The sum '48.60 euros' was written on the top ticket. While it didn't make any sense that we had to enter a raffle on our arrival, the reality was almost as incongruous: the lady who drove the bus was also the treasurer for the canteen and unless we handed over cash for a month's worth of tickets, the girls wouldn't get their school lunch today.

I would grow to appreciate the bus driver over the next few months, although I'd never understand a word of her powerfully-projected, heavily-accented French. Lorette was truly a colourful character. She was married to the town's one remaining distiller, whose copper pots, I heard, were in a small shed behind the school's back fence. Lorette always wore a bright sweater and cut her hair short, highlighted with a red streak or two. Best of all, she was always smiling. From my experience in Australia and the US, I had the understanding that buses, taxis and especially heavy trucks could only be operated by males. For some reason the situation is very different in France.

My mum was quickly comfortable, sharing a relieved laugh with Lorette, while I was negotiating a bigger challenge: with only a sliver of face still visible, and with faint voices that came from deep inside their shells, both girls were begging me to carry them into school. One limp seven-year-old is almost more than I can carry and transporting two girl-sized rag-dolls required super-parent strength I no longer had. Embarrassment impacts the functionality of many parents; for me, it's kryptonite.

I felt that the pressure of our being late to school compounded the responsibility of us being in France in the first place. Behind me, children were flying out of the bus and into the school, adding to the pressure I was applying to myself.

There is an immutable law of physics, something I learned in high school, which states that as you increase the pressure on anything its temperature increases. (Since leaving school, I'd learned that the rule also applies to the human heart.) Increase the pressure enough, and it spontaneously combusts. That point of combustion, different for all substances, is called the temperature of auto-ignition. I don't know what the temperature is at which a human auto-ignites, but as the pressure grew on me, I felt like I was fast approaching it.

Trick number one in the unwritten *Twins' Handbook of Parental Disarmament* is for one twin to make a reasonable request that, when added to the otherwise reasonable request of your twin, combines to make the situation impossible. Together they had created a perfect impasse. I wasted at least a click of the car's clock trying to plead with them, until I remembered my strategy. Breaking the task into chunks, I outlined a compromise plan in excessive detail: I would separately pick each of them up from inside the car – first Elsa, then Madi – and lower them to the ground with their bags still attached. I would hold Elsa's right hand with my left, Madi's left with my right, and we'd march together to the school.

A hand-to-hand connection is one of humankind's most useful links, opposing thumbs make a palm-to-palm bond that is highly functional and deeply emotional. Elsa's hand was thin, wiry, warm, and she squeezed tight. Very tight. Madi's grip was looser, softer and cooler. If I close my eyes, my hand knows how to read my daughters' heart-rates through their palms. Both of the girls' little brave hearts were beating at the cadence of a track sprinter.

My final push was successful, and we safely made the fifteen steps through the exterior door of the school. I'd made it, but could feel the rising tension coming from the girls. The most difficult part of my day was complete, but theirs was about to begin. My focus had been solely on getting them to school – all my energy, manic distractions and fumbling miscommunications had worked merely to suppress their stress. It hadn't gone away, and by working to push it down I could see I'd been priming a charge.

The first room we passed through was a sort of indoor play-area-cum-arts-space. To our right were large windows to an outside play-area full of coarse sand and industrial-grade scooters. To the left was the courtyard with the *mairie* building and the canteen for the children who didn't get picked up by their parents at lunchtime. For drop-off, I was allowed to bring Elsa and Madison inside, help them hang up their coats, their scarves and an extra jumper or two. I did it with exaggerated precision and then led them to the classroom door, where regulations said I must pause.

Aimée taught eighteen students from the ages of five to eight which meant that – allowing for one boy distracted with a building project – there were thirty-six eyes on the girls when we reached the doorway of their classroom. All activity stopped for a moment as I looked towards our destination, a joint desk that Aimée was indicating was the girls' to share. Immediately, and without appearing to take any steps, a group of girls formed a line next to Elsa and Madi's desk where they stood eagerly, but orderly, keen to be among the first to introduce themselves.

One or two boys looked instantly smitten, although in most cases they went back to what they were doing; swapping cards or pulling them from the hand of a classmate. The boy in the corner still hadn't noticed anything and continued to build a sculpture, which I could now see involved balancing sharpened pencils on other sharpened pencils. Aimée beckoned me in, suggesting that the rule preventing parents entering the class-room didn't apply to the first day for those bringing twins from Australia.

It was a pretty standard school room: three rows of three double tables facing two blackboards. There was a large wooden desk at the back that was Aimée's, stacked so high with papers and books that it resembled a horizontal filing cabinet and vertical library. A computer from the last century was against the back wall, which might have been some use had there been a cord to plug it in. Around us were the familiar items of classroom decoration: cut-out letters, drawings in primary colours and writing samples in simple script. The only difference from other classrooms that the girls had visited was, not surprisingly, everything was written in French. Neat, carefully displayed, utterly incomprehensible French. There was a big map. Of France. There was one framed photograph – of the President of France – and examples of the three types of approved handwriting styles. All in French, and, worse, much of it was in the tangled government-approved cursive that they'd have to soon learn. My last French lessons had been twenty-two years earlier, so all I could recognise were half-a-dozen of the words, plus the man posing as the Republic's twenty-third President.

My immediate impression was that the children of the class were shorter than I was used to, mostly dark haired, and with more intensity in their gaze than I was accustomed to in humans of their size. I knew they were just little kids, but we may as well have been under an x-ray. Elsa, Madison and I shuffled across the room as one, a six-legged beast, clinging tightly to each other, heads in a fog of emotions. Fortunately, there was lots of natural light streaming in from the plentiful windows behind Aimée.

Maîtresse Aimée had her long brown hair pulled back, and she wore a tight, short-sleeved, and perfectly professional, cotton dress. Already in demand, *Maîtresse, Maîtresse* was the constant call from her charges. She was the sun around which all the activity of this room orbited. Her arms showed a strength rarely seen in amateurs that, I later learned, came from training four horses before school each day.

The girls and I were each coping in our own individual way. In situations like this I tend to smile a lot and look everyone in the eyes for encouragement or signs of danger. Elsa can steel her resolve for the most difficult task, shutting herself off to outside

influences and just staring, blankly. Madison does a version of
the opposite: letting all her emotions show through her face, in
its colour and in her moist eyes.

Aimée cut a path towards us. I let go of Madi's hand and
extended mine to shake Aimée's. I had added my own heat
when I'd been holding Madi's hand, and our grip had long gone
past clammy. As my palm met Aimée's, I immediately apologised for the perspiration by blaming it on Madison. While
Aimée might not have understood me, I knew Madison knew
I'd tried to blame her, and I tried to take back my Judasian
betrayal. That didn't come out clearly either. It didn't matter.
Aimée hadn't noticed my hand at all, her eyes down and kind
towards the girls.

She looked up and smiled and, with a nod that I took as
being recognition for my bravery and excellence in the line of
duty, indicated that I must leave the classroom now that the
girls had made it to their desk.

I turned on my heels and headed for the door. Up to now
I really hadn't done anything too tough in France; standard if
slightly confused consumer activity and meandering tourist-
level travel. But as I turned my back, I realised I was about to
desert the girls and my heart sank. Fortunately, Madison wasn't
letting go so easily, and I welcomed her lunge: a perfect rugby
tackle to my legs, two arms preventing my progress, her head
buried into my belt line. However, Aimée had anticipated the
move and arrived to prise Madison off me, then pointed to
something she wanted to show her. I made for the door without
turning around to see how my children were doing, holding
in my mind the images of them safely under the watchful eyes
of President Sarkozy and in the caring arms of a teacher who
looked like Julia Roberts – or perhaps more appropriately,
Juliette Binoche. Like the brave captain that I imagined myself
to be, I made sure the troops didn't see me crying.

I walked to the school door and into the bracing air of the
parking lot. It had drained almost completely, leaving only

the parked school minibus – its driver off depositing our money – and my car, inside which Mum was calming herself down by needling a message onto her BlackBerry. I closed the school door behind me, and it was done: the girls were 'in school' and I was 'in France'.

It wasn't quite that simple, of course, as I still had to return to pick them up at the end of the day. Shortly after 4.35 pm, the school door would partially reopen. Aimée stood just inside, blocking the urgent flow of backpacked children. Beside and between her legs peered out the straining faces of children who would be released as soon as Aimée sighted their parents. On the first day of school the girls had secured first place, a pole position they never relinquished that term. I made eye contact with Aimée. She smiled faintly, which I took to mean *J'ai fait de mon mieux*, or 'I did my best', and then she said their names, *Mar-di*, *El-za*, and out they popped.

With a touch to the top of their heads as gentle as their names were spoken, the girls were released, and they shot towards me. The dam of tears that had been held back all day burst, and rivulets were already halfway down their cheeks by the time they slammed into me. I held them tight, nearly as tightly as they held me. Then, without any trouble, I lifted both of them up and turned to carry them back to the car. Perhaps it was that my strength had returned, or perhaps it was just that a weight had been lifted off all of us.

The next day there were, again, salty tears on three sets of cheeks. The following Monday, only two wet sets, and when the girls left school on the Friday of that week, they had their hands full of things they'd painted and broad smiles across their faces. Mine were the only wet cheeks that day, giving me the chance to notice that the tears of a father's relief are a tasty mix, something like salted caramel.

X

Success Is What You Make of Falling in a Lake

Lake near Rillé. Cold, but not freezing.

With the girls into school, Mum's work was done. She and Frits stayed on for a few days, got us through the first week and showed us sights that would be more inviting when the weather warmed. On the morning she and Frits departed, we all drove to school and dropped off the girls, before I continued to Tours where she'd booked tickets on the 10.44 am TGV, the high-speed train to Charles de Gaulle Airport. Mum's flight home was in the afternoon, but as she likes to arrive at all airports well in advance, we'd be getting her on an early train to Paris. It's a genetic disposition that she had not been able to pass on to her son.

While technically she had come here from Australia to help the three of us get settled, we all knew that I was going to be a longer-term project. There sadly wasn't a school drop-off for dads, no government-mandated daily routine, or anything like the supportive arms of Aimée for me to be placed into each morning.

The mother/son time had come as an unexpected pleasure for both of us. The circumstances had opened a window, a chance connection in an environment that brought emotions to the fore. It had seemed quite natural to talk about life's multi-decade transitions while doing the shopping, ordering lunch or folding the washing. We discussed our work lives, our relationship with our respective children, my mother's relationship with her husband and my late father, as well as mine with my increasingly absent wife.

Mum wasn't sure she'd made all the right choices: she had traded a close relationship with her four children for a thirty-year global entrepreneurial adventure with her husband. She'd packed us off to boarding school while swashbuckling business occupied her and my father. When he died suddenly, he robbed her of the time they'd both planned to enjoy with the spoils of their years of sacrifice. His death was sad, a financial calamity, but most of all it was a breach of their personal contract for which there could be no recourse.

Frits had taken a very different path in life, living and working in the same part of town in which he was raised. He'd worked for over forty years for the same employer, a large insurance company, the same company that my mother's father had worked at for over forty years. Frits had two daughters, loved France, was a passionate cyclist, but had never had the opportunity I had been presented with to take a break from work. For very different reasons they both hoped I'd spend my time here wisely. Mum wanted me to slow down long enough to appreciate the place she had fallen in love with. Frits hoped I would ride a lot and, with practice, speed up a bit.

After picking up their tickets we found a table in the station's café. It was a coffee bar and toasted sandwich vendor that did a brisk trade despite its brusque waiters. We ordered a round of strong cappuccinos, but could only managed a stilted conversation. We headed to the platform well in advance of the scheduled departure, even though we knew the train would be precisely on time.

Walking through the tunnel to the platform began a ritual I knew well – mother and son at a juncture in their respective lives, marking the moment by hugging, saying goodbye, and at least one person shedding a tear. The difference was that, this time, I was the one staying behind. On previous occasions it had been the adventurous son heading off – the first day of my primary school, all the way down the end of our street, then boarding school on the other side of Australia, then university halfway around the world.

We both knew we were toting multi-generational emotional baggage here. My father had been deposited on a platform at the age of seven. Long legs, short pants, he was being sent by his mother from a small town in what became Zimbabwe to a boarding school in South Africa. Travelling at an average of thirty miles an hour, the bone-rattling trip lasted three days and he only came back once a year. By comparison, Mum's train would glide at nearly 300 kilometres an hour and complete the trip in just fifty-eight minutes. Give or take thirty seconds.

The TGV is the world's second oldest very-fast-train system. Only Japan's Bullet Train has been running longer; only China's fleet is faster. The T in TGV initially came from Turbine, the type of jet-fuelled engine that was designed to power the pride of France's national rail system.

When, in the mid-seventies, fuel prices spiked, France took dramatic steps to reduce its reliance on fossil fuels and became the only large country in the world to get more than 75 per cent of its electricity from carbon-free sources. With an abundant supply of nuclear electricity, the French rail network was electrified, and the T of TGV was changed to 'train' as in *Train à Grande Vitesse*, Train Very Fast. Its carriages are thin and good looking, as you'd expect of the French, although the design was actually done by Jack Cooper, the Englishman responsible for the Mini Cooper.

The service is famously punctual, which isn't something seen as particularly Gallic. It was just a little younger than the Concorde, another sleek French/English collaboration, and its superior safety record has made it a mainstay of French regional transport. It could claim to be the fastest train in the world until the arrival of Shanghai's Harmony Express, the maglev train which had whisked me to the airport. Like the Chinese train, the TGV is designed to go in either direction, and is completely symmetrical. It has large pointy-nosed locomotives at each end, which makes finding the correct carriage more complicated than I expected.

With some assistance we found the right doors, and, saying goodbye to Frits, I promised, promised, promised to look after the bikes he'd said I could use. He went onboard, racked his bag, and took a forward-facing seat in the second-class cabin. I hugged Mum for a long time and then she rolled her suitcase just inside the train doors, placed her handbag on top of it and turned to look back at me. I thanked her again for coming halfway around the world to help me. In retrospect, the tasks we'd done together seemed quite rudimentary, amounting to shopping for school supplies and basic groceries, working household appliances, and finding the one local restaurant. But I was deeply appreciative for what she'd *really* done: soften the landing of my heart; brighten the nights of my girls. I focused on what was behind me, not what was ahead. I knew I'd been helped with things I knew something about and was now going to be left alone to deal with things I had less experience with.

I'd started to carry my camera everywhere and while Mum looked back at me I snapped a quick photo. My Canon was a full-sized digital SLR, which had been the top of the line professional model about ten years earlier. It was a remarkable machine, and was lightning quick, the benefit of which was that it could focus and shoot in less than one-thousandth of a second, much less time than it took for the subjects to compose themselves. The photograph it took showed a tear or two visible below her sunglasses, and had it been advanced enough to capture the face of its operator, it would have documented similar rivulets beginning to form down my face.

Be okay, she said.

I will be, I said to her.

I will be, I repeated, this time with some conviction.

We both knew there was no risk of war or famine and the only physical danger was perhaps me falling off one of Frits' bikes. Her concern was for the little boy inside of me and how he would do once he was left on the platform.

Precisely on time, the train's doors slid smoothly closed and the glass and steel carriages slid smoothly out of the station. The TGV passed the end of the platform and rapidly accelerated away, leaving me to look at a rear that was identical to its front. For a moment, it was unclear if it was the train that was moving forward, or, perhaps, it was fixed and I – and the world on which I now stood – were the ones going backwards.

I took a cursory look down the platform and shared a moment of solidarity, a feeling of collective intimacy, with the other bye-wishers. Each of us had waved to people on a train of which there was no longer any evidence. For a moment I wished someone would shout out 'Who wants to grab a drink? Let's go to the bar and talk about the people we just farewelled!'

Maybe I would learn of lovers separated by employment choices or parents saying goodbye to children who'd visited for a time that was insufficient. Leaving aside the obvious language difficulties I'd share my story of my mother, weave in the images of my father leaving his own mother more than half a century ago. We'd talk until we'd released what we were holding in, articulate what we wished we'd said on the platform. Perhaps we'd get to text our Paris-bound loved ones with the words we couldn't express in person. But there would be no such gathering of left souls, no chance to share what we should have really said. Instead we all filed through the tunnel and as soon as we walked into the light of the day, our bond was broken, and we all went our separate directions.

On the way home, I drove a slightly longer route to stop at a café Mum was confident was the nicest on the Loire. This is the land of nice cafés, so while that's a big claim, and I knew it meant 'in the summer', I headed there anyway.

I'd picked up a copy of the *New York Times* international edition at the train station, black-and-white evidence of the world in which I once strode. Tucked under my arm, it gave me a bit of extra swagger as I entered the unimaginatively named Café sur Loire. In the local style, it is a true café from 8 am, a restaurant for lunch from noon, and a bar for all the times of the day. I sat outside on the wide deck facing the Loire, drawn by the calm of the river and the gentle tugging of the flat-bottomed boats that were tied to the bank. Small signs suggested they were available for rent in the summer months. The sky above me had started to fill with clumpy pale grey clouds that were divided down the middle by a thread of perfect white.

France's oldest operational nuclear reactor, Centrale, sits across the river from where I was coffeeing. Building the reactor in the historically significant Loire region was controversial, and the compromise was a series of specially-designed, low-profile condensing towers. It was these that were adding the perfect white streak of steam in the middle of nature's greying sky.

I lasted half an hour outside until the cold forced me indoors to finish the paper. I noted that while I hadn't finished my second coffee, and not even halfway through the details of the world's growing turmoil, Mum and Frits would already be pulling into the airport terminal.

I was eager to fit in a bike ride before having to pick up the girls from school, so as soon as it was noon I went to the back of the café for an early lunch. The waiter/chef/barman/co-owner spoke virtually no English, but I gathered that there were two options for lunch. As I didn't recognise either from his words, I indicated that I'd like him to point on his body to the part of the animal the meat came from. He understood me and to describe the first dish he pointed to his lower back and, with an awkward twist of his face, I guessed he was miming his liver being poked. I waved no, smiling that it was not for me, and said *l'autre*, or 'the other'.

What I didn't know was that today was gizzards day: I'd turned down the liver only to get tripe. I am not well trained in eating these parts of animals, but I ate enough to be polite, using the trick that with enough mustard everything tastes like mustard. I wasn't able to finish the paper either, it too was harder than expected to digest – the second decade of the twenty-first century was shaping to be an interesting ten years. I composed a heartfelt thank you to Frits and Mum which could sit on my computer until I was again tethered to the internet. I hurried home, rushing against the twin pincers of the deteriorating weather and the school pick-up clock.

Frits had carefully shown me the two bikes I could ride. I got changed, and headed to the dark cave under the house that was inhabited by a small gang of second-hand bicycles. During his visits to France, he had scoured the local *brocantes* and the outdoor markets of Paris for particular frames and spares. Looking for quality but buying on price, he has accumulated a small collection of pre-loved bicycles. Frits is the type of cyclist who can repair anything on any bike, usually with what he has in a workshop drawer or from a piece pulled from another bike within reach. Like many Dutchmen, but very few other seventy-four-year-olds outside the orange nation, he rides a racing bike, frequently and surprisingly fast. It's no surprise that he's in better shape than most men twenty years his junior.

He clearly loves bikes but had no time for bike fetishism, the riders who worship bicycles just for their looks, people who ride with poor posture, who can't repair them themselves. Frits also has little time for the newbies to the sport, the MAMILs, 'Middle Aged Men In Lycra', the crowd that discovered cycling as the modern replacement for golf.

Many of the traditional gatherings of men have become socially frowned upon during my adult life. Throughout the ages, men have used complex structures to ensure they can convene: secret orders, fraternities and games that take an inordinate amount of time (cricket, golf etc.). I'd played a bit of golf and I understood why it was appealing to men, as it followed the pattern of these rituals. It started with talking about, then buying, expensive stuff. Better still if it was something high-tech or made of exotic materials.

In these rituals, you frequently get to wear clothes you wouldn't wear elsewhere and have an excuse to spend time in the outdoors in the company of fellow males. Often a business imperative is added to give the argument further weight. The growth of cycling as an upper-end activity has been driven by the same factors: men getting the chance to talk about expensive things they can buy, much of it made out of carbon and titanium, wear clothes they wouldn't be seen dead in any other time and be in the company of other men in the outdoors. Its advantage as a sport is that, unlike golf, it is good for your heart, and it only takes half the time.

One of the only acts of organisation I did before coming here was to sign up for the chance to ride a day of the Tour de France. The *Étape du Tour* is the one stage of the professional event that amateurs are invited to race in a few days before the pros. This year the race would take place on the section called Alpe d'Huez, still seven months away. When I'd first told Frits I was going to ride it, I'd added 'Not with Cadel', referring to Cadel Evans, the Australian cyclist racing this year, just in case there was any confusion as to whether I was competing in the professional tour or not.

I was impressed that Frits had not only heard of it, but was familiar with exactly that year's specific course. Only later did I learn that anyone who knows even the slightest bit about the Tour de France knows the leg. Alpe D'Huez is so famous that nobody bothered to translate it for me. It took me nearly six months to work out it was the *étape* (stage) of the Tour that goes up the Huez mountain. The route is selected for amateurs by the sadists who organise the professional race because it is notoriously difficult: three high mountain passes, one very fast downhill, and all at altitude where the weather en route can vary on the same day from near freezing to a baking 100 degrees. At about 100 kilometres long with three kilometres of vertical climb, it was a legitimate challenge.

Not that Frits was the least bit impressed. To him it looked like a pointless outing for expensive bikes and owners who had too much time on their hands. You could, he pointed out, ride the exact same route the day after, without paying the hundred Euro entrance fee.

I was one of those cycling animals Frits made fun of, but family ties forced him to accept me into his world. I hadn't told him the story of the last puncture I had got. I was out riding in Sydney without a repair kit, as it seemed pointless to carry something I didn't even know how to use. I was miles from home when I realised the reason I wasn't making better progress was because I had a flat. Instead of fixing it myself, and wearing my carbon-fibre-soled bike shoes, I clip-clopped down the street to a nearby bike store. I left my hobbled ride to be repaired and slipped into a cab to take me home.

It wasn't that I was completely hopeless with practical things, I was just fully captured by the convenience loop, in which it's increasingly hard to repair our products ourselves, and increasingly easy to outsource the task. I could fix my first car and my first bike, but part of the attraction of the modern versions is that they require someone in white gloves to adjust them.

Frits knew that I'd arrived with none of the prerequisites to get to the starting line of the *étape* – neither the bike, nor the legs, nor the repair skills. Even though he disapproved on so many levels, he was going to ensure I was prepared properly for it. I'd need my own bike eventually, but in the meantime he showed me two I could use, and had taken me out to introduce me to his favourite routes in the area. And he'd given me a puncture-repair kit.

The first bike he'd left in my care was a 16-speed 1983 Peugeot racer in metallic grey, with neat purple and blue accents. Until about 1985 this had essentially been the bicycle that professional riders would ride in the Tour de France. It would have been perfect for my training, if not for the issue of its size. Proper bike sizing is essential for high performance. Like a pair of thongs on your feet or trousers around your waist, while you can wear the wrong size, you just can't go fast in them.

In the simplest terms, bikes are sized vertically by the length of your legs, and horizontally by the combined length of everything above your waist. For both measurements, Frits is below average for even a Frenchman, while I am abnormally long for even Australians of my age. Frits raised the seat as high as it could go, pumped up the tyres and, voilà, I had a French bike to ride in France. The slightly forced geometry meant that my butt was sticking high in the air, my upper torso curved forward and down to the handlebars. While this might look aerodynamic, I had to be careful not to send my knees kicking into my chin.

It was on this mid-eighties Peugeot that Frits had taken me on my first training ride. Frequent cycling around La Briche had given him a detailed knowledge of every town, café, bar and business within a 30 kilometre radius. Just north of Hommes, he'd discovered a bicycle factory, doubly rare as there were no other manufacturing businesses of any type in the radius of his cycling circle. He'd visited the factory and learned that they made handmade cycles for professional riders and aspiring amateurs. He was determined for me to commission an expensive one from the factory. His personal frugality didn't stop him wanting me to spend money. I suspected the more expensive the bike, the better. He even got me the card of the *Directeur de Fabrication*, Aymeric le Brun, and put it by the house phone for me to call.

With respect, I told him I wasn't sure I would understand or physically appreciate the differences between aluminium, carbon-fibre and titanium. That was before the dizzying complexity of the other parts – the twelve, eighteen or twenty-four gears, tubeless tyres, clipped pedals, carbon-fibre rims, disc brakes, aerodynamic seat posts, terrifyingly thin seats – that were all subject to expensive customisation.

My bike in Sydney was an off-the-shelf aluminium model, marketed as the same model that Lance Armstrong had ridden to win a slew of Tours de France. Including all the ones he cheated in. I used it to get through the bike sections of triathlons, the three-discipline races in which I was much more comfortable with the swim and run sections. When I once racked it alongside the 6000 other bikes at Australia's biggest triathlon, I realised just how low end it was compared to the graphite weaponry others were using. I found an odd source of pride having the cheapest bicycle in the race. I'd brought a knife to a gun fight, but at least in the inevitable defeat, I'd be able to claim some moral high ground.

On our first and only ride Frits had pointed out a local lake, Lac de Rillé, and my plan today was to explore it on the other bicycle he'd said I could use, his mountain bike. The all-terrain bike, or VTT for *vélo tour terrain* as the French call it, is the most popular bicycle on the planet today, outselling road cycles by about three to one. Its basic elements are a sturdy frame, thick tyres and plenty of gears. It is America's greatest contribution to the world of cycling (apologies to Lance Armstrong) and it didn't appear commercially until the early 1980s.

The particular model Frits lent me could easily be dated to this period when it was thought reasonable to paint things fluorescent orange and add silver and green lightning bolts as accents. It had three gear rings on the crankshaft and eight on the back axle, giving it, in theory, twenty-four gears. However, as the front *derailleur*, the little mechanism that moves the chain from one ring to the other, was stuck on the biggest ring, and the back *derailleur* was only partially moving, I was warned I'd only have five gears at my disposal. Frits suggested that this might help a bit: given that I had to train for a mountainous ride along the gradient-free tracks of this region, being stuck in a high gear would provide my legs with an extra challenge.

Out of the basement I pulled the mountain bike. By now, Mum's flight to Australia should be boarding. I turned right out of La Petite Briche, rode into a slight breeze and failing light, and past the ruins of Cail's rural adventure. The afternoon here seemed to arrive just before lunch and today's timid sun was little match for the broken cloud cover blowing in from the north. I picked my way around the potholes, as my mountain bike was a rigid-framed version, built before shock absorbers were a common addition. The silence was noticeable, as was the stillness. The scrolling skyscape above me was the only hint that time hadn't frozen, the solitary indication that I was not a sleepwalker, or rather sleep-rider, slicing through a pause in time.

I rode parallel to the furrows of the farming tracks until they connected with the main road just outside the town of Rillé. I joined the smooth road for about five kilometres until I reached the turn-off to the lake. After a short detour to the right, I found a single lane track that led towards, and then alongside, the lake. It was getting a little darker and a little colder and rain spots were dotting my untinted, plastic cycling glasses. A small cluster of cows paid no attention to me, and despite the narrow throw of the lake, small waves were lapping at the edge. Winter rains had filled the lake to overflowing and parts of it spread shallow fingers over the track ahead of me.

The track was very firm, so I rode on, pedalling quite success-fully through water sections that were only a few centimetres deep. Eventually these fingers spread until the track disappeared completely under a wide, but shallow expanse. The surface below seemed firm, so I was able to keep cycling, even though I was technically up to six metres into the lake. Mum and Frits would be in the air by now and, depending on their route south to Australia, they might be somewhere over me. Perhaps they'd look down to check on me and, between the scattered clouds, it would look like I was already able to ride on water.

Success – something I had at times pursued with laser focus, at other times stumbled upon – has no universally accepted definition. Unless you have your world upside down, what other people define as success should be of no relevance to you, except perhaps as a reality check between you and them. Some part of me was aware, as I was riding on water, warm from all the activity, calmed by the quiet surroundings and appreciating the soft lighting, that what I was doing was pretty special. I know that if Frits had looked down from his seat he'd be reminded that he never had the luxury when he was my age of riding a bike in the middle of a weekday afternoon. But I was finding it hard to see what I was doing here in France as success. I might be good at balancing on a bike, a quick learner in the ways of French retail, and I'd got the girls into a good routine. But the truth was I didn't feel I was well adapted for this environment. I had no experience of living in this degree of isolation, less of not officially working, and none at being the sole provider for two young girls.

I had been a company director, businessman, entrepreneur, and was well adapted to risk taking. For the entrepreneur, the reminder of the risk of failure is an almost daily occurrence. Fear of failure is what keeps others away, long enough for the risk taker to make money. I had taken risks and won some, lost some. Perhaps I'd gone too fast up to this point, taking whatever opportunities arose, overfilling my basket. Humans didn't evolve to avoid low-hanging fruit – on the contrary, we grab at that which is easily in reach, and I had certainly taken many of the opportunities that appeared on my path. I had moderated myself slightly to ensure that while I was following some of my father's footsteps, I didn't follow them all the way to an early grave. Unlike him, I had kept fit, but like him I had frequently bitten off more than I could chew. Often, when I already had a mouthful.

The submerged track was getting a little deeper and was arching ominously towards the centre of the lake. I hadn't thought this through well and now had to make a decision: do I stay on the firm track or jump off the path and try to dart towards the shoreline? The water got deeper, and quickly, which made the decision for me. I prepared to make my exit by adding a bit of leg speed, knowing I'd have to accelerate across the softer grass to reach the edge of the lake. I lifted out of the seat, pedalled harder, turned right, but came to a sudden stop. My front tyre had found a sizable rock below the water sending me up over the handlebars. I hadn't been going very fast so, as I flipped over, I had plenty of time to think about my accident and its context.

Had any cyclists ever drowned in stationary water?

If a cyclist fell in a lake and nobody was watching, did it really happen?

To my surprise I was able to twist through the air and landed on my behind. More unexpectedly, the lake was a pleasant temperature, significantly warmer than the air. My bicycle shorts, the padded butt of which had further cushioned my fall, were now letting in water at the seams, giving me a spongy base on which to sit. The lake looked bigger from down here, and the cows remained unperturbed by my gymnastics. I had hit a few bumps in business and I always seemed to be able to get back on my feet. Now I was sitting in a lake, mid-afternoon, midweek, worrying if my mother could see me from 40,000 feet.

I stood up and realised it was going to be a very cold ride home. It was four degrees Celsius, before windchill, before the fact that I was soaking wet. I pushed the bike to the edge and rode off across a paddock towards the sealed road. I tried riding really fast, as the exertion warmed my legs, but the increased wind speed through my wet shirt wrapped frozen currents around my upper body. I experimented with riding slowly, which was a bit warmer, but meant I'd be going for a lot longer. Either way I was set to freeze, so I decided to sprint home. When I arrived, I rushed into a hot shower which took some of the cold off, before driving to the school to pick up the girls. Over dinner I told them the story, leaving out the parts about my personal doubts. After I had put the girls to bed with a smile on their faces, I sat down to write an addendum to the note I had started for Mum and Frits over lunch.

When I'd finally resigned myself to come to Europe and agreed to follow my wife (at a distance), I had sat with friends and business associates to explain myself. Their reactions fell in two distinct camps. The first (and larger) group were people who said excitedly that I was living their dream. All their fantasy French sabbaticals featured lots of warm weather, plenty of wine and the hint of romance.

They frequently mentioned the same two books that I promised to read (and hadn't) about city folk learning to love European country life, bravely tackling renovation inefficiencies, laughing off otherwise maddening misunderstandings, while falling for the improbable beauty of a local, conveniently unattached, woman. I had resisted coming here, whereas it was apparently a widely held aspiration. It was the type of fantasy that was acceptable for one's partner to announce at a dinner party. 'I would love to live in rural France for a year!' The more people had a capacity to do this – the wealthier, the already successful, those with fewer ties – the more prone they were to add, 'But I know I never will.'

The other reaction I got was from people who thought I was crazy, and assumed I was being deported to some sort of foreign mental facility, a self-prescribed treatment for an ailment they weren't aware I was suffering from. Some even apologised for not noticing. Out of contact, away from phones, away from the office, surrounded by that much silence, sounded to this group of friends like such an extreme hardship that I must be in a serious bad way for this to be the remedy.

To the first group I had to water down the description of where I was going. Letting them know the reality of the weather and that I would have important things to do, like looking after my two girls. It didn't help: my plans sounded like the movie version of one of the books. To the second group I assured them that there would be good parts of it – the cycling in the summer months, the local foods and wine, all the reading I would get done. I'd be writing a book, I'd add, to ensure they had sufficient tasks to keep me self-defined.

In neither camp did I find anyone wishing to visit. One friend did offer something concrete: he assured me he would be there for me whenever I needed him. He said that, no matter how hard it got, if I sent him a text he would commit to texting me back.

I'd steeled myself for this to be a lonely journey, even if I hadn't prepared for the cold. I would put my energy into my girls, and I would work on my book, which I'd begin as soon as I finished my thank-you note to Mum and Frits.

Returning to the note, I resolved to admit what happened between me and the lake, just in case they had looked down at the exact moment and seen me. I assured Frits that I'd doused all the bike's moving parts with oil. For good measure I'd also sprayed half a small can of WD-40 on the whole thing, turning it into a shining, bright-orange trophy to the perils of thinking too much while you're riding in a lake. I also let Mum know I hadn't caught a cold, thanked them once more, and promised to make the most of my time here.

XI

Easy to Digest, It Was Not

Outside the Bouff'tard.

About two per cent of the world's population live in France, and it has five per cent of its cars, but about half of the planet's roundabouts. This was something I had once read, and now something I believed. An excuse has been found to impose them on many of the intersections around here. So adored are these traffic moderators that many have been carefully decorated by the local councils, festooned with well-chosen shrubs or decorated with recreated scenes of times gone by. Driving here in the Loire, at exactly the moment when I was supposed to be concentrating on indicating and carefully taking my exit, I'd been distracted by a variety of *mise-en-scènes* featuring neat vineyard tableaux and elaborate pastiches of traditional village life.

The central junction of the town of Hommes is not one of these decorated intersections. It is a utilitarian version of the circle of traffic, a simple concrete ring surrounded by a painted white collar, the discolouration of which shows the tyre tracks of the district's short-cutters. Looking down on the roundabout is a white, freshly painted two storey building with 'BAR Le Bouff'tard RESTAURANT' neatly painted in dark blue cursive across its front. Further emphasis is provided by a border of blue neon tubes around the sign. Inside there are two rooms open to the public, the bar with wood panelled walls of overlapping pieces of rough-hewn timber, and the dining room with seats for about twenty, walls of warm yellow and chalkboards for menus. Through the dining room and outside is the neat white-and-orange-tiled bathroom with an all-in-one light/heater/extractor fan on the roof that turns on when it detects your arrival.

The combination bar/restaurant/community hub was the only colour in town, the only open venue in three towns, and the only neon in a thirty-kilometre radius. Mum and Frits had introduced me to this bright place, and as soon as they departed I went every day, moth-like to its flame. After morning drop-off I'd turn right out of the school parking lot and drive the five kilometres to Hommes to start what I was calling work. Arriving just after sunrise and often before it opened, I'd sit waiting in my car or walking circles in the parking lot behind the village hall. Sometimes the neon would still be on from the night before and on frosted mornings it would paint the remaining crystals in cartoonish tones of blue.

January here had been jarring and intense. I had great hopes for February. The girls were buoyed by the realisation that school wasn't going to get worse each day. I was invigorated by early progress in my writing. However, the second month of the year turned out to be a lot like the first, but with none of its freshness. It was also colder, giving the impression that the seasons were going in the wrong direction. Parts of me were too. By the time I'd crossed the Ides of February I understood why the creators of the modern calendar – based as they were in the northern hemisphere – had ensured we spent as little time as possible in this month. It has none of the celebrations of December, nor the optimism of January, nor the spring hints of March. Its only unique proposition is a reconciliatory wink every four years that, hey, at least I'm not very long. As this was not a leap year, all I had to survive was exactly twenty-eight days of what was, so far, the coldest, darkest, quietest period in my life.

If I'm going to have a nadir, I may as well reach it during the shortest month in the calendar.

I'd quickly developed a workmanlike habit to my writing: clocking in at opening time, organising my work station (a seat in the bar area by the windows), firing up my machine, and earnestly building paragraphs in a Word document. I positioned myself in the bar of the Bouff'tard so as to have a split-screen view of all the action. Left and outside, infrequent street traffic; right and inside, intermittent commerce around the cash register. Whenever I sensed movement, my attention would be drawn to the traffic spinning around the Hommes village roundabout.

The title for 'largest on the route' was a tight battle between the eighteen-wheeler trucks and the ungainly farm equipment. The trucks, few of which stopped, were neatly tied down and determined in their gear changes, brushing dismissively through the town. The farm machinery was unwieldy and wide, mostly tractors towing apparatus that had been designed to be pulled slowly through dirt, not whisked through narrow villages. These machines were built to rip through hardened soils, or slash fields of corn, but when set for transport their sides were folded up, resembling awkwardly bound praying mantises. They leaned out as they were dragged around the turn as if reluctant to be moved from one field to another, dropping small clumps of dark earth. Perhaps this is so they can find their own way home.

Then there were the cars: a selection of small cars and even smaller cars. All compact, and with just enough style to let me know they were European. When they nipped through, shoulder to the turn, most passed by with intent. Finally, with surprising regularity, as I'd never seen them before, were the two-seater micro cars, powered by a two-cylinder engine that is (Frits told me and I'd confirmed on the internet when I doubted him) significantly smaller than that powering the ride-on mower I'd left in Australia.

These very, very small cars came putt-putt-putting through with a distinctive sound that meant I could hear them coming well before they could be seen. Sold under the Microcar brand and other equally descriptive names, these were the cheapest vehicles available for purchase in France. Frequently these were driven by some of the largest people in the region. Despite the French war on McDonald's, the myth of the always-skinny French women, and the appetite-suppressing impact of a much higher rate of smoking than Anglo-Saxon nations, it was apparent that this part of the country was not immune to the correlated difficulties of low-income and obesity.

I went to the Bouff'tard to work. It felt good to have a routine. When I had publicly announced my resignation from my job in Sydney, I'd done my best to give the impression that this was all part of a plan. At times I might have even believed it myself. I said I'd be 'taking a sabbatical' and 'writing a book'. This sounded like a reasonably plausible detour: twenty years in business had surely given me a bookful of easy-to-digest wisdom.

I had brought with me my folders of notes – pages upon pages of scribbles. They started during my time as an entrepreneur in New York City, a public company CEO in Sydney, and business partner to a Hollywood star running one of the highest profile sports teams in Australia. My task would be of distillation, which didn't sound too hard, as I already knew the subject. Perhaps, more importantly, my plan to 'write a book' ensured that I had a job to go off to each day. I had a title, I had a plan. The problem was that with each day, with each circulating vehicle that took more of my attention, it became less clear what – besides a career-smoothing, resumé-filling attempt to get published – I was writing for.

I'd given myself credit for getting off to a good start. In the first four weeks I'd watched my word count rise to over twenty thousand. I was proud of how fast I could type, which I owe to a short training course from a secretarial school I had attended with Mum in the late 1980s. Back in Australia my mother is a big deal in the business world, and she's been rewarded with just about every honour that non-military personnel can collect. The fact that she also holds a speed-typing certificate from the Perth Secretary School is not so well known.

I had trained as a financial analyst so I could never resist putting numbers into a spreadsheet and plotting them against a trend line. I recorded the days at my 'desk' in one row and below it entered the total words as shown by Microsoft Word. Using the graph function of Excel, I was able to visually track my progress.

Using a simple formula, I extrapolated out my word count to calculate what I was on track to write over different periods of time. I knew full well the folly of this practice, having worked through the financial crises of the last few decades. In each case, I had seen the dangers of simply extending a trend without questioning whether what was a mathematical possibility was even remotely likely in the real world. If there is a bigger criminal for each of these disruptions than spreadsheet extrapolation, I don't know where they are doing time. Despite my experience, I googled the number of words in some of the books that had inspired me and added them as targets in my graph. Following a straight line out, I proved that I could finish a *Moneyball* page-turner by July, but my *A Tale of Two Cities* would not be ready until November. *War and Peace* was simply not possible this year.

When I wasn't being distracted by the traffic, I watched the slender bar and its constantly revolving, but everyday regular morning inhabitants. Behind the cash register stood the sparkly-eyed, unnaturally-blonde Colette who from 9 am managed the best business in town. Also the only one. To her left were her liquids. There were two taps for beer – one light, generic tasting, and made by a multinational beer giant, and one darker, much stronger and made by monks. Or so it said in its advertising. In a large ice-bucket she holstered capped bottles of sparkling and non-sparkling wine. There was also an oversized espresso machine which, with a press of a button, produced very small coffees.

Behind Colette, like the dry good shelves of a general store, were the cigarettes. There were the brands the world knows, Marlboro and Camel, plus the French classics, Gitanes and Gauloises. The one brand I didn't recognise was a product of the British American Tobacco company, which entices smokers with an ochre red package and a picture of a kangaroo on a yellow road sign. The colour was a good representation of the middle swath of the Australian landmass and the image is a genuine sign seen frequently across the country. If you've driven enough in Australia you know it really means: 'Here is where many kangaroos get hit by cars'. While it's hardly the sign that I'd think of to promote cigarettes, I'm such a proud Australian that an English company using our national marsupial to sell French people cigarettes doesn't bother me at all. Although perhaps it should.

The fastest trade inside the Bouff'tard seemed to be done from the glass cabinet in front of Colette. Shining like a butcher's fresh meat display, it was where she kept a collection of brightly coloured scratchy lottery tickets. Between my bursts of typing I watched Colette do her nicotine refilling, beer tapping, wine pouring, coffee dispensing and ticket vending. She was the master of the cash register, commander of its buttons, determining its display and controlling the flow of customers with her quick moving fingers and their small rings. To the early morning drinkers, her bright eyes must have been as intoxicating as the beverages she served. To the early morning gamblers, I imagined she was as attractive as the lottery prizes themselves. It didn't matter, I was coming to believe, that the chance of scoring was equally low with both – the excitement was in *la chasse*. And with both you could always come back and try again tomorrow.

I'd been educated in law and economics, followed by twenty years in businesses of all sizes, and believed I understood the processes of commerce. I was confident that I could dissect its multitude of transactions and know where to allocate the gains and losses in the global game of market capitalism. Using the tools I had arrived here with, I could tell you that buying lottery tickets makes absolutely no bloody sense. It's a losing game for everyone but the State. Worse, such games are disproportionately played by people in the lower income quartiles. The drain caused by these purchases is why their enemies see them as a regressive tax, a further impost on those who can least afford it.

In an economically rational and well-meaning world, so great is the scorn poured on this trade that you would think I'd be witnessing a mill grinding down the already downtrodden. The assumption is made that, because the players know that the average outcome is a loss, they must have a dependency, an addiction to disappointment, to play the game. But as I'd observed these rituals over the last month I had seen nothing of the sort. Admittedly I'd missed some of what was said, as my understanding of French was very limited, but there is more than enough in the universal language of tone, expression and body language to make it clear that this was no factory of repression, no hospice for dreams. It was no revivalist church either, as emotions were kept well in check, but with whatever the chosen poison, moods were lifted, tiny sanguine tales were being created inside each person.

With each purchase of the lottery tickets I could see a few coins change hands, a small investment of an amount that I knew wouldn't significantly change a person's net worth. Yet a win, changes that moment, perhaps that day and, even though it is a very long shot, perhaps a life. It appears to be a ritual that is some part escape, some part enriching the recurrent actions of the everyday. All can be achieved in some way by the buzz of an espresso, the ticklish mix of toxins from that day's first cigarette, the bubbly uplift from something sparkling, or the titillation of holding a ticket that is perhaps a pass to a very different life. Each gives a tingle of excitement to the otherwise mundane – and this has value. The few coins that go missing won't be noticed. From a distance, relying on just the data, I had been confident I could prove this to be 'mathematically' illogical. With proximity, these actions were perfectly 'humanly' logical.

At my back was the entrance to the dining room. From midday on, lunch smells drew me towards what I'd decided was the best twelve euros of food in all of the developed world. I had followed Frits' advice to come here for lunch only. I had learned that the more I followed Frits' advice, the more I saved.

The Bouff'tard is a remarkable little restaurant that takes its name from the colloquial expression for a simple meal, *bouff*, which is to be enjoyed slowly, '*tard*, itself a contraction of *en retard*. For about half the cost of a main course at a mid-priced Sydney restaurant, lunch is three courses and includes a small carafe of cheerful local wine. It was a mystery to me how the Bouff'tard exists in Hommes: not because it is unclear how it survives (it has no shortage of clients) but there is no context to explain why it exists in a tiny town of no other commerce.

Just like the village in the story *Brigadoon* that emerges mysteriously from the fog – for only one day every hundred years to save it from being changed by the outside world – it seems as if only magic or mistake could have placed the Bouff'tard here. Brigadoon-like, it appears each day, but then Brigadoon-unlike, it appears the next day too. Similar-sized towns in the area are lucky if they have a cafe. It isn't on a tourist route, it isn't near a concentration of workers, isn't the hometown of either its talented chef, Patrick, or his irrepressible partner and front-of-house manager, Laurence. I'm not aware of anywhere else on the planet with paved roads where you can make your choice of a delicious three-course lunch, plus cheese if you wish, a carafe of excellent house wine, chilled water and endless fresh bread, for twelve euros.

Today felt different. Or rather I was feeling the day differently, because today, for the first time since I'd arrived, I'd made a reservation for lunch for two. *Déjeuner, pour deux, aujourd'hui,* I had said to Colette as I entered, showing off my French and that I had a friend.

I might have eaten more restaurant meals sitting alone since arriving here than I had in my entire life. I'd spent my working career taking lunch meetings at white-tableclothed restaurants or in the office, dropping crumbs into my keyboard. The meeting I was waiting for today gave extra purpose to my purpose. It helped me feel like I was fitting in, it proved I was someone, and I wouldn't feel awkward eating alone. Not that I was the only one eating alone, far from it – more people ate alone than I'd ever seen before. But they all seemed to be so much better at it than I was. In the places I've lived, solo lunching is a sign of commercial or social failure, something that deserves an excuse.

The more I studied, the less I understood this world and its people. Their practices started at pleasantly cordial – which itself was against everything I had been taught about the French – and extended to so polite that I found it slightly threatening. The customer mix was impossible to categorise. From doors open to the end of lunch, they were as balanced as I'd ever seen in the one establishment. On one day it might be a mix of farm workers, house painters and brick layers, a wine merchant with samples, a postman in his uniform, a man of business in his suit, the bank staff from the next town east, a gay couple, a goth girl and her non-goth boyfriend, a number of retirees, and one foreigner (me).

Then there was the habit of everyone who entered the bar greeting everyone who was already there. Sometimes it was just a simple *bonjour*, to which everyone looked up and returned the greeting. Some men would continue from their greeting and go around and shake every single person's hand. Once, after joining in a *bonjour* chorus, I had put my head down and kept typing, only to realise a few moments later that the new arrival was standing above me, waiting patiently, with his hand out. I've lived in a society in which you can now sit on a bus, ride the train – or for that matter fly halfway around the world six inches from someone – and it's perfectly socially acceptable to not even make eye contact, let alone say a word to the human next to you. I participated in the greeting rituals with gusto, wondering if anyone understood how the quite normal to them was so foreign to me.

Things got even more weird when lunch was served. Small groups of people would interrupt their work day to eat together, taking time for three courses. Nobody had a book propped open in front of them, a laptop bent towards them, a smartphone in one hand, a fork in the other. None of the groups spoke at a volume that ensured you heard every word. The most confronting of all were those people who dined by themselves, happily. Sometimes customers would leave their wine unfinished. Included-in-the-price is very close to the definition of free, and where I come from lunchtime alcohol, particularly free booze, would never go unfinished. I'd also not seen groups of grown working men eating lunch together, unless it had the earnestness of a business meeting. Nor tradespeople. In Australia, carpenters were more likely to eat a meat pie by themselves on a job site, farmers to stop only long enough to eat a home-wrapped sandwich and continue on with the ploughing.

Each day, I would be sitting alone, and while I'd be able to put away my computer, I couldn't resist scribbling thoughts on my paper table mat, underlining key words, sketching diagrams. Each time Laurence came to collect my plate, she would glance over my work product, a scrappy battle between determined ink lines and careless oil spots, and give me a smile that suggested she knew I had been unable to completely down tools.

After the first month of great progress, I'd been slowing down and widening in my focus. Increasingly my notes were about where I was, and less about the book I was supposed to be writing; more about gaps in my understanding of myself and this world, and less and less of the certainty of the world I had been paid to know. For as long as I could remember, the world around me was understandable: what something cost to make, what it should sell for, who did what to whom, how work worked. I felt I understood why one country did something to its neighbour – *it'd done a similar thing before* – what drove a company to release a certain product – *we've been waiting years for this* – or why one person left another – *he's been playing around for years*. If there was one job of my education, it had been a binary understanding of the world, teaching me this was right, that was wrong, this was logical, that was not, this better, that worse. Indeed, working stuff out was my principal job and I thought I did it better than most. Everything around me made immanent sense, and what humans did in the system made sense. In this context, I made sense. And the more sense I could make of the world, the more sense I made to myself. Certainty was a self-reinforcing upward spiral. Or so I held.

Here, however, in this little corner of commerce and social ethnography, I was struggling to understand how things operated.

How much of the individual excellence was supported by collective, highly-regulated labour policies?

To what extent was the agriculture here subsidised by the European Union?

What were the returns on state lottery tickets?

How can cars so small carry people so large?

But it was the people here and their behaviour that was completely baffling. Not understanding here was undermining my understanding of me. And without this certainty, my high-conviction book of business tips began to stall. By the sixth week the graph of my word output was suggesting that after six months I would still not produce enough for *Of Mice and Men*, be a *Great Gatsby* or even provide a *Hitchhiker's Guide to the Galaxy*. I had my routine, my word count, my 'job', but there was a problem in the system. I could no more write here than type underwater. My desire to understand what was here was coming at the cost of achieving my goals.

Not that I thought I really did know everything. I was aware of the idea that at one time all of Mankind's knowledge could be held by one human, and of the debate as to who was the last person to know everything Man knew. Whether it was economist John Stuart Mill, or philosophers Goethe, Bacon or Kant, at some point the knowledge in each field bloomed so quickly that it has become impossible today to even know everything in your respective specialty. Rather, I thought I knew how to find the answer to anything, from a well-established hierarchy of experts in their respective fields. I was in a position to be able to reach an ordained expert on the orthodoxy in about one or two telephone calls. Knowing this, I enjoyed the comfort of believing that no knowledge was beyond me.

In a hope that through learning the language I'd understand this world better, I had started to take French lessons. Two or three times a week I would visit Marie-Françoise, a retired Air France hostess who taught French informally to new arrivals. She lived nearby in a nondescript house but dressed like she was a first-class passenger walking through Charles de Gaulle Airport in 1984. Everything felt peculiar here – the local restaurant, the mysterious Marie-Françoise, but most of all the language itself. Some sounds are pronounced, some not, some letters added to the next word, but just dropped if there isn't a next word. At times it felt like a choice had been made to include things that were intentionally redundant. Without question I was Marie-Françoise's worst student ever; although she did think I asked interesting questions.

Most days I would resist the lunch-scented breeze at my back until 1.30 pm, before finding a table. I'd eat the required three courses, drink my small carafe of *cabernet franc*, and finish an espresso. Then I was ready to ride. I'd drive back towards the school and park nearby, but not so close that anyone would see me getting changed. I'd pull one of Frits' bikes from the back of the car and take off for a training ride. I'd work out the time until the end of school, divide the time in two, and ride as fast as I could for half that time, before turning around. I rode fast for warmth as much as for my training. I'd try to arrive back in time to throw clothes over my bike shorts, but frequently did not. I'd prepare a short story or two from my day for the girls – something I'd seen, something that had happened on my ride.

When the girls arrived in my arms, I tried to open quickly with the story, preempting any outpouring, heading off tears from the intermittently difficult days. I tried to learn what I could about the girls' days, but they held their cards close to their twin chests. Sometimes they'd share a short story, an unidentified lunch item, a surprising way to serve cheese, a boy who had done something dumb, a girl who had tried to be nice.

Since phones got smart, I had carried one of them in my right hand. Now, untethered from the telephone system and having nobody to call (and nobody calling), I had taken to carrying my large camera with me everywhere, except when riding. Besides its technical prowess, it felt good to have its thick pistol grip curl comfortingly into my right hand. It was a cross between a paint brush and a weapon, triggering an ancient warmth that comes from feeling armed.

Most importantly, it manifested purpose when I wasn't at my work station.

I'd stop to take photos of anything that caught my eye, which things increasingly were. Even inside the Bouff'tard. I learned that if you sat still long enough to become part of the furniture, you could take photos without anyone blinking. I'd pull over and watch a farmer at work, introduce myself to house builders, stand and watch a gaggle of cows leaning over a fence, photograph a horse with its tail against a tree. Then every night I'd put the camera and my computer on the kitchen table and upload the photos. While I prepared (or reheated) dinner, and the girls did some homework, the photos would slip up the cable and flash onto the screen, each image lasting for just a few seconds. It was the closest thing to television and the girls watched it like it was their favorite show. When that day's batch would start to load, a couple of hundred each evening, I would hear the girls' pencils clink down, and they would comment – not only on the shots they found interesting, but also on the photographic fails, the blurs, the out of focus, the boring, and the 'Why did you take that, Dad?'

My photographs became the final piece in our house's daily routine, a strict regimen designed to get us through this time here. Get through each two-day block of school days, get through the term, get through living as a half-family. None of us brought up what would be happening in the future, whether we'd be one family again, or where we'd live after this term or this year. We'd learned early on not to talk about where we had come from, of Australia or summertime, and stayed well away from where we were going. The girls' mother was *not* to be mentioned, as they'd go all gooey eyed. Nor their brothers. It was a delicate limbo that was sustainable, I felt, as long as I held it together.

All that mattered was to throw structure at the day and help the girls eat as much as possible when they understood the food. After dinner, the girls would shower (well, most days, anyway) and change for bed. I'd cuddle them in their room, tell them another story from the day, making a long story out of some small incident. I worked hard to invite in a calm in the hope that when our eyes closed, a fragile quiet could settle on our hearts.

Tonight's story was going to be about the lunch meeting I anticipated with rare joy. Tonight, I would be able to give the girls a detailed image of me at a meeting. It would make our life here sound like our life before.

At five minutes to 1 pm I checked the card in my hand. Mum's parting gift had been a small book, a little pamphlet detailing Cail's rural construction, printed in 1867. Frits' parting gift was the business card now in my hand, also in French, with the name and email of the boss of the CYFAC bicycle factory. I had no idea what to do with the pamphlet, or if history would help me at all, but I knew well what to do with the card. I had typed a polite email to Aymeric du Brun, *Directeur du CYFAC*, and set up today's lunch meeting, a ritual of modern business that I was, by virtue of having had ten thousand of them, an expert at.

It felt, in a way that was very comfortable, like I was back in business.

XII

Centre de Nulle Part

Down this road, I am reliably told, is a
bicycle factory.

My lunch guest had arrived at speed and stood over the table
I had taken in the bar to do my pre-lunch writing. Aymeric was
carrying a small, long-strapped leather bag over one shoulder,
a type of man-bag that European men somehow make look
masculine. Just.

What are you doing here, living in the middle of nowhere?

He didn't wait for my response.

I guess I shouldn't speak: I run a company here.

He then left me to greet the pre-lunch bar crowd, but mostly,
I think, Colette and Laurence.

In this part of Europe, the standard greeting kisses are a
pair of mid-air pecks, but for close friends it is doubled to four.
Sometimes when Laurence greeted a large group of regular
customers it would go awkwardly silent while she'd make her
way around every person, cheek-smacking four times on each.
While she did this, it appeared that it was polite for the rest of

the group to stand silently awaiting their turn. Into this other-wise silent orgy of air kisses, Aymeric slipped in to take his turn. It's a French ritual that is finished with everyone bursting into laughter, an explosion of jolly I could not translate.

Aymeric declined a pre-lunch aperitif. I had observed people ordering drinks that came in specific glasses, poured from bottles I didn't recognise, or mixed with wine in combinations I'd never seen. I wished he had ordered an obscure French liquor so I could join him and learn how to order something other than *un bier*. I grew up thinking that the sophistication of the French was something that was innately urban. Perhaps I developed a bias that for one group to be sophisticated, another would have to be labelled the opposite. In Australia, it's the divide between city folk and those from 'the bush', the English mind a gap between London and 'those from the North' and the US has the growing chasm between the coasts of America and its 'middle'. French culture, with its choreographed greeting rituals, obscure drinks and ritualistic dining patterns, appears all the more sophisticated when it is found here, in a village restau-rant, the equivalent of which in Australia would be a roadside truck-stop, in England a country pub, America a highway diner.

As Laurence led us to our table, Aymeric let me know he had a meeting to return to, and that we'd need to order without delay. We did quickly, and Aymeric started talking, setting a stiff pace. I could see that he would not be meandering through our three courses and small carafes of *cabernet franc*. He set out the meeting agenda: he was going to tell me the history of his firm, while in parallel explain the development of bicycle technology and the interrelation with professional road racing. I kept to myself that I intended to carefully bluff that I understood the references he was making, nod at the appropriate times, and take it easy on my wine.

CYFAC is pronounced 'see-fac', not 'sigh-fac', I learned immediately. The name is made from a creative contraction where the 'CY' comes from 'bicycle'. The 'F' is from '*fabriqué*', like 'fabrication' or 'to make'; the 'A' is from '*artisanale*', referring to production by a craftsperson; and the 'C' from '*cadre*', the French for 'frame'.

The business is owned by Aymeric and an American called Eric. Aymeric told me that both he and Eric had been professional riders and explained their level in some detail. Sadly for him, the complexities of European cycling meant that unless he had won the Tour de France I didn't have any idea whether what he told me was impressive or not. Either way, his body currently looked more like an office manager than a cyclist. (His words not mine.) Even his legs, he told me, carried the hair of a sedant. His face showed the scars of a nasty crash, which he talked about just enough for me to know it was a cycling accident and to detect that some of the pain was still there. He ended that part of the conversation with a well-rehearsed joke and quickly changed subjects.

I got it now: it was a factory where retired professional cyclists worked with craftspeople to make custom-sized bicycle frames. Bicycle makers, the penny dropped, don't make bicycles – they make frames onto which bits are added to make them bicycles. 'Frame' is one of the more versatile words of the English language: it can structure an argument or delineate a picture, a pair of them can be put on your face to help you see better, or it can describe being wrongly accused of a crime. For man-made structures, the frame can either be something that is built upon or something that contains what is there. For a person, whether we take the experiences that framed our early years and grow out from them, or use them to box ourselves in, is entirely our choice to make.

Bicycles, like all wheeled vehicles, have a structure at the centre, to which the same pieces are arranged around it: the circles on which to roll it, a place for the human to sit, a way to steer it, a way to power it and a way to stop it. To the frame made by one manufacturer are attached the parts from other manufacturers: the wheels, seat, handlebars, two pedals and brakes. Remove any of those and it's either not a bicycle or impossible to ride safely. Add more of any one of those and it is something else – rideable, possibly, but not a bicycle.

It's been this way since a Frenchman invented the modern *bi-cycle* (as he originally wrote it). For over 120 years a bicycle has had a frame of approximately the same geometry: essentially two triangles that share one common side. While every other wheeled vehicle invented in the nineteenth century (the automobile, the train) is almost unrecognisable from its great-grandfather, once the *bi-cycle* was invented it proved fundamentally unimprovable.

Geometry class over, now for the history lesson. I hadn't paid attention when I had driven past Aymeric's factory, but he said I would notice the unused brick chimney that rose directly across the road from CYFAC. It had once been the site of the Mural Cycle Compagnie. Its foreman, Francis Quillon, was a professional cyclist who spent his weekends riding for various professional teams. Sometimes he even got paid. Races typically started early on Saturday mornings anywhere up to halfway across the country. It's no Australia or America, but France is still large enough for that to mean that sometimes Quillon's pre-race preparation was to drive the *autoroute* through the night before a race. Riding as part of the Bic team, Quillon won a few stages of a number of big races and was a member of the French Olympic sprint team. I knew enough to nod and show I recognised that this was impressive.

Quillon was what is called a *domestique*, which didn't mean he was either an immigrant or a house cleaner. Like their domestic counterparts, cycling *domestiques* are frequently underpaid, and certainly do the dirty work. Their job is to make it possible for the stars to fly towards the finishing tape even though they have ridden 100 kilometres that day. Up to fifty per cent of the energy required to cycle is spent pushing aside the air in front of you. For the best rider in each team, the *domestiques* take care of much of the pesky friction, and essentially 'carry' their team's star rider. With a few kilometres to go, they part, releasing their leader, fresh legged, to dash to the finish. Having helpers take care of the headwind for you is so great a benefit that even someone like me, Aymeric says, could ride at the pace of an elite professional pack. I think that was meant to excite, but I felt my pride pinched.

When elite riders are joined with their bicycles, they move as if the two are the one creature. As a young boy, when anyone was watching, I showed off by sitting high on my seat, my hands off the handlebars, and was just able to stay upright. Experienced cyclists effortlessly sit upright, guiding the bike with just their legs, arms languidly by their sides, or removing layers of clothing, cleaning their glasses, lighting a cigarette or taking a selfie with the stability that us mortals only have when walking on our own legs.

If need be, these professional cyclists can also hit each other. When a team crosses some ancient line of cycling etiquette, justice is meted out by the *domestiques*. While it is often made to look accidental, retaliation is always done by the *domestiques* on the *domestiques* of other teams. Rarely are the commanders involved – it is the foot soldiers who are at risk of a gloved fist flying in their direction, or of having a wrench suddenly jammed into their spokes. As impressive as it is that an elite cyclist can fully punch another rider in the face while riding at pace, it's another level of skill for the punchee to take the hit and stay upright, gather himself and catch up so as to swear at the other through a bloody lip.

Aymeric was periodically getting off track, more dreaming than selling, but there is nothing more effective when you're selling a machine than to be selling a dream.

Cycling, I was learning, was more of a contact sport than I knew. From the accidental crashes to the crashes that were made to look like accidents, there was a constant need for repairs to the frames. Due to his work at the Mural factory, Quillon had access to the machines of the trade. After work, he began by fixing damaged cycles for fellow elite riders. Soon came requests to customise frames with whatever simple methods could be (legally) used to get even a minute advantage. From this, he graduated to building entire frames.

With a racer's knowledge of bicycles, and a master-craftsman's skill with machines, Quillon was soon in demand to build the frames for cyclists from many teams. In the early eighties, the Mural factory was bought by a larger bicycle manufacturer, and immediately closed to consolidate production in their existing facility at Le Mans. Quillon was reluctant to relocate as he lived close to the factory, so close that his stone garage lay in the afternoon shadow of the factory's chimney. He approached the new owners to buy some of the machines that weren't going to make the trip to Le Mans. Quillon then asked a few friends to help out one weekend and they manually relocated the machines twenty metres across the road and into his garage. Therein began CYFAC – just another start-up in a garage, this one beside a French country road.

For nearly two decades, custom CYFAC frames formed partnerships with hundreds of cyclists on the professional European tour. Quillon's frames helped riders collect Olympic medals, six yellow jerseys on the Tour de France, and countless victories in the lesser known races that were run on the roads, over the cobbles and around the velodromes of Europe. Not that you would know by looking at those bikes for the CYFAC name, as they always carried another bicycle company's logo.

A few years earlier I'd run a professional sports team, the main task of which was getting us out of bankruptcy.[1] One indelible lesson from that time is that what spectators see is

---

1   The team, the South Sydney Rugby League Football Club, is considered to be the greatest team in the history of Australian sport. Although, most frequently, that is said by supporters of the Rabbitohs, like myself. I was just part of the team that helped turn it around. Much of the credit goes to people like Nicholas Pappas, Shane Richardson, Christopher Green and my partner Russell Crowe.

never the full picture. Sometimes it is to protect the privacy of an athlete, other times it's to surprise the competition, and still others it's just a case of pleasing who is paying the bills.

The same was true in cycling: while up to a third of the professional teams on the European Tour once rode CYFAC frames, the viewers were not meant to know it. Before they left the factory, every frame was repainted and re-logoed under the brand of the big bicycle manufacturer sponsoring the team. As an example, Aymeric mentioned the name of the last Frenchman to nearly win the Tour de France, Laurent Fignon. Fignon was riding for the Super U team in 1989 and lost by just eight seconds to Greg LeMond, the first American to win it. I recalled LeMond, his handsome all-American looks and later his line of eponymous cycles, but I was completely bullshitting when I acted as if I remembered Fignon and his Renault bicycle. The truth was that his Renault was really a CYFAC with Renault painted over the steel. This bit of corporate sleight-of-hand was news to me, and I was meant to be wise to deception of this type.

I wished I knew more about Fignon because he was a talismanic figure in many ways. He had entered the last stage of the '89 Tour with a theoretically unassailable lead, an advantage he had built riding a ruthlessly fast climb up the Alpe d'Huez. A young LeMond had once ridden as one of the *domestiques* for Fignon and helped him to one of his earlier Tour victories. Now they led opposing teams. To win his third Tour de France, everyone expected the Frenchman to ride the final stage, a 125 kilometre time trial, without incident. Fignon cut a stylish profile on his brightly coloured Renault and on his head he wore only a normal set of glasses – large square frames that earned him the nickname 'Professor'. His only nod to aerodynamics was that he'd tied his long blond hair back in a ponytail. By contrast, LeMond arrived at the starting line for the final *étape* wearing a streamlined teardrop helmet, wraparound sunglasses and rode in a new position, extending almost prone on aerodynamic handlebars – so called triathlon bars – a blur of carbon-fibre led by his chiselled chin.

The rest is history. LeMond rode the ride of his life, CYFAC lost its chance to win a Tour de France, and professional cycling was changed forever. What had been, at times, barely professional, a month-long journey through the French countryside, dominated by wonderfully eccentric Europeans on romantic bicycle brands, transformed into a battle for scientific advantage, a high-tech war led by ruthless corporate teams. It says something about humanity that Fignon is better known as the man to have lost the Tour by the smallest-ever margin than as the man who'd won it twice before. The heroic battle of 1989 was a story of Fignon the master vs LeMond the apprentice, of Europe falling and America rising, and, to some degree, the end of the romantic age of cycling. In the first ninety years of the Tour, European riders had a 100 per cent success rate in winning the race. After LeMond, with the arrival of new technology and better supplements, the continent's success rate fell to below 50 per cent.

Aymeric was doing a good job: I was simultaneously learning a lot and starting to feel like I understood more. Six weeks ago I'd thought 'Super U' was just a bold compliment and I still hadn't looked up where Alpe d'Huez was on a map. Yet I felt like I was a member of an elite rider's club – soon I would be on a CYFAC, riding the what's-a-Huez mountain. Even if I didn't have access to the supplements of professional riders, I could have the unnatural benefit of the CYFAC between my legs.

Aymeric knew what he was doing. I wouldn't be here in a country restaurant, surrounded by fallow wheat fields, if I wasn't the type of person who is drawn to the imagined stability of the past, the type of person who, if they had the choice, would be more excited at the prospect of buying a hand-made locomotive than a titanium jet fighter. But I could feel the story was about to take a turn for the complicated and I could sense that the crush of progress was about to get very personal.

When Quillon started building bicycles, it was still a trade employing the materials of the first bicycles: steel for the frames, metal pedals, rubber wheels and cotton shorts on leather seats. Caffeine was the stimulant of choice. But the 1990s saw an explosion of new technologies and new materials for the frames: aluminium arrived, then titanium, then carbon. Soon it was spandex on plastic seats, anabolic steroids in the veins. Quillon used whatever he could to get an advantage for his tiny factory, pushing to the limits what was allowed by the cycling authorities.

While riding a bicycle is one of the most liberating feelings one can get, the sport itself is rigidly controlled. The governing body, the Union Cycliste Internationale (UCI), might sound like a workers' cooperative but it is really a board dominated by the big bicycle manufacturers. Storm clouds were clear by the turn of the millennium when Quillon delivered to the Tour the first *monocoque* (one piece) alloy super bike frame. Lighter and faster because it didn't have thick welds joining the pieces, production was only possible in a hand-made factory. It was put to good use and won two stages of the Tour de France, whereupon it was summarily banned by the UCI. Building beautiful objects out of metal is one thing. Designing bikes so fast they get banned is another. Doing both is a rare and a wonderful achievement and drew top riders to seek out Quillon's isolated factory.

Then, in 2004, the UCI abruptly banned all independently produced custom cycles from the professional tour altogether. Just, I guessed, because they could. The theory was that the fans of the sport deserved to be able to buy bikes they saw on TV. I got that: back in Sydney I'd bought a Trek bike, in part because I'd been sold that it was the same model bike that had helped Lance Armstrong keep winning the Tour. With the stroke of an administrator's pen, Quillon's business was no longer a business. As much as they wanted to, his elite customers couldn't buy his bikes, and his business steered towards insolvency.

To help with the bankruptcy, the State appointed an administrator to run the firm. They selected a younger, thinner Aymeric, who was working at the time as an accountant to supplement his modest income as a semi-professional rider. His job was to ensure the company paid its staff their entitlements and to make a plan to close the business, selling off the remaining equipment.

Of all the temptations that men readily yield to, the rescue fantasy may have the strongest power over the male of the species. Whether it is a real-life damsel in distress, or a company in receivership, the draw to save what others could not has a special attraction. I've watched many pursue it, some be ruined by it, and been drawn to it myself. I know well its telltale signs. The first is that, unlike other pursuits of the male, it is not driven by obtaining great wealth. The goal is not simply to get a large pot of gold – more likely it is to save a particularly important pot, or, better still, save a pot-making factory that supports an entire town.

Neither is it primarily about getting the girl or procreating. Sure, there may be a lady involved, but the act is to seduce an entire village, not just her. Even when it is a business venture it is no less romantic; a battle for what is right, even if it is an idealised vision of what used to exist. It's a challenge of fighting for good over evil, of small-and-close vs large-and-impersonal. The more the odds are against you, the better. It certainly was for me when I chose to get involved in the sports team I ran. For alpha males it has a siren's call that is almost impossible to resist, but it's more likely you'll lose your lady than get one, more likely it'll wreck your home than build you one.

As nobody was around to tie Aymeric to the mast, and with some room left to mortgage his house, he joined forces with CYFAC's US distributor, and together Aymeric and Eric bought the company out of administration. The conclusion to the Business Studies section of my lunchtime lesson was that CYFAC was then bought by two formerly professional cyclists, who had a dream and a dangerous level of debt. Aymeric didn't say that, but it's what I heard.

The closer Aymeric got to the present day, the more confident I was that my nods were being correctly timed. The key to bluffing, I have learned, is to finish well as the blank stares at the beginning are likely to be forgotten.

The next trend Aymeric explained was one I understood from personal experience: the increase in the number of cyclists amongst middle-aged men. The reason given is most frequently its health benefits, but we both know the main reason is that it takes about half the time of a round of golf. Men could no longer plausibly tell their wives that they 'had' to play a round at the club to ensure the right professional progress. A weekend cycle, it could be argued, would at least keep one trim and stave off a heart attack. Men desperate to find a safe male-only domain, having lost it in the office and at the club, could now pursue it on two wheels, travelling at a pace they hoped would make it hard for the ladies to sneak into this domain.

Suddenly these MAMILs were driving an explosion in the demand for high-end bicycles. Added to this was the 'Armstrong' effect. When people in different professional sports point to the times when their sport's popularity soared, they will inevitably talk of a time when an American (or better still, two Americans,) were at the top of the game. For golf it was Arnold Palmer and Jack Nicklaus, then later (the pre-disgraced) Tiger Woods. For men's tennis it was Jimmy Connors and John McEnroe, women's tennis it was Chrissy Evert. Johnny Weissmuller did it for swimming, even Bobby Fischer did it for chess. For cycling it was first Greg LeMond and then (the pre-disgraced) Lance Armstrong. With his all-American looks, executive-like ruthlessness, private-jet-flying, rock-star-dating, Oprah-appearing celebrity, Armstrong was the lycra-suited image of a man in his prime. Even when he suffered a painful cancer, he came back to win the tour for a seventh time.

But for the fact he was a one-testicled (anyone would have sympathy for his loss) drug cheat (no-one should for this), he was the ideal male role model for a world that valued success, regardless of what you did to achieve it. Any transgressions would be forgiven, as long as you looked good doing it, gave a bit to charity, and didn't get caught. Sadly for Lance, and fortunately for us, he was only able to do the first two of these.

Now, like herds of colourful livestock, these mammals would slow weekend traffic, wearing the full body outfits of the pros. Riding on authentic professional machines, they could belong to cycle clubs, raise money in long charity races, and even ride parts of the Tour de France. Aymeric knew I was doing the latter, yet was kindly encouraging. If it wasn't so ridiculously gruelling, he might be more open to mocking. My ride was only about 100 kilometres, but it was up and over three mountains he knew the names of, and I had to avoid running into over eight thousand riders, every one almost certainly better students of the Tour, and every one unquestionably more experienced at cycling races than I was going to be.

By this stage Aymeric was running well behind schedule. He had left a third of his carafe; I had drained mine. I showed restraint by not finishing his remnants. He suggested we take our espresso standing at the front bar, while the bill was prepared. The conversation turned to this year's Tour de France, its route, and specifically its return to the Alpe d'Huez. He said he believed the route would benefit Cadel, the only other Australian Aymeric was on first-name terms with.

I'd met Cadel before coming to France, as I'd participated in a charity race with him, riding side-by-side across the Sydney Harbour Bridge. I couldn't resist doing a little name drop. But my name dropping didn't work: Aymeric simply assumed that Australia was so small, of course I'd know Cadel on a first-name basis.

Alpe d'Huez still sounded to me like another canal the French had dug, but it was really a three-star ski resort at

1500 metres in the French Alps. The reason for ending a race there is that the climb up goes through twenty-one switchbacks, an upward climb of 1000 metres. All under the afternoon sun.

He added that Cadel would be riding with the BMC team, on a bicycle made in a Chinese factory. At this point it would have been quite easy for Aymeric to get stuck into Chinese factories, mass production, or make a jab about a male cyclist from the town of Katherine, or the prospects of someone from the pancake flat Northern Territory of Australia having success riding up and over the French Alps. But he didn't. When he talked about racing, he was on the side of the cyclists and wouldn't begrudge them for the bicycle they had to ride or the sponsor who paid their wages. Nor did he care where they came from. He was part of the international syndicate of cyclists – he felt their pain and their injuries, and sided with them against the Union Cycliste Internationale and powerful corporate interests. He longed for the peloton, spoke affectionately about smooth surfaces, and was romantically drawn up steep hills. He might be an executive today, but he had the heart of a professional pedaller.

I was now completely charmed. I didn't care that there was a sales element flowing through our lunch. It wasn't as much man-man love as it might sound; rather the promise of a man-man-machine *ménage à trois* with a bicycle that was yet to be built. Aymeric paid our bill – to my surprise – and we quaffed our very small coffees at the bar. He asked the question I'd been hoping he would ask all lunch: would I like to come back with him?

I jumped at the proposition; after all, he was offering something that a lot of men find rather titillating: a factory tour.

XIII

Factories of My Youth

I was pretty good with a mic, but never 'Make
Sammy Davis Jr laugh' good, as Dad was.

Aymeric's compact, French-made car scooted out of the parking
lot of the Bouff'tard, just like its owner had entered the restaurant. I rolled out behind him in my Land Rover, feeling more
like a truck driver than ever before. We'd spent a lunch talking
about men propelling themselves at fifty kilometres an hour, for
hundreds of kilometres, on bikes weighing seven kilograms or
less. Just the seat of my car was heavier than the bikes CYFAC
had been building for decades; my car heavier than the largest
of the machines used to build them.

I grew up around factories, and knew well their sights,
their smells and their place in the lives of men. I can't say
I ever powered up a lathe (except to turn a set of candlesticks
that won the thirteen-year-old me a third prize in the Royal
Melbourne Show), nor pushed a wheelbarrow (except in some
sort of childish race), and the closest I got to joining a union
was playing rugby union (which was once a real union but

stopped being one more than a century ago.) But thanks to the role they played in my father's business, and the time I'd spent in them as a young man, I, at least, knew how to read them.

Like the maps made by early explorers, the memories formed at a young age are not always the most reliable of guides. Often they tell us more about the cartographers than the world they were plotting. If nothing, a boy's memories are accurate maps of the young heart at the time they were etched, patterns woven into the fabric of the man that would come.

When I was too young to be trusted to form accurate memories, my father left his law practice, and bought, out of bankruptcy, a manufacturer of woollen yarn and blankets. Dad had immigrated from Southern Africa, some combination of seeking refuge from the region's white governments and looking for opportunity in Australia. He boarded a boat bound for Melbourne. During the trip, a fellow passenger convinced him he'd have a hard time breaking into the structured business community of the East Coast, and should try his hand in the 'wild' West. When the ship docked to refuel in Albany, he got off and caught the bus eight hours north to Perth.

He talked his way into the local law school, was never a stellar student, but proved an excellent commercial lawyer before entering business. As an entrepreneur and investor he experienced a meteoric rise to the top. In corporate battles and takeover attempts, he took on the entrenched forces of the Establishment and is remembered for cutting a high-profile swath across the stock exchanges of Australia, the UK and the US. But it was his first business, his smallest, the Albany Woollen Mills, that he would remember as his hardest. It was these factories that formed the basis for my childhood ideas of people at work.

The Woollen Mills were in the port town of Albany in the very southern tip of Western Australia. Albany's two largest businesses were the Southern Whaling Station and the Woollen Mills. The former speared whales out of the Southern

Ocean, the latter spun lower grades of local wool into carpet yarn and made thick blankets. The top grades of wool had always been exported to the garment-quality mills of Italy and England. The whale trade was in its final years, and when the Mills went into bankruptcy, the State Administrator allowed Dad to use borrowed money to buy control. Soon the blankets became an omnipresent feature of our lives: they were on our beds, the back seat of the family car, and spread over the grass at all family picnics. In the seventies, when modernity finally reached the west coast of Australia, other kids at school had access to the fleecy spreads made of polyester, while we always had the sturdier, locally made, woollen blankets.

Wrapped in coloured paper, Mum made them the perfect present for any occasion. She'd always have a few in the boot of the car just in case she went past a store that might like to sell them. She'd pull the car over and say she was just going to 'pop in'. She'd find the owners, drop a blanket off as a sample and pitch the store-owners that locally-made woollen blankets could still be 'surprisingly soft'. No matter what she said, I still remember them as prickly and longed for the uniformity and lurid colours of man-made fibres.

I remember the Mills vividly as an imposing factory carved into the dark rock of Albany's tempestuous coast, a stone fort of commerce braced against the hostile Southern Ocean; above a curtain of wind-bent trees, wet by the spray of the turgid waters that ran black. Inside the factory, merino fleece was boiled in giant copper vats, the cross-drafts mixing the scents of ocean mist, sweet smoke from the burning eucalyptus wood, and the stink of wet wool that has the pungency of dog farts. Rattling machines stretched the wool fibres and spun it into long lines of thread that crisscrossed the factory until tartan rugs and army blankets materialised at the other end of the building.

At least that is how I imagined them, as I was never actually taken to the factory.

Such was the importance that the Woollen Mills possessed in our family that I'd needed to create images to accompany the stories I heard from my parents. In reality my pictures were a child's pastiche formed by combining images pulled from the hymns we sang at school ('was the holy Lamb of God . . . among these dark Satanic Mills'), BBC television programming with its authoritatively posh accents, and from the fact they were down there in Albany – a place so tough that men were still going out in boats to fire harpoons into the skulls of fifty-tonne whales, before dragging the carcasses back to town and then, with long-handled cutlasses, slicing off the meat and boiling the blubber.

Perhaps I wasn't taken to the Mills because it was not the type of thing parents did for seven-year-olds in the 1970s. Or perhaps my father didn't think it was the future. He went on to different businesses, always bigger, mostly further away, and seemed to be working all his life. I remember the most played activity of my childhood was the almost silent pastime of 'waiting for Dad'. Throughout his life he left his office, his desk, or got off a phone call with great reluctance. As kids we'd wait at home, wait in the office, or wait in the car. Once I waited on the cricket oval in my school's annual Father-Son game for him to arrive. Every passing car could be delivering the evidence of paternal love. Eventually a teacher kindly offered to play my dad so I could have a turn at bat.

No, it's okay, Dad always runs late. He's probably just finishing up an important call.

Of course he never did arrive, and I spent the day in the outfield, watching the cars drive past.

Not all the waiting was sad, and the best waiting was when we got to wait in his office. When the Mills had returned to profitability, he'd used the shares to buy a trucking business, this one servicing the mines in the far north of the state. I would play on his secretary's electric typewriter, seeing how quickly I could press the buttons before it would jam up. Then if I was really, really lucky, somebody would be found to take me into the truck workshops adjacent to the offices.

None of man's enterprises are as large as open cut mines, single pits of which are kilometres wide, often just as deep. At the bottom, giant digging machines with buckets that pick up house-size mouthfuls of dirt fill thirty-tonne trucks that drive up the circular perimeter, spiralling towards the surface, before rolling back down to be filled again. The mines of Western Australia are the world's biggest iron-ore deposits and are large enough to be seen from space. They had to be serviced, financed and staffed from Perth which, while nearly 2500 kilometres away, was the closest town of any size. Dad's business serviced these mines with spare parts, retreaded tyres and rental equipment. His trucks also ran a delivery service for anything else the miners needed. His facilities were a series of neatly white-painted sheds, with 'BELL' written on one side in large red letters with a black outline for impact. It was there that I was able to form actual, rather than imagined, memories of modern factory life.

I was given amazing freedom to walk through this adults' playground, though Dad would always find someone to look after me. Mostly they had another job to do, and they were merely asked to ensure I didn't set fire to anything. I'd shadow them, or they would give me a small task to do. One way to understand your absent father is to see how those around him talk to him, how he talked to them and how they talked to each other about him. The other way is to experience how they treated me as his son. While Dad was in his office, or on the phone, 'finishing up some work', I had plenty of time to learn from these one-off uncles. I was entrusted to a deputy, a foreman, or to a long-serving truck driver. Over those years I was the beneficiary of so much reflected love. Society made it hard for two big men in an employer-employee relationship to express their full emotions, certainly not to hug, and so many times I was the recipient of the unspoken respect, the other-wise-unrequited man love.

The sheds that repaired the trucks were without doubt the coolest place imaginable for a young boy to be invited into. Like most boys I loved trucks: at five I would push yellow pressed-metal American-made Tonka trucks through a sandpit, and I don't think I ever found better playmates: hard working, durable and able to withstand any load (including my younger brother). But when I was able to discover real trucks, they were much, much better.

The main route of Bell trucks was a drive up and back from Perth to the open-cut mines of the Pilbara, which took a driver nearly five days. The only turns on the way up to the mines were a right turn as the driver left the Bell yards, and a second right turn two days later in Karratha. The haul was undertaken in American-made Mack trucks, sixteen-gear, 600 horsepower diesels, twenty-tyre monsters that were hitched into road trains. Behind the cabin, three trailers were attached, making a thirty-metre-long, 100-tonne road hazard of spare parts, small machinery, retreaded tyres and slabs of beer.

In the cabin of these proud machines a man would live most of his life. The insides were pure distilled 1970s Australian manhood – or at least those bits I could understand. The edges of the driver's seat had been polished by the tanned shoulders of its singlet-wearing inhabitant. A mat made of towelling with the local beer brand would typically adorn the dashboard. The steering wheel, three-spoked and almost horizontal, required wide arms to hold, broad shoulders to turn. It was silky smooth to the touch, with finger-width undulations on its underside. Countless small lights, switches and assorted dials faced the driver, only one of which I understood the need for: the speedometer. A large CB radio hung from the roof, its handpiece hooked onto the box with the black spiral cord hanging casually below. I couldn't imagine anything cooler than the captain of this red-and-white Bell truck – late Johnny Cash or early AC/DC pouring from the eight-track – communicating in the expressive, coded, quasi-American vocabulary to other truckers as he dragged his load half a continent north.

Behind the two front seats, if you climbed carefully over a
gearstick proportionate in size and complexity to the task asked
of it, lay a narrow bed. A soft mattress, a collection of sleeping
covers, a tiny window on either side with incongruously delicate
lace-edged curtains. What went on in there, a young man could
hardly dream. But I sure tried.

The repair shop for these monsters resembled a giant's toy
box; one with an oil stamped concrete floor and a high roof
of corrugated iron, where, under a patina of red dust and iron
filings, I discovered tools fit for nation building. Strewn across
benchtops, or neatly arranged on the walls, there was at least
one of every conceivable utensil, only larger, thicker, heavier
than seemed right for human tasks. Should you need to keep
Australia from slipping into the Southern Ocean, here hung
the spanners that could tighten the bolts for the task. There
were hammers if you chose nails for that job, screwdrivers for
screws that would have to be delivered by crane, and an assortment of levers that would enable you to dislodge Uluru.

I relished every visit to the workshops. I felt like I'd been
invited into a men's club. The workmen were always kind,
generous and warm. In the Bell workshops, even a trip to the
bathroom was thrilling; there was bound to be some tattered soft
porn in poster or magazine form, and the stench would give me a
chance to demonstrate the strength of my constitution. After an
embarrassingly short pee, I could wash my hands with the men's
hand soap that was designed for removing sump oil from the
deep crevices of work-hardened hands. It was rough, sandy, like
the contents of your swimmers when a wave had dumped you at
the beach and it smelled like the laundry room at home. I loved
to vigorously wash my hands, pretending my hands needed it,
enjoying the sting as I removed the top four layers of skin.

As I pursued my career in business, I rarely had my hands
properly dirtied. I suffered more paper cuts than any other

work-related injury, and my lower back pain was from poor seated posture rather than any actual heavy lifting. Through his life my father's work was our family's religion; discussed at every meal, the household's purpose, the justification for long absences, late nights during the week. It was even practised on Sundays. My father had the brightest eyes, quickest smile, sharpest brain, largest hands and the best sense of humour of anyone I'd ever met. But above all else, he was absent. Away 'up North' at first, then away 'interstate', before being away in England or America. By the middle of the 1980s he was a world-beating businessman, and as most of the world was a long flight away, he was away a lot. Mostly, though, he was just away in his thoughts.

When I did see him, I would observe everything, inhale his presence. I loved being near him while he worked. First it was sitting at his feet, buttoned into my polyester pyjamas, amongst the leathery tannins of his study at home; then it was a chair near the uncluttered desk of his office, later in an Italian wool suit in the seat next to him on a corporate jet, leaning in to hear his every word. I'd listen to the stories of his adventures, try to get a detailed picture by unpicking the combination of smells; his inexpensive cigars, bergamot from his tea and remaining scents of whatever industry he'd visited that day. I knew he spent most of his time in an office, and later in his career he mostly shuffled papers, traded shares. He even owned his own plane eventually, and while I can't remember if he ever said anything about it, he said lots about its captain, his skill and experience. It was the way he spoke about the men and women, their work sites, factories and giant machines, that ensured I had a lifelong attachment to the places where man and machine worked together. Even at the time I knew that while most were looking at the newspaper headlines, the stockmarket highlights, I got to see the way he greeted everyone with the same kindness, appreciating those who worked hardest, and had the least time for those who traded on any form of unearned privilege. Dull, he would call them. All our family knew that four-letter word was his biggest insult. He knew of no bigger sin than being unaware of one's good fortune and then not using it well. He reserved that particular insult for boorish, entitled business leaders he met, from the east coast of Australia to the east coast of the US. *Dull*, he said, *and probably a crook*, he added, after meeting a certain hotel owner and property developer at a bank-sponsored soirée in the late 1980s in New York.

Thanks to my father I developed an appreciation of work that ensured I found the processes fascinating, the purpose apparent, the tension palpable. Man and machine, brought together by capital, working together under the same roof. He taught me so much, and my first apprenticeship in business was being taken into the factories and worksites that he let me visit. I got a brilliant start, but it ended too soon.

I was twenty-one when my mother woke me up in the middle of the night to say she thought Dad was dead. We'd just had a long and happy day; in retrospect it might have been one of his best. Surrounded by family, books, horse races playing on the radio. As a young man I hadn't brought home many medals or ribbons for anything athletic, still trying to grow into my lanky body. That day he watched me play squash and beat a local champion, sweatily playing my heart out, looking up to the gallery for his approving eyes. Dinner had been simple, quiet, with a bottle of red wine between us.

Calm cracks like glass – suddenly, and with no chance of repair. When Mum's screams pierced that night's silence, it was clear that things would never be the same. We found her running through the house in her white cotton nightdress calling for help. We dragged Dad's body off his bed onto the floor and tried to resuscitate him. Our combination of mouth-to-mouth and desperate heart massage was futile. My sister, who always has her shit together, even remembered the right combination of breaths and chest pumps. But it was already too late: Dad was away and not coming back anytime soon.

In business he had achieved more than imaginable, getting off a boat before its destination, rising to an early disrupter, a fine-suited marauder of the bastions of the Establishment. He achieved so much in work; in life he only failed to make it last. He left me half-formed, having only absorbed part of the lessons I should have. Soon after he died I took off in business myself, always moving in a manic rush for success. I'd learned a lot of his secrets but hadn't taken in the lesson about moving at a sustainable speed. This was ironic, as I was now driving towards the CYFAC factory, distracted by these thoughts, and I had slowed to half the legal speed limit.

During his life, my father had lived in a cloud of his own thoughts, even when driving. One day when heading to work, deep in thought, he was pulled over by the police for going too slowly. It became an oft-told family joke, but was no surprise to us. On the morning of his funeral, we all drove to the cemetery, coincidentally taking the same route he took to the office, in a convoy that moved at the appropriate funereal pace. Dad, we all joked, would finally be happy that we all were driving at the speed he liked.

Now it was my turn, moving slowly in one of the slowest places I had ever found myself, amongst the fallow fields, worn-down farmhouses, driving towards the only factory for miles. I felt a little like I was getting a second chance. Going back to a factory, now as an adult. Maybe this time round I would get the full lesson.

XIV

Fait à la Main *Is Not Fate of a Man*

CYFAC, where 'made by hand' means exactly that.

The indications that I had reached the CYFAC factory were limited to one sign with two bicycle frames hung either side of it. Light, fast and sleek, the frames may be perfect for a number of races, but they make crap signposts.

The factory was really a series of white metal sheds that had been joined together into one structure about the size of three tennis courts. Closest to the road stood the stone garage I recognised from Aymeric's story; it was the building in which Francis Quillon began to craft frames. It looked to have been built imprudently close to the road, although I guess it was the road that expanded, rather than the garage that encroached.

Next to the garage were a series of unassuming sheds of different shades of fading, suggesting the distinct stages of this business's life. It was surrounded by a wire fence, more to delineate the boundary than for security, and a dozen or so employees' cars that snuggled against the building. Facing the road were two doors, one metal and one made of tinted glass, which I correctly guessed was where visitors should enter.

The front edge of the reception desk was just inside the door, leaving barely enough room for me to wipe my feet on the company logo'd doormat. The long, narrow desk served as a work space for the receptionist, Katia, as well as the dock for deliveries going in and out, and a place for piling of all types of papers, invoices, letters and more paper. Next to Katia's computer was a vase which didn't appear weighty enough to ballast the two enormous roses extending from it.

Katia had obviously been told I was coming and said that Aymeric was on a call in the adjacent office, and she'd send him an email to let him know I was here. I was offered a coffee and invited to wait. I was not offered a seat, as there wasn't one. I leaned against the glass doors, holding my cup of steaming instant, thinking the plastic sleeve might soon melt.

Aymeric had warned me about the coffee, and it was worse than he'd prepared me for, burning my tongue before insulting it. Everyone else carried on as before. A package was delivered, one removed, a sparkling fresh bike was wheeled through by a man who paused to say *bonjour* and shake my hand. The telephone rang at least twice, somebody came in to ask Katia a question, then shook my hand and said hello – in heavily accented but nonetheless English – and carried on his way. I liked the place already.

I still spoke very little French, but I understand enough factory to know what to look for. Is the factory fastidiously organised, reasonably orderly, busting at the seams, or chaotic? Dangerous even. Is it organic, well planned, slightly confusing or inconsistent? When the rubbish area is orderly, you know a certain pride extends through a factory. But when it is spotless and smells of cleaning fluid, the owners knew you were coming.

A factory floor is arranged by thousands of deliberate actions. Everything is where it is because somebody has made a decision to put it there. Viewed from the outside, workplaces project their history; from the inside, it is their personalities that are revealed. The residue of the hours worked is collected in the cracks in the concrete, wrapped around the handles of tools, displayed on noticeboards, written on the backs of toilet doors, and the neat semi-circles scratched into concrete floors by the arc of a door's path and a thousand openings.

What is the relationship like between workers and management? Does the boss's office have a view to the factory floor or to the showroom? Is their door open or closed? Since 'open door management' became *de rigueur* in the 1980s, almost all managers keep their office door open. So, sure, it's technically open, but is it open like a book, or open like a crocodile's mouth?

What other subtle messages of management-employee communications can be found? And whose side does the State appear to be on? Are there messages about employee rights, or messages about compliance with company policy? Regulation rarely has an invisible presence in the workplace. Do announcements concerning company social events dominate the noticeboard, or is it fluttering with careless photocopies of new safety requirements? What is the role of safety? Is it a series of perfunctory actions to comply with the law, or the efforts of a caring manager who feels an employee's injury like their own?

I also knew how to look at the people in the factory for what they wanted to tell me. How do the men wear their sleeves? Are they at similar lengths, or is there a great variety in how they bare their arms? Buttoned at the wrist, rolled tight above the elbow, halfway up the bicep, or cut off at the shoulder? Of what generation are the tattoos? Blurred marks of identification like a sailor's forearm, gang symbolism or neo-hipster ironic? How do women socialise in the factory? Do they huddle in small groups, always sitting together at lunch, or do they mix freely? Who's texting on their mobiles while the staff can see the boss is concentrating their attention on a guest?

Aymeric was off his call and walked in to start my tour. Before we could move, a young man entered, ear to the factory's cordless handset, mid-conversation. I'd been told about Fabien, CYFAC's engineering prodigy, and his studious expression and techie glasses fit the description; but I was a bit surprised by his good looks and shoulder-length hair. Fabien was muttering 'Oui, oui' into the phone, apparently in agreement with the person at the other end. The engineer then passed the phone to his boss, the problem now firmly in his hands. Like the effortless reordering of cyclists in the peloton, Aymeric had seamlessly taken over the *problème* and he silently indicated that Fabien would lead the tour.

I was guided through a door towards the factory, leaving Katia's domain, her office's papery smells, its abundant natural light and the tools of accounting and office administration. Only now I noticed her perfume, conspicuous by its absence.

Fabien was starting the tour in the storeroom where the raw materials were kept; for a bicycle, this was where life began. Fabien, whose English was fortunately better than Aymeric's for the more technical task ahead, began by introducing me to the raw materials of bicycle fabrication.

From these stores, nine tubes of different diameters, tapers and profiles would be cut and joined to build the frames. The pieces were arranged in countless cardboard boxes labelled with the appropriate chemical symbol: Fe for *fer* or iron, Al, for *aluminium*, Ti for *titane*, and C for *carbone*. On the same level as the tubes were two boxes filled with another important component of factory life: individually wrapped *mademoiselles*, small chocolate-filled bakery items that I would learn were shared in an all-factory morning coffee every day at 10 am.

Fabien explained the process with an engineer's clarity. The material for a bicycle's frame was selected, and then the geometry determined by the customer's proportions. A 'spec sheet' was produced and placed inside a plastic pocket which would follow the frame through the factory. It was like the small sheet that follows a human child when they are first born, identifying its blood type, date of birth and so on.

When George and Robert were born, Robert spent the first few days in a humidicrib, his oxygen carefully monitored, with a page of his details hung on the outside of the Perspex box. As he was pushed around the hospital the only proof you had that the thing inside the box was your son was the paper on the outside.

We moved to the first room, its grey tones and machines making it quite familiar as a workshop. If the bicycle was to be made of steel, the work was undertaken here. The machines in this room were for working steel, and I recognised some of them as part of the original collection that had been shunted across the road twenty years earlier. A giant lathe, grinding machines, drills, rasps, and hammers small, medium but none large. The worktables were metal and appeared to have been cast from one piece of steel, legs and all. On the surfaces lay tools I didn't recognise but assumed were specific to the trade of building bicycles.

French pop played from a small stereo, which was audible except for the deafening interruptions when metal was being sliced, bored, polished, or sanded with assistance from one of the machines that stood at the ready. The metal lathe was a product of a time when Russian heavy-machine making led the world. A small copper plate read *Krasnyĭ Proletariat 1964 Moskva*, which meant it was made in Moscow in the Red Proletariat factory four years before I was born. The large drill was held in place, its polished bit positioned menacingly over the plate below. Across the room, a circular saw spun to its terminal velocity, its whir turned to a whine and then it spun almost silently. Even though it was a safe distance away, I instinctively pulled my fingers back into my pockets.

Against any of these giant machines, the thin metal tubes didn't stand a chance. Today the steel used to build elite bicycles is less than half a millimetre thick – an incomprehensible .01 of an inch at their narrowest – and it seems unfair to shape them with something resembling a four-tonne Soviet tank. I watched as the operator carefully measured and then made a few cuts. When the job was done, mercifully quickly, its operator turned off the machine and walked away to perform another stage. The machine slowly wound down and then stood silently, ready for action at the push of a button, the flick of a switch.

It was easy for me to understand this room. The tools were intuitive, the actions were mechanical. It felt like one of my father's workshops, and I was comforted by a familiar patina of dust, metal shavings and fine oil covering everything.

As soon as Fabien explained the basics, he introduced me to Bernard, the foreman and chief frame builder. By the respectful manner in which I was introduced, I knew this was a place in which people worked in concert with machines, rather than a place where machines were simply operated by their attendant humans. I've toured factories where the machines were clearly in the leading role and the people merely operators.

Bernard was mid-task and his hands were well oiled. I introduced myself, using a little French and outstretching my hand. He offered me his forearm. I gripped it, unsure of the protocol. A small nod was his only greeting. He knew the language gap made his words pointless and carried on with his work without breaking his rhythm.

This felt like Bernard's room, and Bernard felt like this room.

I was told that in this room, over the past thirty years, he had measured, cut and joined the frames for 10,000 bicycles. Bicycles built here had gone on to dutifully serve one owner, then been sold to another, then another, or perhaps passed down in the family. You could fill a medium-sized stadium with the people who had flown down a hill on one of Bernard's creations.

Fabien kept the tour moving and pointed me towards the room in which the frames made of carbon were assembled. It was hermetically sealed with bright neon lighting. Inside, we encountered two young men wearing full-length, white chemical suits with hoods. They breathed through face masks, their eyes protected by large clear goggles. On their hands were latex gloves and they were delicately using small instruments, tweezers and paintbrushes. This room was separated from Bernard's by a thin sheet of glass but at least a hundred years in appearance: the two men here might as well have been doctors performing delicate surgery.

Everything about working with carbon fibres is different. Once the tubes are cut, they are placed into a frame that looks like the type of traction device for holding bodies that are being reset. The carbon tubes are joined, not by a giant force, or by the application of some infernal heat, but by carefully layering the joints with sheets of woven carbon cloth and then applying some sort of smelly goop with a paintbrush. It is like joining limbs with bandages soaked in glue. The carbon cloth itself is cut using a standard pair of tailor's scissors before it's placed over the desired joint.

How strong could anything be if it started out as material you could cut with scissors designed to shape a dress? When it set, Fabien assured me, it would be five times stronger than steel and only half the weight.

To ensure that the goop – technically an epoxy coating – dried evenly, each frame was attached to a small machine on which it slowly revolved for twenty-four hours. It was also successful as a piece of kinetic sculpture. While Fabien answered the surgeon's questions, I was staring at the rotating frame, its shiny black tubes shaped and then reshaped into triangles as the newest creation circulated. As it dried, large viscous drops of excess epoxy plopped to the floor, hitting a paper covering at a random but ever slowing tempo.

Watching paint dry had never been so hypnotic. I must have been staring for a while, as Fabien had to call me to continue the tour.

In truth, this world appeared more medical than manufacturing, and the operating theatre confounded me. When I can intuitively understand the things around me, I feel stable. I know wood: it's something you can drive a nail into, cut with a saw, shape with a chisel. Similarly, with metals and the concrete that make up most of our built environments. But with the arrival of things made of complex compounds, I'd stopped trying to understand the things in my world. The problem with this is that progress is an accelerating force, which leaves you further behind with every day, with each new invention, each new update. I stopped looking under the bonnet soon after my first car, and when I looked again twenty years later all I could see was plastic.

There was a time when you could pull something apart and understand it. Someone else may have made it, but a standard screwdriver or spanner was all you needed to be in a position of power. You might not be able to fix it yourself, but you could at least start a conversation with it. And if we open something today, can we do anything with what we see? As a result, we rely increasingly on trust, a blind faith in the manufacturer. Perhaps this is why we give over more and more to the corporations who sell to us.

Throughout our tour, Fabien was constantly being asked questions, or asking a question himself. Everyone at CYFAC, it seemed, had a question for everyone. *Problème*, which was how most interactions were started, wasn't always a cause for consternation – more like announcing the challenge. It might concern the thing in their hand, be about tubes laid out on the trolley that they were pushing, or the spec sheet they were holding. A tilt of the head, a point of a finger or an elbow (if their hand was otherwise engaged) might indicate that the question related to a frame they had worked on earlier, something that was drying, or something that had been returned for repairs.

It was a highly sophisticated conversation, not because I could understand the complexity of the questions – far from it – but because the communication was immediate, purely functional, without any indication of hierarchy. It was a factory-wide interchange that wove through air, a dialogue where the content provided the equality between the participants.

Bicycles might be painted in fancy stripes later, but at their core they must be extremely functional. They have no time for anything superficial; they don't care for the distracting strata that humans create for themselves.

I was taking photographs as we walked around. I was trying to respect the space I'd been invited into, the relationships I was observing. It was clear the workers were used to a degree of *voyeurisme*. At the start of the tour, adjacent to the official noticeboard, I'd seen a wall of articles from cycling magazines. Amongst the photographs of fully painted bicycles were plenty of images from the factory floor, including faces I was now beginning to recognise. I was learning that what this business had to promote would not be found in any marketing materials, and certainly not by their exterior signposting, but here on the factory floor.

Fabien finished answering the questions relating to the carbon frames, I tore myself away from the spinning thing, and he walked me into the painting quarter of the factory. The room was clean and well organised. The air was fresher here than in the carbon room, a product of extractor fans rather than access to open windows. Once again, we were with futurists, everyone here was in bright blue suits, face masks hanging like necklaces.

Just inside the entrance, a young woman was tangling with a web of images on a computer screen. An oversized printer was dropping sheets that were the inverse of what she was studying. They were stencils of logos and names, the decals and patterns that would guide the painters. Fabien asked her to adjust an object on the screen, using the corner of the nail of his little finger to point to the offending shape. She saw it, and would make the change. The seamless exchange continued.

It is here the naked frames were given their uniforms. In the first of three booths they were given a coating of an off-white powder – some sort of protective dusting that might as well have been their underwear. Here, the frames were dangled by their necks and they looked far from dignified. It seemed I'd caught them off balance, as if they were in the act of getting changed.

Next to a library of paint colours were three spray-painting booths. In the first I was introduced to John, who appeared to be a magician of the painted arts. He was using an air-powered sprayer that blew paint at the frame so fast you couldn't see the paint travel through the air. The effect was that as he waved his hand the frame miraculously changed colour.

Sara, in the booth next door, was removing pieces of the stencils with the point of a scalpel, with the same precision I only wish I could have when called to remove a tiny splinter in the finger of Madison or Elsa. In the corner was Stephan's office, a small airtight room in which he added the final touches to the frames and, after verifying every detail, applied the varnish cover. I was told he was the *patron du syndicat*, the employees' union representative, but I didn't need to be told that to know Stephan is the boss of this area. He was tall with a bronze dome that reflected the bright lights, with the type of smile you'd wish on a friend. But he was all business.

At the end of the room, a line of finished frames glistened in a neat row. I doubted they'd ever be this shiny again. A bicycle frame at this point – no wheels, seat, steering bars – was akin to a baby ready to leave hospital: smooth to the touch, warm to hold, but utterly useless. The shining new frames were all dressed up, but had no way to go, and they waited silently to be taken somewhere else to be turned into a bicycle.

The task of *assemblage* fell to the softly spoken Hugo, the youngest member of the team. He stretched out his hand to meet me, the first time I'd been able to shake anyone's hand inside the factory. Noticeably strong and with no wasted mass: muscles, veins and bones that appeared as if they could take me apart. His eyes, in contrast, asked questions. With an impressive intensity, he attached box-fresh parts to give the frames their much-needed functionality. He was dressed in fresh blue overalls, suggesting he straddled the worlds of the nineteenth-century metal workers and the graphite and paint spacemen. Each day he assembled three to four bikes. He made rapid progress, without ever looking like he was moving quickly. A good workman makes his job look effortless, a great one makes it hard to even notice the work. I turned away for a moment to listen to Fabien and when I looked back, a bike had moved one appendage closer to realisation.

Hugo's job was to take a frame and join it with the bits that would make it a bicycle. He attached the wheels, added the cranks, fastened clipless pedals, connected countless rings of cogs, ran brake and gear lines, and wrapped tape around handlebars. When he finished the build-up, he lifted the bicycle onto a calibrated stand to check that the final result matched the designs of the spec sheet. Measuring every dimension, he confirmed that from the black-and-white schematic, a shining piece of road-riding technology had been built.

Behind Hugo, leaning against the wall, I noticed the bike he rode to work each day. Ironically, on his daily commute, he chose not to utilise any of the modern appendages that he spent his days attaching. His steed was a prototypical 'fixie' – for fixed-gear bike – that wouldn't look out of place parked outside a café in Redfern, Sydney, or padlocked to a parking meter in Williamsburg, Brooklyn. The bike of choice for the world's most style-conscious cyclists has sharp velodrome geometry, flat handlebars, a handmade leather seat from London, and is free of the convenience of hand brakes and gears. Somewhere you are likely to find a sticker that reads 'ONE LESS CAR'. On Hugo's it was written in French as '*UNE VOITURE DE MOINS*'. The hipsters' fixie has become so synonymous with urban culture that, at first, I thought Hugo's bike looked out of place here, and wondered why such a cool ride was leaning against the side door of a factory in rural France. Of course, it's precisely the other way around: the hipsters of the world are modelling their rides on the real thing, and Hugo was the real, real thing.

After the assembly room, I'd completed a circle, a clockwise lap of the factory, and was at the end of my tour. Dr Fabien had covered at least 100 years of manufacturing history for me; twice that in demonstrating the origins of European artisan excellence. I'd been reminded of the modern approach to industrial relations and people management, and seen the future of the trade: young graduates in spacesuits and the unpretentious cool of apprentices pedalling the French countryside on custom speedsters.

Aymeric appeared again, effortlessly demonstrating the precision of the two-man management team. No mention was made of the *problème*, and the phone was passed to Fabien to continue the conversation. Aymeric was back in charge. He led me into what appeared to be another storeroom. From the jumbled line of recently finished bikes, I realised this was their version of a showroom. The table in the centre was strewn with new products, different types of gears, countless metal and carbon tubes dropped off by local reps trying to get CYFAC to add them to their offering. Against the wall was a machine that could only be a measuring board for potential customers.

CYFAC built its reputation on the frames they constructed, relying on word of mouth, as riders told other riders what was really under the paint. Marketing in their own name didn't come until much later and they appeared to be lagging a little in the promotion business. I am okay with this, as it's better to be great at making, and average at marketing, than the other way around. As a potential customer I felt I'd be paying for the bit I needed (a good bike), not something I didn't need (a fancy brand).

The factory tour, its people, its history, and the evident teamwork and pursuit of excellence, had suitably softened me. I was now going to be asked to make a purchasing decision. Isolated, small and purveyor of terrible coffee CYFAC might be; uncommercial they are not.

Before I made any decisions, however, Aymeric told me I'd have to be measured for my bicycle. And that meant I'd have to get undressed. I hadn't come with my own cycling gear, so he offered to lend me a pair of cycling pants, the type of lycra tights that come with attached shoulder straps; like shorts with suspenders. He passed me a new pair in a plastic wrapper small enough to fit in one of my hands and, sensing my awkwardness, left the room for me to change.

XV

I Am Changing

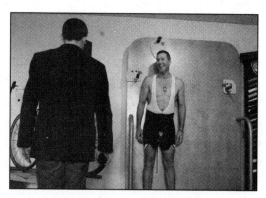

Measuring all of me; well, almost.

Getting naked in a factory is something I hadn't done before. Not that they are impersonal spaces – on the contrary, they're very personal – just that they're someone else's private space. Protected here under a roof that repelled the rain, shaded from the burning sun and sheltered from the cold by pressed steel walls, there was a stage on which a human drama ran for the life of the factory. Sometimes it plays for decades, sometimes centuries. Every shift, every input and every output are imprinted in the factory itself. People shape things, and things shape people.

I slipped into a pocket-sized storeroom to change, hanging my clothes on the stacks of bike parts and neatly arranged cleaning items. When I stepped out, Aymeric had returned and his face let me know a strange shape had arrived. I'm larger than the average cyclist, and the shorts he'd provided were sized 'medium' for that small subset of athletes. Shirt off and shoes gone, socks kept for warmth, my legs were hairy and my chest had lost its summer tan. The shorts were really much too small, and the built-in mesh suspenders were hiking the pants up high. When worn under a tight cycling top, the riding shorts would be part of a sleek athletic outfit, but as I stepped out of the cramped change-room – socks on, top off – it must have looked more like a combination of lingerie and a safety harness for my testicles.

'An Australian might win the Tour de France this year,' Aymeric blurted to immediately break the tension. I was just narcissistic enough to have a momentary flirtation with the idea that he might be referring to me. I'd spent countless hours of my childhood sitting through school assemblies where medals and ribbons were handed out to winners who were not me. As a result I'd developed a habit of imagining my name added at the last moment for awards I knew I hadn't won. So it wasn't such a stretch for me to insert my name on the podium when Aymeric mentioned the Tour de France. For just a millisecond I let the feeling wash over me that perhaps I'd get a call one day to say that a team needed another rider from Australia and, given that I was living down the road, could I join the real Tour de France at short notice?

Such overactive imagination is one of the particular developments of children who are separated from their parents at a young age. It is seen in refugee children, the so called 'street kids' who raise themselves in slums around the world, as well as those 'fortunate' enough to be sent away to boarding school. There's even a name for that version: Boarding School Syndrome, a condition described by an English psychotherapist Joy Schaverien. Kids who are taken miles from home, plonked into an artificial environment with little adult supervision, develop a strong habit of working out things themselves. Even if they get it wrong. With nobody to ask, no parent to explain, children over-develop the skill of making up explanations for the world. Inside your head becomes your only really safe space.

It can be a very helpful skill, also developing fantastic imaginations and independent thinking. However, when you catch yourself half-naked in a French factory, barely contained by a pair of cycling shorts, as you dream about winning the Tour de France, it is an embarrassment that I hoped wasn't showing on my face.

Of course, when he mentioned the 'Australian who might win the Tour de France', Aymeric had been talking about Cadel. For good reason, Australians are dreamers when it comes to sports. From our horses to sailing yachts, golfers to surfers, we've been world beaters. An Australian even won an Olympic gold medal in speed skating – on ice, something we haven't had permanent deposits of for more than ten thousand years. My victory in the Tour de France was orders of magnitude less likely. I had yet to learn how to ride one of these bikes in a manner that matched the standard of the machine itself, and had yet to even attempt the shaving of my legs.

I'd made an agreement with Aymeric that if I was going to build a bike with them, I'd be able to get a complete photographic record of the process – from the moment I walked in the front door, to the time the bike rolled out the back door. It also meant I had to photograph the part of me being measured. For my fitting I had to stand against the large measuring board and be held in place by small red protrusions that slid under my arms to prevent me from moving. They were effective but ticklish, giving the impression I'd been pinned to the board. Photographing this section was a technical challenge. While I was being splayed against a board, and gently touched up by a man and his tape measure, I'd have to use my camera's self-timer settings. I sat my camera on the conference table and propped the lens up on a thick marker to get the correct angle. After each measurement I dashed between the camera and the measuring board.

In the rest of the factory a small team was building the ideal bicycle in an infinite variety of lengths and angles.

But here, where each customer came in only one size, it was Aymeric's job to work this out. He set a laptop to his left and entered each dimension into a spreadsheet. Thanks to the sports science department at a French university, 60,000 other human-bicycle fittings had been analysed for their posture and performance data. I was promised that, *if I stood still long enough,* the computer would be able to rapidly spit out the design for the perfect bike for me. The building of the bike would take six to ten weeks, the measuring of me twenty minutes, and the bit where the computer decided the essential geometry, all lengths and precise angles, a fraction of a second.

If the process was intimate, it was for both me and Aymeric. We were building a machine to fit my particular body. More than a tailored suit that fits neatly as you walk or sit, a bicycle is a machine that you hold in your hands, move with your legs, join with your groin. What we're trying to achieve is a long-term relationship with a machine, but this part starts as prosaically as entering your details in an online dating site.

The first measurement, of both online dating and bike building, is height. No need to measure, I knew it well: 191.5 centimetres, or six feet three and a half. As to my weight, I sheepishly offered 95 kilograms. It was more than I'd like, and I said it under my breath, even though what we were recording was only between the two of us and a computer that sat in the basement of the Université de Lyon.

While this part of Aymeric's lesson was more technical, it was based on some very easy to understand principles. The man-bicycle combination moves forward because of the force the cyclist applies with his lower body, the biggest constraint being the wind friction created by the upper body. Expert riders are able to crouch low over their handlebars, tuck their elbows in and form a sleek dolphin-like curve with their backs, their helmets an increasingly streamlined extension of this one aerodynamic parcel. Less experienced cyclists ride more upright, pushing their chest into the wind like the bow of a lycra-covered barge, their helmet interrupting any wind that might have otherwise flowed past smoothly.[2]

When I'd found myself the focus of the bullies at my boarding school, I became determined to build some upper-body mass. I once had the idea that if I did ten push-ups for every punch I'd got that day, I'd be strong enough to withstand the next day's barrage. It didn't work, and I didn't shake the nickname 'Bones' for all of my teens. As my muscles didn't come as quickly as I called for them, I instead cultivated an ability to withstand pain. Strength in the chest and arms eventually came, but ironically around the time the bullies lost interest. For certain sports it came in handy – it helped me swim faster and defend myself on the rugby field. In business I had a frame on which I could hang a wide-shouldered suit, which helped give the impression that the wearer was more confident than I felt inside.

Aymeric's final task, possibly the most intimate way of getting to know your customer in the manufacturing world, was to extensively measure me below the waist. The legs create the drive, a form of mechanical lever that the cycle sizing must get right to get the most out of. The largest and most powerful lever is the thigh, which departs from the hip joint inside the body and is most accurately measured from the top of the inner thigh, the pubic bone.

Aymeric warned me we were about to get a whole lot more personal, and I stepped off the measuring board – partly for a break, and partly to reset my camera. As the camera blinked

---

2 The simplest version of the formula governing the potential speed of a bicycle is: S (velocity) = F (force) – μ (friction). The F is applied by the legs sharing the rotation duties, while the μ is the friction from the wind resistance of the man/bicycle pushing through the air and that coming at the tyre/road interface. Road friction is no more than one-tenth of the total friction. The thinner the tyres the less there is. The bicycle itself is responsible for another one-tenth of the friction. This means the human is responsible for 80 per cent of the drag, which is why posture, or fit to the bike, is so important. The more you can comfortably bend your upper torso into a smooth bullet, the better. Sadly you can do nothing about upper body size and weight.

down from ten to one, I got back against the board and assumed my position with the shoulders held in place, thinking Aymeric would be coming at me with his tape measure. Instead, the measuring device has its own piece of equipment for this part: without warning, a ten inch black rod that had been hanging limp off the measuring wall automatically lifted up into my groin with hydraulic resistance. Just then the camera snapped, capturing the moment when the most vital of measurements, in the most delicate of places, was accurately recorded.

I was trapped, pinned to the board by my shoulders and raised by a mid-groinal protrusion, which Aymeric took as the perfect time to ask me what material I'd like the bike to be made of. Each material would have a cost implication.

'Carbon,' he asked, 'titanium, steel, aluminium, carbon or perhaps carbon?'

I'd already decided to get a bike made of steel, although it was clear what would be a better choice for Aymeric financially. I had nothing against the other materials, but I understood steel. I knew where it came from, what it looked like, and why it worked. Aymeric was disappointed I'd chosen the cheapest option, but when it became clear I was not budging, he offered that the benefit of steel was that it was durable, and would survive a crash or two.

'Thanks,' I said, and then added 'I think' as I had not yet thought of coming off this rocket at the speeds he was encouraging me to train for.

With the work done, I asked him to pass me my camera so I could get one last photo of the thing between my legs. Photographing down my body is not the most flattering. Muscles of cyclists seem to expand below their waists, thighs billowing out of their shorts, whereas mine seem to go into hiding. My hips are my widest point and as I looked into the camera I could see the muscles on my thighs narrow to my knees and then disappear behind the calf bones. They terminated on slender ankles from where my feet took off at right angles: feet that are long and thin and at the very top end of the sizes regularly available in shoe stores. They work really well when I'm swimming, but on a bike I look a bit like I'm pedalling with flippers on.

I told Aymeric that I had six months to get cyclist's legs, including learning to shave them. His only response was to make sure I knew the race was closer than I had thought.

'Peter, Les Alpes d'Huez is in four and a 'alf.'

XVI

Measuring between My Legs

'Madi, go back, go back.'

That night at dinner I had lots to tell the girls, and lots of photos to upload. I excitedly told them about having lunch with Aymeric, about the factory, about each room I'd visited, about each stage of the bike being built, about how they were going to build not just a bike, but *my* bike. I explained to them that Aymeric had agreed I could photograph every single part of the process of its construction. They were quickly and deeply fascinated by the images that were materialising on the screen.

'It looks serious,' one said.

I agreed and added sternly, 'I know I have a lot to do.'

I was hoping that this was a so-called 'teaching moment'. If I want the girls to grow up as something other than consumers, I must somehow help them understand the work that goes into the things in their life, how they function, and even how you can repair, not simply replace, them. I had not always been the best teacher: when I'd taught them how to change a bike tyre over the previous weekend, I noted that they were able to do it at the age of seven, something like thirty years earlier than I learned that skill. This would be an opportunity both to imbue in them the passion for the slow process that goes into making a fast bike and the work one must do on oneself to deserve an object of such precision.

They are at an age where they will soon have their own computers and smartphones. Dropped into their careless palms will be the computing power that was unavailable to some nations at the time I was born. Inside those machines will be minerals that kids their age have scratched out of African hills, parts that young women have assembled in cramped Asian factories. There is no context in our society for them to readily understand this – everything arrives complete, finished, cooked – so perhaps seeing the process of one bike being built can help them understand the work that humans put into things.

I can pretend to myself that I'm not one of those always-trying-to-teach parents, but my kids know better. As a child, the lessons of my father were delivered in the format of 'watch what I do; I won't be saying much'. It was a masterclass, for sure, but a version of life that my instructor proved could be lived brilliantly, but not for long. I was going on a different path, seeing my role as parent as dedicated to the intergenerational transfer of happiness. I couldn't much change the world my children would inherit, but I could adjust how they saw it and leave them to decide how they would live in it. All of which meant I had to give lectures like tonight's. I'm used to the tell-tale signs of eyes starting to roll when I talk of the impact of the air-conditioning in a public place, the food miles of the ingredients of a meal, the political reason why it's easy for some people to get through customs in some places, but not for other people. This time, however, I had photos, and they were already gripped.

'I know I must train hard . . .' I intoned with suitably fatherly gravitas.

The second part of learning about value is to understand yourself, and what you have done, or will do, to earn the thing.

'. . . and lose ten kilograms . . .'

I knew they didn't really know what that meant, but I added the detail because complexity is a card that adults often play if they sense the simplicity of a child's view will expose them.

'. . . and shave my legs.'

I had no idea what they'd think of that last bit, but the images they were transfixed by had rendered them speechless. After a few hundred photographs of every part of the factory – the roses on the desk, the tubes in storage, the sparks flying from the lathe, the hand-worn tools, the men in white suits, the shining epoxy, the spray booths, and finally things that looked like bicycles, fresh painted and even some with wheels – they were stuck on the series of images of their father half naked.

Once the images uploaded to the computer, I watched the girls furiously hitting the back arrow until they arrived at the one that had piqued their attention.

They silently studied the photograph and I uneasily repeated what I'd said before.

'I know, I know, I will train a lot, and lose a bit of weight, and shave those legs.'

All of which sounded like adult priorities, leaving Madison to comment:

'And buy a shirt, Dad.'

XVII

On Ice, Thinly

If the activities didn't exhaust them, another
château visit would always finish them off.

The next day I woke to an email from Aymeric to say I should
return by 9 am to the factory to watch the cutting of the steel
tubes. As it was a Wednesday, the French day of parent/child
interaction, I had to beg that we postpone. A short, grumpy
email came straight back to remind me that he couldn't be held
to the delivery schedule if I kept moving dates.

'We have a factory to run, Peter.'

A short, humble email went back from me, excusing him of
all responsibility, and we agreed the tube cutting would take
place on Thursday.

I hadn't heard of the midweek, school-free day before
arriving in France. When Aimée first told me about it during
registration, I looked at her with a combination of cognitive
dissonance – *like, no school for anyone?* – and some fear – *what
about my schedule?* She told me there were lots of activities
I could do with the girls in the local area, including horse riding

lessons in Saumur, ice skating in Bourgueil, and even going to the heated indoor pool in Avoine. Consulting a map, I found that a circuit of Saumur–Bourgueil–Avoine would be most logical, and allow a visit to the Hyper U supermarket on the way back. So every Wednesday I embarked on a three town, multi-activity-plus-pantry-restocking triathlon that had the desired effect: fill the fridge and exhaust the girls.

After the first of these Wednesdays I returned to the school with the girls by my side and told Aimée how well it had worked and thanked her for the suggestion. She laughed and let me know they were the complete list of activities in the district, not meant to be packed into the same day. 'One each week,' she said. However, once the girls were hooked, they weren't having anything less of a midweek adventure.

We found the horse riding behind the home of Dominique and Sandrine, a warm-hearted couple who were equally large in both personality and size. Dominique was a handsome man of Algerian/French descent with hands the same size and colour as a baseball mitt. Sandrine had been a professional tennis player and as I had arrived in mid-winter, she welcomed me as the human embodiment of the Australian Tennis Open, the blue-courted vision of searing temperatures that plays incongruously on European TVs every late January. We were able to talk tennis before I could talk French, as the vocab was mostly made up of players' names that I knew.

Their small plot was better loved than well kept, full of animals, their twin boys, a rotating supply of foster kids they looked after, and horses of all shapes and temperaments. They shared a political philosophy bordering on revolutionary, but ran a business that catered to the children of the château'd class. I had come for the riding instruction but would have returned for the chance of their company. As a bonus, the instruction was exactly the way I thought it should be: incredibly respectful towards the horses, steady steps of confidence-building risk-taking, and lots of cleaning up and grooming for the kids to do. Should any child leave manure uncollected or a mane unbrushed, the full force of Dominique's voice would shake the small barn as if the artillery had arrived. The girls loved it, instantly.

Ice-skating took place in a grey-sided community hall that showed no external signs that inside circled the most vibrant youth gathering for miles around. On our first visit, I had held the girls' hands for support, but soon we held hands only for fun. With one or more by my side, we lapped round and round, skating circles to the radio mix of international pop. It was a dreamy state for all of us, something about being completely in your body, moving at speed and having Katy Perry in your head. There weren't many parents on the ice, never any dads, and certainly none who brought a big digital camera on the ice to photograph their girls.

For the swimming, we went to the pool that Aimée promised she'll take the whole school to (and hopefully, I thought, me too) *en printemps*, in the spring. Frits told me he suspected that the three pools were warmed by water from the nearby nuclear power station. It was large and very warm, and had a great slide marked *enfants seulement* – children only. I very much doubted that the girls and I were swimming in radioactive overflow – Frits' commentary of the area was least reliable when it got close to anything vaguely political.

What it gave the girls was a chance to show off. Natural water creatures due to an Australian childhood, they made the French kids look like terrified landlubbers. They developed a game of retrieving the other kids' water toys, which got to the point of local kids throwing things in just to see how deep the girls would go to get them back.

Between activities, the girls and I surfed radio stations on the Land Rover's rudimentary radio. Initially, a song sung in French was Madison's cue to shout 'Change!' from the back seat. For her, French was a pointed reminder of being away from her mother. It hurt her to hear it and would send her down an emotional path that none of us wanted her to go on, partially because one or both of us were liable to join her. So I would quickly change the station.

Gradually, as French accompanied us for each small roadtrip, Elsa would step in and ask that I leave a song on for a while. Eventually they both warmed to a number of French pop songs, including one they even started to sing along to. It helped that the chorus was in English. With the crossbred song now in their heads, more and more French songs were accepted until the genre no longer caused Madison to turn her head to the window, stare out and pretend not to cry, tears betraying her stoic gaze.

Perhaps the reason I loved Wednesdays so much was that it evidenced my good fathering so clearly. Aimée might have meant for us to do only one activity, so I wore doing all three as a badge of honour.

The most dramatic impact of our midweek day of activities was that it put the girls to sleep early. The cold, the changes of clothing, the rushing to get to the ice rink before it closed, the giant pool and slide that I could go on when no attendants were looking, took a toll on all of us. The girls would fall asleep in the car on the way home, in their bellies a meal we'd found at a café on the way. Inside this car I was, undisputedly, a good family man. I had my community and it was warm.

The girls' mother had come to visit in the first six weeks, breaking her European adventure with the boys in their rented Renault. It hadn't been easy for any of us. They represented choice, and showed it in how they dressed, the long hair that the boys had grown over their collars and their wake-up time being well after ours. If life could be taken at your own speed, how could I explain the precise routine I held the girls to? If cities that the girls knew of were only a day's drive away, how could I explain our isolation? And if Mum and Dad were sharing a room when they were together, how could I explain our long periods apart? Little of this last part was easy, less of it said. We were trying to do our marital separation with the dignity that the children deserved. They could see, in fact anyone from outer space could see, that our circles had grown wider and wider over the last decade. That I was stuck in a farmhouse and my wife was free and on the road was only the latest manifestation of us growing apart.

During their visit, the girls had excitedly pulled the whole family out of bed and made everyone join our weekly Wednesday ritual. The photos I took that day told a story of the girls full of pride showing their France to their mother and brothers. Inside the skating rink the light is artificial and insufficient, so the images were moody, even without being able to show the teenage hormones that hung in the air. The boys wore leather jackets, their hair flowing and blond, better dressed and better looking than they were at skating. I was so proud of these little men, missed them deeply, and was more than a bit envious of their long locks of carefree hair. Their trip would be rather an adult experience – of museums, of old cities, of places and history that they'd one day appreciate more. But no-one was anything but a kid when they had skates on in a roomful of other kids, as chattering blades flew over soon-rutted paths to the beat of tweeny pop.

The photos show two happy girls, arms outstretched, the right mix of confidence and regard for gravity. They are travelling away from the camera, and, in one, their mother is watching them as they swing around the curve of the rink. They will one day spin away from both parents and take their own path. Our job will be done if they do so with a mix of confidence and suitable regard for gravity. Katy Perry may still be playing then too.

XVIII

Still Water Runs (Deep)

The toys we made, the things we played with.

After dropping the girls at school the next morning, I rushed to the factory to be there for the cutting of the tubes. I was excited, thinking it was a good day for me, not such a great one for the tubes. I'd lost valuable credibility at the factory by not showing up the first time, and when I arrived they told me they'd assumed I'd be late and had scheduled another three frames in before mine. Not to worry, I said, I'd just continue my tour of the factory, self-guided this time. While my tubes sat waiting their time before the blade, I took photos, happy that nobody seemed to notice me or my large camera. Just before Bernard was to begin the cutting of my tubes, they got a stay of execution: a bell rang, machines wound down, tools clanked onto benches, and the radio was once again audible. It was exactly 10 am, which meant it was time for the break.

I followed the flow of employees to a table in the storeroom, next to the supplies and the two boxes of sweets. The table was long and narrow, and full of plastic coffee cups. Katia had been busy in my peripheral vision. Each person had clearly established their order in advance and their version of instant – with or without milk powder; one, two or three sugars – was waiting on the table in 'their spot'.

Around the thin table sat a half-dozen metal stools, not nearly enough. A crate served as one, while others brought makeshift seats from across the factory as they arrived. I recognised the stools as a product of IKEA, as I'd purchased a few myself. I knew that under a large adult they were unreliable at best; emptying their cargo by either tipping over backwards or collapsing forward when one of their three legs buckled under. The weak limb could be bent back into place, but never more than a few times before it came off in your hand. In the CYFAC factory, somebody had welded an extra support to the underneath, a small piece of metal that made them perfectly sturdy, even under me or Bernard.

I am a believer in the flat-pack system, but while we enjoy its low costs we forget the short life span of many of the objects we consume. These IKEA-purchased stools prove that no-one, even a handmade cycle factory, is immune to the low-cost culture. At least at CYFAC they had the tools to add the metal that its makers decided was unnecessary, a sliver of support that must have saved its manufacturers – the Swedish-founded, now tax-haven-registered, multinational – pennies per stool.

The all-factory coffee break was the closest to a meal with a group of adults that I'd had since coming to France. The conversation rolled easily, the characters of each person more apparent for the fact that I didn't understand a word they were saying. There was the joker, the smart-arse, the quiet one, the polite one, the goofy one, the boss, and the person who makes fun of the boss. Aymeric had a very gentle style as the leader, perhaps understandable as he was three decades younger than some of his team and half the size of one or two. Around the table, everyone was equal.

I was asked a question by one of the men, which Katia translated. *Did I know Cadel Evans?* I answered, and Katia translated. There was some laughter at my response, possibly at my expense, but it didn't matter, as the conversation took off again. I felt accepted, but not understood, and happy that that didn't matter. No sooner had the break started – and just before I was going to attempt to ask my own question – than people began standing up, saying their polite *mercis*, and dismissing themselves. They were clearly eager to get back to their tasks. I stayed until I was the second to last person at the table, gave my cup to Katia and then I was the last.

In my first job, as a junior associate at a Manhattan investment bank, I relished the weekly meeting of all staff. Coffee, Thursdays at nine, in a south-facing conference room on the fortieth floor of an office tower, the corner of 53rd and Lexington. The partners sat either side of a long, highly-polished table in deep leather chairs, the rest of us silently leaned against the walls and floor-to-ceiling windows, listening to tales of deals done and deals coming, stories of global significance and intrigue, always with a strong undercurrent of competitive name-dropping. Later, when I was playing the role of boss and running my own coffee catch-ups, I did what I could to create less hierarchical gatherings. However, none of it was as successful as the workplace *égalité* that Aymeric achieved.

Not that any of the experience from my previous world mattered here. Deep in thought, I hadn't noticed that Bernard had been standing to my left for some time. In front of him was a trolley on which lay half-a-dozen steel tubes, of three or four different diameters, and my bike's spec sheet. He paused and, without words, asked me if I was ready to watch them be cut.

Bernard removed each tube from the cart, ascertained the length that was required from the spec sheet, and, with a metal ruler and a white marking pen, carefully indicated where the incision would take place. He turned on the circular saw, and as it wound up to cutting speed, he positioned the tube under its spinning blade. When the machine reached a constant hum, he held each tube down with his left hand, and brought the blade's handle down with his right. I saw none of them struggle, but it would have been futile, his arms like trunks pinning them to the apparatus. Each of my tubes released a weak squeal of protest, a spiral of glowing embers spurted out in all directions, and the end piece dropped to the floor, falling into a bucket of other innocent offcuts.

As Bernard repeated his process he didn't pause or pose, or even slow down for my photography. I missed the cutting of the first and second tubes, and when I was crouching below the saw for the third cut I caught a shower of embers, some on my hands, and one on my lens. The small burns that blistered on my hands would be gone in a day or two, but I learned then that molten metal leaves an indelible mark on a camera's glass lens. I never got the shots I wanted of this stage and was still sitting on the floor below the circular saw when Bernard had moved onto another stage, having switched on the old Soviet lathe.

It wound up slower, with the soft whir that comes from machines of real power. It had the bulk of a midsize car and seemed vastly out of proportion to its job, which was to fine tune the cutting by a fraction of a millimetre, each turn shaving tiny metal curls off the tubes, taking them to the precise edge of Bernard's markings. After the pieces were trimmed by the lathe, the edges were polished smooth with a sanding belt that also owed its heritage to the old Soviet Union and had spent its childhood in the factory across the road. In less time than I felt befitted the significance of this stage, the cutting of the tubes was complete.

Bernard pushed the cart aside and took another set of tubes, silently regarded the next spec sheet, and, with constantly unemotional professionalism, began another cutting. I had come in support of my tubes, but was soon, even though I was in a crowd of one, cheering for the man doing the cutting.

At CYFAC, around 12.01 pm, machines across the factory wind down again, the hammering dies off, and the factory goes quiet. People walk, drive or cycle home to be with family, or take a boxed lunch to eat with others. I formed my work habits in countries that don't stop for lunch, and kids rarely leave the grounds of their school. I hadn't yet discovered that the midday meal with your children was by far the best time to spend with them: breakfast is always rushed, semi-asleep infants inhaling food while semi-asleep parents stress about the impending day; dinners are recurring recovery sessions, as exhausted adults stressed by the work not finished and children exhausted from trying to remember everything from the school day sit and try to talk politely. Often the responsibility of conversation is sheeted to the man on the TV. Lunchtime, I would soon discover here, is great family time: bubbly kids mingling with still optimistic adults. It might even be healthier, as it gives the body the main meal in the middle of the day, not right before it tries to sleep. It certainly provided a mindful break from work while there was still something you could do to change your day.

Madison and Elsa ate lunch at school, so I had nobody to eat it with. That was okay, as I had an errand to run. Madison had developed a minor skin rash, which I'd been told the hard water here can do to the inexperienced. I had a bit of my own below my new beard, a red backing to an otherwise greying stubble. Madison's was in a more delicate place. I was going to drive to the *pharmacie* during lunchbreak, and I went out to tell Aymeric that I had something important to do. Aymeric said that nothing more would happen to my tubes today, so I had no reason to come back.

Ouch. I had just started to feel at home; now I felt unwanted.

I drove out, turning left towards Rillé, alongside the wide ponds of the Plan d'eau de Hommes that lay just north of the factory. There are seven ponds in total, the largest a few hundred metres long, most with steep sides that drop straight into the water. When the châteaux and other houses of this area were built, the stone was cut from large open-pit quarries. With a few hundred years of disuse, they eventually filled with water. I have been told that since people learned to swim for leisure (which only happened in the last fifty years), they've become a popular summer gathering place. It took some imagination to picture this now, as all the light that a midwinter sun could muster was being absorbed into their depths, and the wind was lifting one-foot high, black waves that moved at the same speed as my car.

Water, flowing and frozen, stone and steel had been the core elements of our time here and I'd had to learn a lot about each since arriving. The rest of today would be about solving a problem that our water was causing Madison and me.

The water at La Petite Briche came from the dilapidated water tower that stood – just barely – behind our house. It was part of Cail's state-of-the-art (for 1867) water distribution system and was now wrapped in vines with a solid covering of moss. It lifted water from an aquifer forty metres down and stored it in a wooden tank on top of its small turret. The water that we drank, cooked with and bathed in started life like all rain water, pure H_2O, but by the time it exited the taps in our house it had developed a particularly local character. As drops fell towards the ground they sliced off enough carbon dioxide in the air to form tiny concentrations of carbonic acid: a bit of the H_2O and some CO_2 made a tiny bit of H_2CO_3. The water that started its path down to our supply was thereby slightly acidic.

Some ninety million years ago, when this whole area was the bottom of the sea, the floor of the ocean was made up of squillions of calcium-shelled sea creatures that were buried under the weight of a squillion other calcium-shelled creatures. Under no more pressure than the weight of their relatives above them, this foundation formed into a type of soft white stone, a member of the limestone family. The stone now lies close to the surface, is soft enough to be cut with a hand saw, but strong enough to be stacked as building blocks. The Loire Valley is known for its nice summers and pleasantly meandering river, but the reason the Loire became the Valley of the Kings with over 1000 châteaux is simply because of the availability of cheap building materials. In a similar way, a reduction in building costs in the US drove the expansion of American house sizes. When the French aristocracy became history's first well-to-do class, they built their houses bigger and bigger, making the Loire the home to the McMansions of their time.

Our problem came from the softness of this stone, which gave away some of its calcium as the slightly acidic water passed by on its way to our aquifer. At very high levels this calcium re-petrifies inside humans as kidney stones, but mostly it passes harmlessly through the body. Until now, our issues with the water had been mostly first-world issues – for example, it had reduced my coffee machine's flow to a dribble, the clothes iron looked like it had been dropped in a bucket of white paint – but what it was doing in Madison's pants was no laughing matter. She originally just hinted at a problem, and I'd hoped it would go away. It was frankly a slightly awkward conversation for us both. She'd said it again just as we arrived at school one day, and I'd rushed her out of the car without resolving it. Then, the previous night, tears tumbled when she told me that the redness on her 'front bum' was making her cry every day at school.

Remembering Frits' advice about the ever helpful Corrine, the area's only pharmacist, I was sure I could find a cream at her store in Gizeux that would do the job. It would salve the bright red rash, reduce the pain she was feeling, and calm the panic that had gathered in my throat thinking about how to do first aid on a body part I had no first-hand experience with.

As I approached the pharmacy, the green neon cross that demarks all such dispensaries across France was dimmed. The clock on my dash showed it was nearly 12.30 pm, indicating I had arrived during the cherished midday hours. Not surprisingly all the parking spaces outside the *pharmacie* were vacant, so I pulled into one next to the front door to read the printed confirmation of my mistake.

Behind the shutters of the houses around me in the village of Gizeux, I imagined families would be *à la table*, breaking that day's fresh bread, sharing cheese and dried meat, *rillettes et tomates*, maybe with a small glass of wine poured, chatting merrily. I, on the other hand, was alone, silently brewing in my car. I was far from appreciating the system here and was still taking it personally each time 'FERMÉ 12–14' was the welcome posted on a providore's door.

I sat in my parked car, considering whether there was some-where I could go close by for lunch and make the trip look like it was intentional. Without any pushing, tears dropped to my lap. The salty drops were close to the surface at all times in those early months. I turned my car around in the deserted street and rolled off slowly. I drove past the corner bread shop which was closed, the town's other shop, a small *boucherie*, also closed, and the town's only restaurant, *Le Bœuf Couronné*, closed, the sign said, two years ago. As if on auto-pilot, I steered a familiar route home. I drove in silence, ate some leftovers at the kitchen table in silence, and then set off again for Gizeux. I planned to arrive right at opening time to make it look like I knew the system and would not be mentioning my earlier fruitless visit.

I drove extra slowly down the potholed road to the D749, turned left, past leafless forests and bare fields that must be tiring of the wait for spring's thawing rays. The heating in the car was still on full blast from the morning's school run and as the cabin began to overheat I moderated the temperature by driving with my window open. I slung my right hand out my window and let it be tossed up and down by the cold currents, enjoying the sensation of gradually losing all feeling in my fingers. It was as if my hand was getting drunk, an escape for my body from the concerns of my head, a path I'd used myself during the hardest times in my career.

The road was deserted, and I drove at the speed of a tractor ploughing a field, using less than sixty per cent of my car's available gears. It was my fourth trip along this path already that day and I was used to the hypnotic tilting of my car as it took the curves of the route. Roads here were either dead straight or illogically curvaceous. The straight ones were thanks to the Italians: a legacy of Roman occupation a thousand years ago that gave France its first 15,000 kilometres of improved pathways. The twisting routes had been shaped by a more ancient force: they originally curved besides rivers and their tributaries, but when the steam diggers of the nineteenth century drained these lands, the water receded, leaving roads that now seemed to serpentine just for the fun of it. All the roads here rang with the sounds of the past, like the cheers that echo in a stadium long after the game has ended, a paved museum of watery events of the past.

At the end of one long right-hand curve, as I approached the village of Gizeux, its château appeared on my left. It is one of the few châteaux that is still owned by the descendents of its pre-revolutionary owners. In the summer months it is protected behind an impressive avenue of plane trees, but in the winter the trees are a skeleton row that make the château appear quite connected to the village. Once it would have been the centre of village life: the aristocratic *famille du château* would have been its largest employer, as well as the tax collectors, the local government and, when it suited them, the de facto judiciary.

During the French Revolution, the Gizeux château owner bravely went off to fight for the losing side, leaving his wife to guard their multi-turreted home. She had little to fear: this part of the country included many who were happy with the system the way it was. Legend has it that the townsfolk helped paint over the friezes in main halls, hide the silver and upholstered furniture, shielding the château from the full brunt of the Revolution, its wealth redistributors and the pyromaniac looters.

Today, the world seems to divide differently: those outside the cities are more likely to want to change the system. Whether from America's 'rust belt', England's north or the countryside of France, the enemy are the urbanites, who are now more likely to be happy with the system as it is.

In modern France, there is less of a job for the château dwellers. Before the Industrial Revolution, the landed gentry were often the town's largest employer, and in the democratic changes of the French Revolution they lost their role as local taxman, and de facto judiciary. Today the owners of the Château de Gizeux are essentially landlords for a small hotel and experts at fixing up their inheritance. The family is still well liked in the village, on a first-name basis with the villagers. Like many of the remnant members of the aristocratic class, they struggle with the responsibilities and bills that come with their crumbling mansion. I'd met them before in the pharmacy and passed them in the aisles at the Hyper U in Bourgueil, their trolley never overly full.

I followed the curve into the village, turned right at the old mill, whose waterwheel once ground the town's flour, past the *lavoir*, a covered section of the stream which once served as an outdoor laundry, and then turned left at the shuttered restaurant. Just past the bakery (now opened) I could see the green cross (now flashing brightly) of the *pharmacie* of Corrine Berthold.

Corrine owned and managed the pharmacy, which was part of a national franchise. She wasn't tall, or particularly thin, but her smile, cracking laughter and confidence made her a natural magnet. She spoke quite passable English but demanded that I talk to her in French, or at least use French vocabulary for key words. I felt that she liked that I was Australian, as opposed to the other English speakers in the area, who were, without exception, English. I'd seen her displeasure when a visitor entered the pharmacy and started talking in English, seemingly unaware that it is not – yet – a universal language. She liked that I was in training for a race up Alpe d'Huez, as she'd proudly told me that she had a holiday house there. I had reacted as if that sounded very grand, so she let me know the apartment buildings were very big, and hers was only a time share.

For a combination of her widely needed services and her unflappably positive attitude, I'd worked out that this was now the centre of village life. Mothers came here pushing prams to buy medicines, cream and age-appropriate diapers for their children. A much older brigade arrived on canes to buy medicines, creams and, perhaps, age-appropriate diapers. The customers were rarely young professional women looking for lipstick or teenage boys sheepishly asking for prophylactics.

I entered the *pharmacie* confidently, now just after 2 pm, and there were already other customers being served by her two employees. When Corrine saw me, she skipped all greetings, and loudly stated her hours of operation. She was somehow aware I'd tried to visit during her lunchbreak. As she took lunch in her house, the building that adjoined the pharmacy, I guessed that while at the table she'd heard a car turning around outside. From the distinctive sound of my engine she'd correctly guessed it was me. By telling me her opening hours, she wasn't rubbing my nose in it, she was offering to help me: if there was a real emergency, she went on to say, I could have simply knocked on her door.

The embarrassment I felt was an amalgam of the two forms of the red-faced emotion: the cold form, a type of self-shame when you've made a public mistake, and the warmer form that I feel when I'm overwhelmed by unexpected kindness. They both come from the same root, but they feel quite different. It is all embarrassment nonetheless and to distract from the blossoming across my face I changed the subject.

Je cherche un rasoir.

I said it with confidence because the French word *cherche* is helpfully close to search and *rasoir* to razer.

On Aymeric's instructions I'd attempted to shave my legs the other night. I'd tried it standing up in the shower, but the water kept washing off the cream. I then tried to use the sink, slinging one leg over the basin, but couldn't keep my balance. My disposable blades hadn't made it through even half the job. The girls had come in a few times to see what was going on and were amused at the sight of their dad, leg whitened by cream, wobbling around the room, in a blood-spotted towel. I'd been left with one leg mostly shaved, half a dozen small cuts around my ankle and knees, and unsure what to do at the top and bottom. *Do I really have to shave the top of my toes? How high do I go? When do I stop?*

Aymeric had left out important parts of the instructions. But there was no going back now – I had to finish that job. Corrine was able to help me get more blades without me having to give details of what I needed them for.

'*En plus?*' Anything more, she asked.

Next, I started to explain that I was searching for some cream for Madison. I hadn't planned the conversation, and I'd never been into a pharmacy to buy lotion for a vagina before. I suddenly regretted not having Googled the key French words for the conversation, something I could have done quite easily over my lunch when I was browsing less useful places on the internet. I might have been able to guess at the French word *vagin*, but it would never have occurred to me that the word took the masculine form, as in *le vagin*.

Lack of preparation be damned: this was for my daughter, so I was going to do this dance in front of a small and increasingly attentive audience of local women. Using very little vocabulary and plenty of awkward hand gestures, I acted out an indiscreet pantomime – one hand showing her height, the other to show the body part I was referring to – that described the cream that I needed, who it was for, and what I had to do with it.

If Corrine was enjoying my display of self-immolation, she didn't show it. She softly smiled and took all the drama out of the situation by simply placing a suitable remedy on the counter and summarising the key elements of the instructions. Then, performing her role as community glue, she asked how I was doing living by myself and if I needed any *assistance*. There wasn't any question in her inquiry; she had just watched a piece of interpretive dance on the theme of my struggles, so what she was really doing was letting me know she was there to help if I needed it.

'*Non, tout est bon. Merci.*' No, everything is good. Thank you.

This was a lie, but at least I'd said it correctly.

I paid, said *merci* a few too many times, and left. I made a note of how different my mood was when I went to the pharmacy during the hours in which it was actually open. Heading home, I turned the radio up, and this time I used all five gears. I put my hand back out the window but this time it felt like I was high-fiving the oncoming current.

I reached for the paper bag of my purchases and held it out the window. Clutching the bag tightly, I shouted to all around what I'd just achieved.

I've got 'em! I have the cream! I have the blades! I've been under-stood by a French woman! Tonight I will fix Madison's rash and I will finish shaving my legs!

I didn't care that the only spectators were grazing cows, and there was no sign that any of them shared my excitement. These real ones even came with mouths, but I suspect few spoke any English.

XIX

Serving My Girls

Two very strong things doing what
they do best: growing.

As a parent, what's for dinner is always emotional soup.

The quiet of your kids as they eat is music to your ears. The calm brought by fully laden bellies is a perfect antidote to the concerns of the day. I'd been attempting to cook local dishes each night and it hadn't been going well. Some of my creations had been met with a look of despair – four eyes desperate to find something on their plates that they recognised. Under this gaze I was more prone to action than reflection, and my response was to jump up and search the cupboard for an alternative dinner. Elsa was easy: she'd inherited her mother's sweet tooth and in the Hyper U I'd found some healthy-looking potted yogurt that mixes its berries with evaporated cane juice. That's how some fancy foods describe their added sugar to appease label-reading parents.

Madison was slightly harder to feed. Since the first time she tried solids (mushed apple that she spat back) she has never been able to swallow anything even slightly sweet. It's not an act, although I've had to defend her countless times against those who think she is just a fussy eater, a high-maintenance glucose-averter. She has been strict – even her birthday cakes have had to be made with bacon-flavoured corn balls. At parties, when the piñata pops, she dives like the other kids on the lollies that come out, even putting them in her mouth to fit in with the other kids. Then she'll leave the room to spit them out. Fortunately, she was born in Australia where salt is impregnated in most meals, where 'a pie' means 'a meat pie', and where overly roasted meat is part of the staple diet. For Madison, I'd search for a piece of bread, butter it deeply and then apply a thin coat of the meaty tasting spread, Vegemite.

Before our arrival in France, a kind-thinking family member had sent us a supply of Vegemite to help us transition to French cuisine. While Vegemite is in every Australian household (or so its producers claim), any international sales are limited to homesick expats. Its only wide-scale distribution in Europe was when it was included in the ration packs of the ANZACs on the Western Front. Vegemite lovers will tell you with pride that it's a 'good source of vitamin B', but the remaining 99 per cent of the world will tell you it's barely edible, as evidenced by the fact that we've been able to export very average beer, Crocodile Hunters, flat whites, AC/DC and countless actors, but never elicited any overseas interest in the national spread.

After many evenings of having to recover with '*pain, beurre et Vegemite*', I'd miscalculated our supply and had recently run out of the rescue spread. One night Madison and Elsa looked across the table at me with unusually wide and wet eyes, and with my shrunken brain I sprang into action. I gave Elsa two tubs of yogurt and promised Madison I'd get some replacement Vegemite from the supermarket in Bourgueil. I checked that Merit'oh and Catherine were at home, put on our one movie, *Toy Story* 2 (or 3), for the twelfth or thirteenth time, and jumped in my car.

The Hyper U was forty-five minutes away, and, driving as fast as I could, I arrived at the almost deserted parking-lot just before 7 pm. Sensible shoppers, I assumed, were at home feeding their children stuff they liked.

Keen to complete my transaction before closing time, I ran towards a young lady stacking shelves, holding up the empty jar of Vegemite, and began speaking passionately in mangled French.

'*Je cherche le Vegemite! Le Vegemite pour ma –*'

I never did finish the sentence. As soon as I looked into her wide, sweet, but clearly terrified eyes I became acutely aware of the folly of my actions. I retreated from the store so quickly that I didn't even think of getting something else Madison might like. Bread, butter and a half litre of milk would be her dinner tonight, as Vegemite was now permanently off the menu.

Both my girls, in very different ways, were winning all of my love and respect, which sadly often I returned with such nonsensical acts. Elsa holds her energy deep inside her. It's the type of heat that hides inside a cooked tomato: it may look the same temperature as everything else on the plate, but the roof of your mouth will tell you otherwise. I've learned to never underestimate how much is going on inside her head. She often looks quite vague, blank-faced, and regularly walks in the other direction from the rest of her class. This might give you the impression that she's not thinking. I've learned that it's exactly the opposite.

Madison, on the other hand, shows you that she is feeling everything: the wind direction, the position of objects, the mood of adults. She shows her happiness along a smooth continuum: starting with a visual sign that she's alert to something she enjoys, then an upward trending curve of her lip, then an open mouth with her teeth showing (or spaces where teeth will soon return), then a steady progression of giggles, laughs and screams of joy.

If there's a scary scene coming up in a movie, Madison has already left the room. All it takes for her to disappear is a subtle key change in the film's soundtrack, a symphonic precursor to hint that something bad is about to happen. When she cries, the tears project outwards, her eyes go red and her lips quiver. It's as if the features of her upper face throw themselves down in grief, a cycle that is replenished as her lip catches her tears and her nose sucks them back in with each sniffle.

If Madison seems perfectly controlled by her emotions, Elsa has them in perfect control. She has a smile that could turn a sunflower, but when she thinks something is funny her face doesn't acknowledge it, she just thinks about it. Sometimes she just furrows her brow and walks off, repeating what she has heard over and over again, softly giggling to herself. She will cry, mainly only upon breaking bones and, as she hadn't come close to that recently, I couldn't remember the last time she teared up.

Individually, and as a colourfully-dressed collective, my girls were changing me faster than I could ever have imagined. Despite their pint size, it was their gallons of courage that were having the most impact. I admired how they tackled school each day, sitting close together in the classroom where they understood little but were always the centre of attention. Despite the challenge that school represented, I was moved by their determination to depart on time each morning and impressed by their ability to rebuild their disposition within minutes of leaving. At home it was their untold creativity that allowed them to make up for their lack of companions in after-school play. But my greatest admiration was reserved for their bravery in the face of the challenges that I knew were impacting their little hearts: being without their mother, without their brothers, being out of the familiar confines of Australia, and perhaps most of all, being cold.

This made each dinner all the more important, and I was trying to make every meal special. I lit candles every night, something we'd only ever done before for birthdays and at Christmas. Between them I'd fill a wine carafe with water as it appeared more fancy, next to what was left of a bottle of local red wine for me. We had big red napkins, which I folded neatly and placed on the table while they played nearby. I set the table with placemats and would announce the menu restaurant-style when everything looked warm and inviting.

Bon Soir, La Restaurant is ou-vere, I would mangle in French. *Le Dinner tonight iz about to be serv-ed.* Often I would sound more Italian than French.

I was struggling to get the food thing right here – it seemed to be one step too complex. I'd kept them on a diet of things they knew for the first month or two, but was sure we were missing the point of living in France. At the pharmacy one day, Corrine had asked what my girls were eating, and, not waiting for a response, suggested I get some help in the kitchen. While I stood there wondering how much pride to feign, she dialled a friend, who called a lady they knew was looking for work. I understood they'd organised for her to show up to my house the next day. Angelique, who I was warned didn't speak English, knew she'd been asked to help an Englishman who had two girls, and would do so by leaving a meal by the back door, three days a week, in return for a few euros.

I'd begun to leave the door open for her, and one day, without asking, she started to do the clothes washing. I didn't complain, as away from the pharmacy I didn't need to pretend I was doing so well. Angelique didn't just not speak English, she spoke her French loudly and at an incomprehensible speed. When she'd notice I didn't understand her, her response was to talk even louder, a method of comprehension-by-force that I thought was only practised by English speakers.

Angelique, Corrine had told me, worked four different jobs, as well as looking after her two school-age children, Laurence and Laurent. She'd pass by La Petite Briche during the day, arriving and departing at the same pace she talked. She was always on her way to another job. The previous year she'd left her husband – which gossip informed me was because he was a drunk – and he had recently died in a machine accident, which gossip informed me he was operating while drunk.

I loved her energy and enthusiasm in the face of a bemused Australian, but the girls were openly terrified by her. Not because she was scary, but her attempts to give the girls some love – all in loud, rapid-fire French – was more than they could handle. She had a big heart, but she heaved like a person who was just containing her pain.

All the meals Angelique prepared for us were local specialties – something I had asked Corrine to tell her to prepare – and I left her to make whatever she wanted. I just nodded when she said the names of the dishes she proposed for the next week and I hoped I'd be able to translate when I saw them in the pot. On one particularly frigid night, at the end of a particularly frigid day, I warmed a dish Angelique had left on the stove. It was *le bœuf*, or beef, normally a sure hit. The girls had been born when I ran a cattle company, and had grown up with the luxury of eating beef in its most tender versions, either steaks of fillet or hamburgers of ground beef. Tongue, however, was nothing they were prepared for.

The tongue is a magnificent muscle to look at, showing all the complexity that enables it to do its job. It is actually a group of eight muscles designed to go up, down, left and right, and curl into a roll. Pound-for-pound, it is among the strongest muscles in the body of a mammal. When cooked and cut down its length in thin slices, it shows the rivers of connective tissue that assist its dexterity and strength. I was keen for the girls to try it, and besides, I figured it would come with lots of vegetables and I'd bury it in tomato sauce if I needed to.

Serving cooked tongue to the uninitiated is one thing, but it turns out that reheating tongue is another, pushing the texture towards leather and concentrating its already noticeable odour.

The unfamiliar aroma was enough to stop the girls in their tracks when it arrived at the table.

I had done it again: after a long day at school, fuelled only by a cold lunch, at the end of another freezing day the dinner I'd organised would be an abject failure. I'm pretty good at a lot of things, one of which is telling myself I've screwed up, and extrapolating it into a rod with which to thoroughly beat myself.

I looked down at my plate, took a bite, and, as I chewed, I smiled and tried every version of encouragement I could come up with. None of these seemed to help: not the details of the vitamins in tongue, the almost humorous stripey pattern, or that eating different foods was part of our adventure here together. The vegetables were also imbued with the *jus*, or at least the smell, of tongue, and they were equally impossible to eat. Each mouthful was a room-temperature, throat-blocking reminder of Dad's failure. We did make the best of every day, we did highlight the good progress when it was made, but we knew we were always on tenuous ground here, emotions just below the surface. I could see the girls were starting to deflate in their chairs.

I jumped up and went into the kitchen to look for something else they could eat. From *le frigo*, I grabbed the pots of yogurt for Elsa, and some salted butter and a baguette for Madison. I sat back down with the substitute dinner and started a long-winded apology to the girls.

I said I didn't know that Angelique was cooking tongue for tonight. This was sort of a lie, as when she'd pointed to her tongue, I could have guessed what she planned to cook. I was becoming enamoured with our surroundings, and as a result I was keen to try everything. Trying them on your kids is another thing.

I explained that Angelique wasn't a cook – she was just a single mother, preparing these meals for us to earn a few extra euros. Let's focus on this detail, I thought, as there was a strong chance it would buy me some sympathy.

'She's divorced, lives alone and has two children she has to look after. One is called Laurent and one Laurence,' a detail I tried to use for humorous effect. It didn't work.

'Don't blame her, blame me.'

My words had seemed to arrest the girls' downward path but hadn't been able to lift their mood. If anything, my stories reminded them of just how pathetic our life here felt at times. We had made just getting through the day without tears a major milestone. We celebrated achievements like buying the right type of yogurt, putting washing powder – not dishwashing powder – in the wash, understanding the homework that Aimée asked them to do. Every day that the girls understood what they'd eaten for lunch was considered a golden day. A good night's sleep was defined as one not interrupted multiple times by Madison's mumblings. We'd learned to appreciate things that we took for granted in our old life.

Most of all, we'd developed a skill of putting the question of our future well underground.

The girls looked at each other, as they often did, and I wondered if they'd developed some of the legendary non-verbal twin communication system. Sometimes, when I saw them playing quietly by themselves, no other kids about, I really hoped that such a system existed. I was trying to emulate their stoicism, but I was sure my real emotional state was plastered across my face. I opened up and finally told them.

'Elsa, Madison, I'm really sorry. I'm not sure why I'm here, not sure what I'm doing really.

'Maybe we have to go back to Australia, maybe we are being silly.

'I'm trying my hardest, I'm doing what I can, and I'm being as positive as I can be.'

There, I'd said it. I breathed in, and the air that arrived was surprisingly fresh.

Then Madison talked.

'We know, Dad.' Her emphasis falling on *know*, reminding me how far ahead of me they are at times.

'We'll be okay.

'Anyway, it's light in the mornings now when we go to school.'

Another small victory that we'd learned to celebrate.

She reached across and we had an awkward hug over the wooden table, which we held for a long time, even though she had the table-top sticking into her chest, and I, in my stomach.

We sat silently while the girls ate their substitute dinner, and afterwards asked to go and play in the next room. We'd arrived with virtually no toys and they had more than compensated by cutting plain paper into two-dimensional dolls, making musical instruments out of sticks, and reimagining a few soft dolls into human children with whom they would organise imaginary playdates. Their favourite pastime, however, was a role-playing game based around their ages being changed through a time shift. Before they left the room they told me the desired destination: Elsa wanted to be raised up to eleven and Madison reduced to three. I waved my fingers in front of my mouth, said a few magic words, added some minor theatrics and then *POW!* – Elsa was empowered to walk Madison out of the room telling her she was going to teach her how Lego worked.

I stayed at the table, got out my laptop, and started to cry. Now I cried tears of relief from having come clean to my seven-year-olds. I cried tears of love for Madison and her bravery, her common sense and for the hug that had confirmed her words.

From where I was sitting, I could see Elsa had appeared in the doorway. She walked up to me and, without pausing, collided into my shoulder, encircling her arms around me. Thin and wiry, and much stronger than they looked, she tightened them around me. Her grip lassoed my chest, pulling my arms in towards my sides. I noticed I was now sitting up straight, one head height taller than before her arrival. My arms were trapped by her hold, and all I could do to return the cuddle was cup her elbows with my hands.

She hadn't said anything, and I thought to thank her. But she spoke first.

'Dad, you are the best dad in the world.'

Despite her lack of objectivity, I wholeheartedly accepted the compliment. Then, without another word, she returned to the living-room to play with her infant sister.

We'd been here now for nearly two months, and I'd been filled with doubt the entire time as to whether we'd make it.

In that moment, I knew we would.

Together.

X X

Bernard's Masterclass

Health and safety regulations deem that this
is the best way for a child to learn.

I'd just dropped the girls at school when I got the call. I didn't
get many – some weeks I wouldn't get any. From a group of
likely callers of one, I guessed correctly it was Aymeric. They
were about to weld together my tubes, he said, today the
bicycle's frame would take shape. Feeling the anticipation of an
expectant father, I turned around and sped towards the factory.
I had been the reason we were overdue; first it was to juggle
around the girls' school schedule, then I'd asked for a delay to
go up to Paris to get a lens appropriate for the task. I needed
something that would enable me to capture the precision of the
process, without getting me burned or my 24-70 mm lens more
damaged. The girls got their promised trip to Paris and a climb
up the Eiffel Tower, and I found a second-hand store that sold
a 105 mm macro lens that was perfect for the job. Essentially
it meant I could stand at nearly twice the distance, but still
capture almost microscopic detail.

I really didn't want to miss this stage, and I knew there was a chance that they'd just continue without me, still sceptical of my commitment to photograph every part of the process. I was excited and drove faster than comfortable in my car. I wasn't sure what my son felt, who happened to be sitting at my side, riding shotgun for the school drop-off this morning.

Robert had been the only one awake when I'd fed the girls that morning; his mother and brother still asleep upstairs. They'd broken their European road trip to visit us, and while it was great to see them again, I could have done without their lack of structure. The girls and I had made ourselves a tight unit, with a tight routine – most of this, thanks to the girls themselves. They got themselves up every morning, dressed themselves, loaded their schoolbags, and were near the door when it was time to leave. At night they played after dinner until they came to see me to say they were heading off to bed.

'Okay, Dad, we've finished our game. Can you change us back to real ages so that we can go to bed now?'

And off they would head, walking carefully upstairs, brushing their teeth, washing their brushes, putting them in the cup by the mirror and then giving me a shout to come and say goodnight. I'd read some small book (probably the same book again, as we only had three) and sing another of my tone-deaf songs.

In comparison to the girls, Robert and his brother may as well have been hippies. I'd missed them greatly and appreciated the stories of their adventurous road trip, but this, their second visit in two months, threatened the stability that the girls and I had created. Both George and Robert, just into their twelfth year, were already tall, and their hair hadn't stopped growing when they stopped getting it cut. It was now well over their collars, on its way to their shoulders.

The young man in my passenger seat wore the hip clothes – mostly black – of someone who'd recently been shopping in a city. Robert is a super-smart, super-sensitive and super-friendly kid, but he wasn't super-happy about our change of plans. I know he had things he wanted to do at home, he wanted to be out of a car for a change, and there was reasonable wi-fi to use. Without giving it any thought, I told Robert that today he was going to be spending the day in a cold factory, helping me photograph the welding of a steel bike.

I'd tried really hard with my boys when they were younger, but the intimacy I'd developed with my girls showed me just how much I'd missed with them at their age. When they were the age the girls were in France, I was CEO of a public company, proudly the youngest to lead a business of that size on the Australian stock exchange. I'd run fast towards a role like that, but when I got there it didn't take long to understand that the seven-figure remuneration was in return for a bit of my soul and most of the time I would otherwise have devoted to my family. I decided to never do that again, and had been searching for balance ever since – a route I never thought would take me to an early-morning dash to a factory with one of my sons.

While I am pretty sure I knew how *not* to live, I wasn't confident that I knew what was the right way to prepare my sons for the world of their future. Working to make money to buy stuff, then disposing of that stuff to buy more stuff, made little sense anymore.

When I entered the workforce it took about ten years to earn enough for a downpayment on a house somewhere near where you wanted to live. Today the number is more like thirty years, and if long-term trends continue, Robert and George might have to work forty years before they can afford a house. If their generation is going to have less, whether by choice or circumstance, then valuing the things they have more may give an equal or greater level of happiness. Until I had a clue, my kids would be getting a bit of everything.

One of my failings as a father had been to not give my sons the introductory course on factories that I had taken. While I hadn't planned it, today would be Robert's unscheduled masterclass, a chance to watch the ancient trade of metal work, using the most advanced metals, as performed by a man at the top of his profession, assembling a bicycle with a precision to the tenth of a millimetre. Essentially, he'd be cramming a couple of hundred years of progress in the metal trades, bicycle manufacturing, alloy development and computer-aided design into a one-day class.

Robert continued to not be so pleased. Not only was this not planned, but it wasn't like anything he'd been prepared for in his previous educational excursions.

'Don't worry, it won't take long,' I lied.

Consumerism only works when the act of consuming, as in using up the thing, is bookended by buying the thing in the first place and buying it again after. Any system of not buying – such as sharing, lending, bartering – doesn't add to GDP, which isn't economic growth and, without that, there isn't progress. Or at least progress as it is understood by the economic and political consensus. Equally, cherishing what we have, fixing things yourself, loving the warmth of a well-worn object, holding onto things, doesn't help our economy either. The only thing that helps is to buy and then buy the next thing, the next version, the newest model. Because my lessons on this subject to my kids are sometimes heavy-handed – Dad-splaining – I was relishing today's visit. Hopefully, along with Bernard's metalwork class, Robert would get a lesson in the opposite of modern economic theory.

The practicum would be led by Bernard, the thirty-year veteran of CYFAC, who was built much better than I was to teach this class. The lesson would take place in his workshop, and as Robert entered I felt him deflate in this world of old tools and ancient methods. Every surface was littered with another small or large tool, all with different depths of steel dust depending on the frequency with which they were required. The only nod to this century was that the radio station played a combination of French folk-pop and Englishy angst-ballads.

The steel tubes were once again wheeled in on a low trolley, with the spec sheet now to describe the angles at which they were to be joined. The steel Bernard would be working with was unlike the material I'd banged as a kid. Growing up in an iron ore part of the world and loving workshops, I relished the few times I'd been allowed to actually hold a welder – watching molten metal join pieces of steel. I thought I knew metal, but it had come a long way since then. Steel, while I wasn't looking, had changed: these tubes were less than half a millimetre thick, yet they are capable of holding ninety kilograms of me, bouncing over stones, flying downhill at fifty kilometres per hour. Or so I hoped.

Whether Robert would pick up the lessons of today would depend on whether he would see the demonstration as creating a positive correlation between the work that went into something and its inherent value. When an object's value is consistently mixed up with its price, the thing ceases to have any value except for the price that the vendor sets for it. It's understandable that people care less for things, as we are trained to see items as having no intrinsic value; only some extrinsic price that is placed on them by indifferent vendors or the incomprehensible gyrations of 'the market'.

Robert has grown up in a price-taking world, accepting what the vendor demands. I doubt he has ever had to bargain for anything in his life, and I'm not sure what would happen if he did. I imagine if he tried to negotiate at an Apple store the staff response would involve a call to security.

Worse for us, as consumers we're increasingly not in a transaction with the producers at all, but intermediaries such as supermarkets and consolidators. They all play the actual producers off against each other, putting further pressure on them, whether they be dairy farmers or phone manufacturers, to lower their costs of production. In an open, transparent market, like the local weekend varieties we were visiting, the consumers talk and share information. A certain solidarity is created. Online, it's the worst. The best bidding sites pit consumers against each other, where success comes from beating our fellow consumers. In a world of abundance, we've been tricked into focusing on scarcity. We've turned against ourselves without noticing. Shopping has got competitive. The doors fly open and we push against each other, elbowing our fellow citizen, not considering who is really on our team.

Rethinking our economic system, a system that is built for progress only when it is powered by consumerism, is a growing field of economic study, closely tied to new political thought. Thomas Piketty, the French economist, has, since the beginning of this century, been telling anyone who'll listen how and why inequality continues to expand in almost every nation. Put simply, when the returns from having capital are higher than the return from actually working, inequality is destined to expand. Robert had a lot to concentrate on, so the Political Science course on the likely responses to a world of increasing inequality would have to wait for another day.

I gave Robert a small job to do for me in the factory: hold my spare lens and be ready to pass it to me as soon as I needed it. I knew from my first trip here that Bernard doesn't break his rhythm for photo opportunities. I asked Robert to concentrate on my movements, and he learned quickly to ready a lens as I moved.

Most of all I was trying to give Robert some direction so as to stop his hands wandering. He has the most delicate of fingers, long like mine, and a mind that causes him to touch before he asks. I knew I'd have to ensure he didn't get his hands into anywhere he shouldn't. After all, we were in a factory of spinning blades that become invisible once they reached working velocity, heat that turned metal bright red at 1000 degrees, but then returned to its original colour while remaining a blister-making 200 degrees. Around us were buttons that came with their own warnings, written across them in red all-caps French, while the jars all carried the universally understandable skull-over-lightning-bolt symbol. The table-tops were full of metal shards and tiny iron filings, and it looked like most of the electrical wires were pretty well insulated. I also knew the greatest attraction for him would be the supply of *mademoiselles*, morning coffee's chocolate snacks that were sitting nearby, unguarded.

Bernard was a professional, I, on the other hand, am an amateur behind the lens. I grew up with a camera that had about five things you could change once the film was inserted. Now my camera has approximately fifty variables, a combination of settings that I make in advance, plus the ones that I adjust for each shot. With my mind so full, I have little or no memory of what I captured and knew I'd have to rely on the uploading of the images to remember what we saw today.

At exactly 10 am, the bell rang, and all work stopped as the ritual of morning-break began. Great! A breather for me and another part of factory life that I could introduce Robert to. At morning coffee he'd get to see the delicate interaction between co-workers and get to officially eat his first *mademoiselle*.

When Robert was seated, I asked Aymeric to ask Bernard if a child had ever come in to the factory to watch his process. Aymeric answered himself, 'No,' but I asked him to ask Bernard the question anyway.

'No,' Bernard said without a pause, with the 'o' being almost silent, giving strength to the nasal 'N'.

I smiled at Robert, and he smiled back while concentrating on acting like he was eating his first *mademoiselle* of the day.

'That is, before you, Peter,' Aymeric said to everyone's amusement, bursting my bubble of self-satisfaction.

There was a time when children did come to factories, but that was to work. Perhaps our perception of the injustice of this is one of the reasons we try so hard to keep them away from the means of production. The factory system grew out of the home workshop system, where families naturally worked together. The workers in the Industrial Revolution's first factories were men paid by the piece they delivered. It was up to them if they wanted to bring their wife and kids along to speed things up. Early weaving machines would jam often, and the only way to get the machine back to work was to have a small child spend their days scurrying under the power loom to unjam the shuttle. Factories and their evil owners, of which there certainly were some, didn't put children to work: parents did. Just like the mines in Congo, it isn't Apple asking for child-harvested lithium, but rather a local mine operator who pays per bucket of ore, and families who bring their children to help out.

Robert appeared to be warming to factory work, as when Bernard excused himself, once again the first to do so, Robert immediately followed him. I stayed at the table for a few minutes, hoping others would notice and reach the conclusion that such an attentive boy must be the product of good fathering. The crew seemed more interested in their sweet *mademoiselles* and rough coffee.

The next three hours was a smooth flow of activity. It was the first time for Robert, me and these tubes, but a process known well to Bernard. While Bernard never lost focus on my frame, he was often called aside by the factory system to simultaneously work on parts of other frames.

One moment he'd be shaving a fraction of a millimetre off one of my tubes, the next he'd be called to slice through another rod being used elsewhere in the factory. He'd put two tubes in place to be joined, but then an alarm would go off and he'd remove one from the oxy bath, insert another. He'd be asked to look over his shoulder at a frame that had been polished to inspect the job or address an urgent fix that was delaying an order that had to go out. True prowess is to make the complex seem simple, and Bernard did all of this without a noticeable change of pace, a rhythm that he kept from the moment he entered the factory in the morning, through the coffee break and lunch, to the time he would depart some nine hours later.

Robert stopped handing me my lenses, not because he wasn't a dutiful son, but because he'd become completely wrapped up in the process. Without a camera to fuss with, he would often move to the next stage before I did. Increasingly he was in my shot. First as something I tried to move out of the way, and then, as I watched what was happening, he became part of the process. I had come to photograph Bernard melting steel together but became aware I was watching an ancient dance of master/apprentice, a father-like figure and an eager-to-learn son.

Bernard never made it easy for me, not understanding the work I was trying to do. While his forearm frequently hid the action from my lens, the images showed that he had opened his shoulders to Robert. With a slight change of his position, he'd opened the process to Robert, letting him come in close. The day had started all about me – I was the excited man driving to the factory. By the end of the day, the relationship that was captured had a longer history, its origin in a deeper purpose. Robert barely makes it through five minutes of a school class without some type of teacher-led refocusing, but here, for nearly five hours, he'd been captivated.

At school, while woodwork was my favourite class, when I signed up others questioned my level of intelligence. The smarter kids were ushered away from anything creative or useful.

The counsellors weren't simply being nasty, it was just that the societies in which I've worked have an assumed hierarchy of happiness that is correlated to the perceived status of one's trade or profession. Somewhere near the bottom were the farmers, assumed to be trapped in an agrarian age and appropriately grumpy. All builders, for example, while above the farmers, were still below all the designers and architects. The account-ants were above them, the lawyers even higher, and so on. The further you are away from actually making stuff, the higher your standing in modern society.

It wasn't always this way. Once the King sat at the high table with the head of each trade group. In England they were called the Guilds, each trade represented by highly respected chiefs, men who sat at the top of society, meaning that no matter what profession you were in, you could rise to the top of society in terms of respect. In France, these Guilds succumbed to the temptations of the elite, grew into exclusive societies with restrictive rules, and when the blade of the revolution arrived, they suffered the same fate as the other representatives of the one per cent.

When trade groups re-emerged, in the middle of the nineteenth century, they took the form of distinctly egalitarian bodies devoted less to excellence, and more united in the fight for fairness and higher wages. Trade unions, as we know them today. The fight between the pursuit of excellence and the protection of fairness remains at the heart of all battles with, and within, organised labour.

That night I loaded nearly a thousand photographs, from the wide shots of the factory to parts of the process in macro details. And most were now in focus. From the carefully distant observations of Robert and Bernard, one in the fresh clothes of urban youth, the other in the timeless blue of overalls, to the microscopic melting of the alloy used to join the tubes, its subtle change of colour as the magnesium burns green allowing the red of its steel content to harden. The wide shots were of the grey on grey of the room, its tones gradually changing through my shots as the lights faded in the early afternoon.

The greatest change, beyond the gradual dishevelling of Bernard's hair, the growing collection of metal filings on his shirt, was in the young man who got closer and closer throughout the day. I went there to photograph a bike being built, metal being cut, melted and joined in a Vulcan's grip of heat and pressure.

As I scrolled through the images again and again, it was clear that I had a study of my son and Bernard. Robert's eyes tell you where he is focused, his posture tells you how open he is to what he is seeing. To my son, Bernard had given a lesson in the love of work, the pursuit of excellence that was physically transferred to the object, permanently welding to the steel frame a value that would remain irrespective of price.

For Bernard, the texture of his hands tells you they are his primary tool, but the complexity of his task and his management of his environment require him to work with his brain. However, in the images, in the moments that pass too quickly for our eye to detect, it became clear that he works with his heart.

XXI

Learning to Ride: Cross Training

The paint design was about the only area
I could add any value.

When Bernard finished the joining of the tubes, there was still enough time for me to get a ride in against the fading light. The bike was still two months away, which I now saw as a benefit.

I'd been riding every chance I had, racing the dead flat roads, competing only against myself and the infrequent traffic. I was eating well and dropping weight fast, but knew it was my head that I had to train. I had a habit of wandering off into thoughts as I rode and had to find small targets to keep up my pace. Sometimes I'd chase down some rumbling farm equipment, and overtake the tractor, proving to myself I was not the slowest thing out here. I was pushing myself hard, but incline-free empty roads were not the ideal conditions to train for three of the steepest ascents of the professional tour, surrounded by eight thousand other riders.

After watching the work on my bike, it wasn't so much the fear of humiliation next to the other riders, or the reverence for the three peaks, that motivated me: it was preparing to be worthy of the bicycle that was being built. I knew I could bluff the other riders by wearing a professional-looking outfit that I'd carefully match to my bike like the rest of them. The mountains themselves were unlikely to notice the impact of my pedalling up their backs, flying down their fronts. But my bike would know the moment I sat awkwardly down on its narrow seat. It would feel it as my feet fumbled for the pedal clips, the grip of hands that rarely left the handlebars. Other riders had better things to do than notice what gear I was in, but my bike would know.

So that afternoon, after seeing the preparations being put into my future team-mate, I knew I had work to do to get the strength, the legs, worthy of my ride.

I went down to the *cav*, or basement, and took out Frits' mountain bike. I had come up with a plan to compensate for the flat roads: to make it more intense I was going to take the seat off the stem and make it impossible to (comfortably) sit down.

In the fading light, I took off from La Petite Briche and rode the network of straight roads across the surrounding fields. They had once been the rail tracks serving Cail's giant barn. The rails long since had been taken up to melt down as steel for a French war effort. The wood sleepers no doubt served closer to home, warming houses through the winter months. The paths of his private twelve-kilometre rail network remained, six prongs heading out in different directions, making a series of perfectly straight sprinting tracks. Standing up over where my seat had been, tempted to sit down but remembering not to, I raced along each of the tracks, easily defeating the stationary remnants of previous crops that lay to each side. In the distance, a solitary tractor was doing the early planting of spring. But otherwise I was alone. The only sign of life was a few fields with a winter crop of some sort of low plant with a leaf like spinach. I learned it was sugar beet, which Cail had introduced, a way to make sugar in places too cold for cane to grow.

My system worked, although it hurt like crazy to stand up for an hour, grinding away in a high gear. I came to the end of one track and met the main road that leads away from the CYFAC factory. Suddenly I realised that if someone from the factory were to be driving home at that moment I might be spotted. It was close to dark, but the lights of a passing car would have exposed me. It would do my reputation at the factory no good to be seen like this. Not only would they think I was training on the wrong type of bike, but also that I didn't have a seat, and must be so embarrassed that I trained under the cover of dark.

XXII

What Are Friends For, Anyway?

Happy, we all were, up to a point.

Once the boys and their mother left, we fell back into our normal state. With our weekly rhythm set, it was repeated with precision every seven days. Wednesday for activities, weekends for free play, and school days that went like clockwork. I'd wake at 7.05 and stumble upstairs to open the blinds in the girls' room, keeping my head low when I turned around. Ever since we'd escaped February, this ritual would actually let in light. The girls would wake easily and start to dress themselves in clothes they would lay out on the floor before going to bed. The result, including hat, looked like colourful shadows of themselves resting on their bedroom floor. I'd tell them they could watch a little TV while they got dressed, one of them clicking a Lego remote for the TV Madi had made out of an egg carton.

I'd head downstairs to start the French toast, which we'd agreed to every single weekday morning. Weekends there was enough time for a Janet omelet. The only modification to the breakfast regime was which bread I used: was it baguette that in one day stiffens to timber that I cut with a knife-cum-handsaw, or pieces of the Freddy's American-Brand bread from the Super U that is sold pre-sliced, with the crusts removed, and remains soft for two weeks after it's brought home.

Both types of bread spent the same time in the mix – four eggs well beaten, a splash of milk, and if I remember, a pinch of salt – and both left the goop equally floppy. Elsa liked hers cooked well done, Madison asked for hers mushy on the inside. It was hard to get the order perfect when cooking all the pieces in the same pan, so I'd learned to cook one side more than the other, and serve Elsa's with the dark side up, Madison's with the less-cooked side showing. I'd deliver the plates to the table with an emphatic 'Just the way you like it'. Nobody had asked for a change, and I accepted this as a small Dad victory, even if they were secretly in on the deceit. We were all just trying to do the best we could, and nobody was in a mood to call out the other.

Madison would always eat all of hers. Elsa would bury her pieces in brown sugar and push them around the plate, nibbling a bit and leaving me the rest to clean up. I'd get their bags and my bike loaded into the car, tidy the kitchen and we'd drive off to school. My cries of 'If we leave now, we'll beat the school bus' have been replaced by the girls saying, 'We must go, Dad, if we're going to beat the school bus'. When things were colder, the potholes filled with water and froze, and I'd drive smoothly over them. Now the ice has melted, and the potholes have returned to the depth we remembered from when they first introduced themselves.

At the intersection with the D769, I'd check for oncoming traffic, careful that we beat – not collide with – the speeding school bus. The drive is less than five minutes, and I'd select the French pop station I'd discovered at CYFAC. The girls had now found favourites amongst the songs on high rotation. Almost every morning we'd beat the bus, even if it rushed up behind me and followed me into the school parking lot. I'd park, something I could do now with confidence, and walk the girls to the school door. Madison always asked if I could hold her hand; Elsa would achieve the same outcome by pushing hers into mine. My hands are large, always warm, but can be a little sweaty. Both girls had told me they didn't mind the moist bond we formed.

I'd walk them to their classroom, help them take off their outer layers, hang up their bags, remove the books they need that day, and walk them to their desks. I say *bonjour* to a few of their classmates I knew by name. The boys liked to approach me and repeat *hu-llo, hu-llo*. I'd smile coyly at Aimée and attempt to slip out. Madison would often circle back and catch me by the classroom door and I'd hug her again.

After drop-off I'd either speed to CYFAC to photograph or make my way to the Bouff'tard to write. Either way the middle of the day would see me united with its twelve-euro *prix fixe*. I'd then head back to the schoolyard, camera full of images, computer full of words, and change into my cycling gear in the public toilet. I'd leave just enough space to ride for an hour and a half. I'd get back just in time, join the other parents and wait for Aimée to crack open the school door. The girls were always the first to be released. They'd fly out and I'd drop down to my haunches and hug them both. I'd carry their bags, and we'd head towards home, all of us exploding in a desire to talk. I'd prepare dinner, they'd watch my photos load onto the computer, we'd eat dinner, they'd play, I'd write, they'd fall soundly asleep, I'd write some more, I'd fall soundly asleep. Then repeat.

Increasingly the photos showed a variety of life here. The girls were following the progress of my bicycle the same way people watch a TV series. They knew the names of the main characters, Bernard and Aymeric, but had noticed the show was starting to drag. I told them it was my fault. I was learning so much that I was slowing things down while I captured more of the process.

In precise detail they were getting the path of a number of bicycles through a factory, the steel versions and the ones in carbon. They were learning about the tools of the trade, but increasingly the people and their relationships. The complexity of making things is something you can write down, put in a manual, replicate to the point of automation. But the delicate flow of interactions between humans – the conversations in which unexpected problems are raised, when solutions are debated without concern for ownership, where different degrees of perfection are subtly negotiated between a group of workers – is less of an objective process and more like a dance, more of a hymn to pride in one's work than an instruction manual for joining tubes. I thought I'd be showing my girls a how-to series on manufacturing, but it became clearer, with every batch of another hundred photos, that the documentary was about people at work.

In addition to the factory photos, I'd discovered a growing number of activities in the area, now that I knew where to look. Behind the houses there were various small workshops; inside nondescript farm sheds, people packaged finished foods. Everywhere here the subterranean network of caves worked as giant constant-temperature storage facilities.

Most were used for wine, but in one, Freddy, a twenty-something man with a well-worn white van, had started a business to supply high-end restaurants in the capital. Every Friday he'd load his van with a specific mushroom and speed up to Paris, stopping at the kitchen doors of a number of elite restaurants. In the barn behind another farmhouse, Franc raised a variety of rare owls and hawks for sale to aviaries around the world.

Behind the stone wall of the school, in a small low-roofed wooden shed, I sat and watched a distiller work with a series of large copper vats. His thick hands, blood red from his mixture, lifted steaming lids, stirred a turgid treacle, and out of the bottom of one of the tanks dropped shiny ruby-like droplets of his high-octane mix. I learned he was the last of his family to be allowed to continue this trade, thanks to a raft of new regulations from the European Union relating to the production of spirits. After him, Hommes would no longer have a local brew with a 400-year heritage.

The life here retreats in the winter, but had begun to peek out in the spring. It had been hidden from me mostly because I wasn't trained to see that which is not promoted. There are no signs that read *Franc's House of Rare Predators and Peculiar Owls* or *Freddy's Cave of Mushroom Delights, supplier to the top restaurants of Paris*, or *Augustin's Family Firewater, lifting village spirits since 1610*.

It was becoming easier and easier for me to appreciate this land as the days grew longer; even as they passed more quickly. I'd met a beekeeper and learned of the ten-week process towards a jar of honey. I'd discussed the twenty-year gestation period of the trees planted by a tree-planting father with his tree-planting son. I had studied Merit'oh's amplifier-building business, his clients willing to pay a small fortune for the privilege of feeding their music through the vacuum tubes that were the best technology half a century ago. I talked basic French to a sausage maker and was invited by an adorable young girl to follow her to her parents' goat-cheese-making facility. I'd even found a shop nearby that became my favourite place to buy fresh bread. I had convinced myself the girl behind the counter had a crush on me. She was rather pretty, with dark brown hair, big brown eyes and one brown tooth. I was falling for this area everywhere I looked.

With every ride my legs got stronger, my lungs larger and my circle of exploration wider. I was still riding Frits' racing bike, doing what I felt was my apprenticeship on this machine until I had the legs to deserve something better. Each day I would ride, but as Aimée was always precisely on time, I had to plan my ride with similar accuracy. With increasing bravery, I added to the outbound route, pushing harder on the return, always knowing I'd need a moment to slip my jeans over the cycling tights. If I got back too late, I'd have to join the other parents standing barelegged in my shorts. I was often the only male, the only person ever in shorts, and about the only one not sneaking a quick pre-pick-up cigarette.

Each of the new villages I reached was marked by the same small blue oval plaque with the village's name and the maker of the label. I'd snap a photo on my phone, and then look at the map that night to see where I had been. The plaques said they were a product of the Michelin company, the one I knew first as a manufacturer of car tyres, then as the company that rates fancy restaurants with gold stars. Turns out, it also labels French towns with its blue plaques. The origins of this odd business diversity are not hard to understand. I learned that among the early uses for their patented pneumatic tyres was people using cars and bicycles to travel to new towns across France in wider and wider circuits of discovery. To increase demand for their tyres, Michelin got in the travel promotion business. As the French won't go anywhere without the promise of a good meal, the company started to rate the restaurants you could drive or ride to. That grew to the international rating system for fancy restaurants – up to three stars for the world's best – although their customers are now more likely to fly in, rather than pedal to these top-rated restaurants.

One day, I was focused on trying to take an interesting photo of one of these town markers when the owner of the house it was attached to barrelled out to see what was happening. Dressed in the attire of a farmer – boots and forearms to confirm it – he had a wide face that set off bright eyes. Had it not been for them, I might have been more apprehensive about the sudden arrival of this large force.

I quickly launched into my usual three-part introduction: '*Je m'appelle Peter, je suis Australien, et j'habite à La Petite Briche.*'

His eyes dimmed, and he looked blankly at me. I was used to this reaction. When I'd first got here I was technically speaking a type of French, but really I didn't know what the words I was using meant – I was just stringing together sounds I had been told to say. But I'd been working on the language and was enjoying weekly lessons with Marie-Françoise.

This was one of the first sentences I'd worked on to get just right. I'd even worked on the local accent. But it still got me blank stares. The problem was that people just didn't get the concept of what I was saying. The man who introduced himself as Phillippe was no different, but unlike others, he suggested I slow down and take it piece by piece.

'*Je suis Peter.*'

'*Oui, oui, oui, je suis Phillippe,*' he said to show he understood this part.

'*Je suis Australien.*'

'*Australien?*' And he then added the universal confirmation: '*Kangourou?*'

'*Oui, oui,*' I responded. '*Et j'habite à La Petite Briche.*'

He furrowed his brow, leaned in and looked like he was going to tackle me. Phillippe then called out '*Maman!*' (Mum) – then '*Something, something, La Petite Briche, something, something, Australian. Something, something, kangaroo!*' He threw up his hands; thanks to the unlikely marsupial, I was in. I'd created a connection by holding my hands up like little paws and jumping a bit. Everyone would laugh at that, and it worked because no other nation has a monopoly on such a well-known creature that conclusively links you to your country.

Phillippe's mother appeared from the kitchen, apron around her neck, walking with some pain, her back arched like a lady who had known hard work. She clearly hadn't been very tall before she started to tip forward and was now not much higher than Phillippe's belt. But when she spoke it would have been loud for someone twice her height. She kept repeating, '*La Petite Briche, something, La Petite Briche, something else,*' and then walked off – I assumed to keep cooking.

Phillippe indicated that this was his house, behind us were his sheds, and on the small rise past the field at the back, his cows. He proudly pointed out his tractor, parked in front of the house in the position that a suburban house has its SUV parked. I'd been in the cattle business and knew enough farming to talk to anyone who worked the land. My job had kept me miles from the actual fields for most of the time, but had given me plenty of time meeting those who are the modern stewards of the land.

It's not hard to tell a good one when you meet them; farmers have one of the toughest professions legally undertaken in our society. It's a given that some will work every day of the year; dairy farmers often rise before dawn 365 days in a row. They are pushed from above by shifting market forces, with more and more power consolidating in the supermarkets' hands, buffeted by the whims of the weather, less regular than ever before, and hidebound by regulations that are drawn up by city folk with little understanding of the reality on the land.

That's before you appreciate that the basic job is to tear up the earth, slash down what is grown, thrash and grind what you drag back, breed animals only to kill them in their prime, or suck them dry of the milk they're making for an offspring you've removed from them. Yet the best of the farmers, and there are many, are calm, kind people, with an immensely broad knowledge required to do their jobs. Most have a love of the land greater than the ones who only visit it on the weekend. It's an irony that even those who raise animals to be slaughtered often have a higher regard for the welfare of animals than those whose involvement is limited to eating pieces of them served medium rare.

Phillippe asked if I would like to *regard*, to see, his property. I was eager for the introduction, and like my other visits to people's enterprises here, very happy for the brief moments of company that it created.

His farm's buildings are half a dozen of different ages, from quite modern to what looks like the Middle Ages. The machinery, too, covers a period from as recent as the almost space-age tractor that sits in his front yard, through well-used ploughs and seeders, to things that look like they'd be more suited to being pulled by an ox, up to its knees in muddy soil. Under various coverings are machines of modern agriculture. The same diesel engine that powers the tractor's oversized tyres also turns a crank at the back that's used to power a variety of choppers and crushers and other mechanical devices. For a farmer, a tractor is not only the moveable office in which he'll spend long and solitary hours patterning his fields, but also the portable power source at the core of his business.

His animal husbandry was the next part of the tour. In a series of old stone barns were two small calves, tied to the wall but happily eating a mixture of roughage and grains. They were friendly and pulled at their ties to sniff my hand. Outside and sharing a common wall with the neigbours is a small cor-rugated iron shed in which I found another three calves, these ones much smaller, drinking milk from bowls. Next to them is a three-level structure of nesting cages, doors ajar, home to twenty or so chickens and some of the geese that I'd seen scat-tered around the house and farm, diligently going about their pecking business.

Behind the bird's apartments are a series of hutches, and I recognised Phillippe's word *lapin* as rabbit, as it had been on the Bouff'tard's menu frequently. His milking shed was in the distance, and his cows were making their own way to it, a single file line of larger-than-average Jerseys, Holsteins and French Browns, drawn out of habit towards their evening feed and their second milking of the day.

Next to the house, in a stand-alone building that looks like relative luxury, I was introduced to Phillippe's best animal friend, his pig. She was already a good size, had his bright eyes, her nuzzling our hands an indication that she was used to finding treats there. He smiled and said that she'd be dinner in another three months.

It's not a straightforward love relationship, that between a farmer and the beasts he will raise and then kill. It's easy to think there could be no bond between the diner and the dinner, but the connection can be as deep as others have for a household pet, the contact more frequent than some adults with their own child, and the tenderness more publicly displayed than some towards their wives. Some people seek to impress you with their position, others with what shiny things they have to show you, or the variety of words with which they shape their stories. Phillippe had none of these at his disposal, but plenty of his own confidence, and was immediately likable.

At that point his mother barrelled out of the house carrying a handful of photographs in her hands. She was talking even louder than before, a volume only exceeded by that of the man I correctly guessed was her husband – a smaller, older, slightly pudgier but otherwise precise facsimile of Phillippe. Also called Phillippe. I have never met two more compact megaphones. The volume is somehow made without shouting, and it is not projecting in any theatrical manner. It just feels as if you are standing on the speaker's front teeth and are being buffeted by the wind and spittle.

In her hands were a few small black-and-white photos, fitting easily in her palms, each with a white border of delicately bevelled edges. She was talking (shouting) and Phillippe was repeating *école*, or school. I recognised the shapes in the photos from what were now the ruins of La Briche. She pointed out the three-gabled front of the giant barn in good condition, and what is now our house. Pointing to her chest, she made it clear it had been her school. She was proud to have attended school, so I asked if her husband was one of the men in the photos.

'*Non!*' They looked at me oddly. The man in the image was *mon père*, her father. Her husband, young Phillippe let me know, couldn't go to school, as he had to work the farm from the time he was a young boy. Girls got to go to school, boys entered the real world. Somewhat like my kids, I thought.

I asked her for *un moment* to photograph them in her hand. The shots I would show that night to the girls would have her hands – knuckles large, skin worn – and the perfectly preserved seventy-year-old photos, one of the three peaked barns of Cail's farm, and another with two men posing next to an early tractor. Phillippe's grandfather had been one of the last to work on Cail's experiment in industrial farming. Turns out you don't need to own a centralised rail system if everyone can have a tractor. Diesel was correct – his engine did give power to the people, the farming people at least, all those with access to a diesel tractor.

The final picture she showed was of two men, on the one bicycle. One – *mon père, mon père!* – was standing on the seat while the other pedalled, a type of circus act, performed in front of Cail's giant barns.

On my first visit with Phillippe, I counted more than twenty trades that he must know to do his job, a series of tasks that has only increased with the introduction of mechanisation. Wishing to show that I appreciated the work that went into all he had just showed me, I pointed to the surrounding area and suggested it must be *difficile*, difficult, to be *un fermier ici*, a farmer here. Without missing a beat, he responded that it is hard to be a farmer anywhere. And getting harder to be a farmer in any of Europe. More expensive equipment, higher capital costs, more complex selling options, increased array of chemicals, new animal welfare rules, restrictions on what you can and can't raise and grow. '*La régla, la régla, la régla,*' he said: regulation, regulation, regulation.

I understood. Increasingly, farms are owned by absentee investors, operated by professional managers and worked by specialist contractors each having tightly defined roles. He told me his son was going to a school near Tours, and that he didn't think he'd return to the land. Perhaps fifty generations of families had worked these farm lands, and his generation might just be the last. It may prove to be that Phillippe is the last in a thousand-year lineage to hold in himself all there is to know about farming.

The introduction had finished, and I was back at the front door. As my bike looked at me, I realised that I'd been attired in my cycling tights for the farm tour. Like stepping out to get the newspaper off the front lawn, and forgetting you sleep in the raw, I was suddenly shy. I made a joke out of my attire, which Phillippe seemed to appreciate. I said I must be heading home, to pick up my daughters from school. That Phillippe warmly invited me to bring the girls to get some milk suggests my outfit hadn't been too upsetting.

Madison likes milk in a way that is close to love, as her aversion to sugar means it's the one thing she can find in any house that she knows will fill her up. Later that week I'd returned with the girls and been given two large bottles of fresh milk, which made Madison happier than at any other time I'd seen her here. Phillippe senior even invited the girls and I back for dinner. Well, I thought it was dinner: after three hours sitting at the dining-room table, I realised that I'd been invited for a drink. Eventually we thanked them and went home for a late meal of bread and butter and a litre each of fresh milk.

I went back many times, photographing his growing pig on numerous occasions. The girls met all the farm's animals, and learned to hug the rabbits and hand feed the calves. I left unexplained some parts of the process; such as the prospects for the cute young cattle, or why the rabbits were quite so large. Phillippe always welcomed the girls, and always asked me to speak slowly. He'd work out what I was trying to say, ask me if that was right, and then encourage me on. His support allowed me to find words that I didn't know I knew, words that I'm sure I hadn't learned, but had heard. I would just insert them in the hope they made a sentence. He gave me the confidence to think I was speaking French, and at times I guess I was.

Months after this first visit, I was invited to come back to see the pig slaughtered. It took place over an entire weekend, and involved twelve members of Phillippe's extended family coming together. I followed the entire process with my camera. The first shots showed the pig trotting out of its house with her tail in the air, wiggling at the side of its owner. Then she gave an awkward look as a brass tube was pressed to her forehead, a stubby, single-shot rifle that let go with a thud. My reflexes now better, I captured the precise moment she looked at me with the gaze of 'Did my friend Phillippe just do that to me?'

There was a moment for celebration confined to Phillippe and two cousins, wide smiles, punctuated by the opening of tiny bottles of beer. Some sort of toast went out. *The pig is dead, long live the pig*, I imagined. I took a beer with my spare hand and continued to shoot while the cutting part began.

For two long days the family worked with only the interruption of a festive lunch. While it wasn't a great weekend for the pig, it was a combination of family reunion and home economics and cooking class. A variety of sausage meats were mixed and then fed into natural casings, and various baked meat dishes were covered with the exotic pieces of stomach lining. If there was any piece not utilised, they must have snuck it out while I was looking elsewhere. The best cuts were individually placed in plastic bags by Phillippe's wife, Karine, marked with a date and placed in a deep freezer. Then, on a whiteboard, where she'd neatly drawn up a calendar for the next six months, she wrote the menu for what would be made for the evening's meal. Karine was a powerful lady. I learned that she worked one of the milking shifts each day, and it slowly became clear that this factory, this small team, was working under her soft orders.

The last photograph of the day, as Sunday's light faded through the kitchen's two small windows, recorded Phillippe's mother, sitting heavily on a low bench. 'Fatiguée, fatiguée,' she repeated.

But that wouldn't happen for another three months after this first visit. For one thing, the pig had another 50 kilograms of growing to do. But meeting Phillippe, having someone draw from me the French that was inside me, inviting me over to his house, sharing his table, his tiny bottles of beer, made it feel like I had my first real friend in the area. And while I knew we didn't understand all we said to each other, I was pretty sure he wasn't about to shoot me in the head.

XXIII

Learning to Ride: My First Cycling Victory

Madison, about thirty years younger than
when I learned to do the same repairs.

Spring had fully sprung, and things were growing everywhere the light touched. With the sun, out came the people and their desire to gather. Beside the road, there also grew small patches of fliers advertising local events. The events were described on A4 pieces of paper, stapled to a stick and planted just outside the entrance to the towns here. They weren't large, and sat low, so I got into the habit of pulling over and getting out of my car to see if I could understand whether any of the events were of the type the girls and I would like.

I'd taken the girls to what I had thought was some combination of livestock show and country & western dance one weekend, which had turned out to be a meat sale. At one point there was indeed a type of country music playing, but mainly we stood around and looked at parts of animals in makeshift display cases. The girls love meat: I'd developed their passion to a point I now regret. But how you experience life is a lot about what you are expecting, and even though the girls seemed to like Frenchy-country music, we'd still got dressed for a dance and left with a bag of sausages.

One series of notices didn't need to be any larger to get my attention. It was about cycling, a race, and it was in a town nearby. They had me at *velo*. Closer inspection showed it was for mountain bikes, for VVTs, as the French call them in an acronym I would never understand. It mentioned the Bourgueil by the Loire, which I guess meant that was where it started, and it gave a date and time that I guessed was when it started. The numbers 10, 34 and 54 suggested there were races over each of those distances. I was keen to get any race experience I could, and this would be my first in France. I would soon have a new road bike, but I figured a mountain bike race could be good training. After all, 'Our Cadel' started his professional cycling career as a mountain biker.

As the race was on a Saturday I arranged for the girls to be supervised by Angelique. It worked well as they were terrified by her, so whenever she was in the house, they played outside. Before I left I showed the girls Frits' mountain bike, freshly cleaned for the race, showed them my 'race' gear, and generally tried to make them proud of their dad. I pointed out how I'd been able to expand the number of gears on the bike from three to about eight (out of the theoretical eighteen) and was proud of my progress in the art of bicycle maintenance, even if it was mostly thanks to finishing a can of WD-40 on anything that looked related to gears.

I was still pointing at parts of my bicycle when Elsa asked if she could leave, as they were, she said, in the middle of a game. I knew they'd continue to do what they always did, the role-playing, making toys from sticks, and drawing things for hours and probably wouldn't notice my absence.

I drove to the Bourgueil Halle, parked nearby and registered quickly for the fifty-four kilometre version. I was given my race number, pins to attach it, and three tokens for some wine and a snack after the race. I slipped the tokens into my back pocket, pinned the number on my chest and cheekily rode into the middle of the large group of cyclists already lined up. I mumbled earnest-sounding apologies that didn't seem necessary, as no-one was too fussed as I pushed in.

When the flag dropped, I took off like the best of them. As it was a race of variable lengths, I used the equipment of each rider to tell me what length I thought they'd be doing, so I could pace myself with the right group. In some sports, the more equipment you have, the more you show yourself to be a novice. Shiny new bike with lots of gears, and large springs at both ends: probably the ten-kilometre ride. Well-used and suspension on only the front, probably the thirty-four. No suspension, fewer gears, even some with just a single gear: certainly the fifty-four. My bike was a bright orange misfit, with green lightning bolts and pre-rusted gears, which ensured the crowd would never suspect how seriously I was taking this. To them I was an Australian on an offensive bike from the '90s; to me I was a youthful Cadel Evans dreaming of the Tour de France.

The leading group made easy work of most of the riders, cutting the few hundred that had started down to a couple of dozen with real intention. The first five or so kilometres was along sealed roads, and the pace quick, which thinned out the lead group. Unlike their road-racing relatives, mountain bikers are less of pack animals, and most were riding alone. I was picking off another rider every minute or two. To allow for the multiple lengths, the last part of the race took us onto a muddy circuit through a forest, each rider doing a certain number of laps depending on the version for which they'd registered. At the entrance to the forest there was a checkpoint where a deskful of energetic volunteers were handing out energy snacks, filling water bottles, and earnestly directing riders. Sadly, not in English. I was left to do the maths myself and I calculated I'd be doing three loops.

I was close to the front of the group as we rode the first lap. We were within sight of each other and the path was reasonably firm, although I guessed it wouldn't stay that way after a few hundred riders circuited. When we got back to the volunteer desk for the second lap, we began to lap the stragglers from the rest of the pack, and the riders became a more confusing mix of both the 34 k and 54 k competitors. The surface had also changed, ruffled by the other riders, and was now slippery and far less friendly.

A few were giving up, walking their bikes back to firmer ground. The lead riders had spread out considerably, and for long sections I'd be alone in the forest. I was steadily catching riders who I'd correctly identified as my competition early on, and by the time I got to the intersection for the third time, I got the feeling I was very close to the front. There was a line for the water and energy bars that would have slowed me down, so I decided just to kick on, riding into the third and last lap with the vigour of someone who knew they were in the running.

It didn't matter that this was a social race, the cycling version of a fun run – I sensed a real chance for an upset victory. *I could actually win this.* Imagine, riding the bike Frits bought for twenty euros at a street fair, the delicious revenge on those with the thousand-euro machines. None of the volunteer-station snacks were needed: I was fuelled by something much deeper.

The path had disintegrated significantly, dirt had clogged my extra gears, so I tackled the muddy grind with the same three gears I'd been practising with. By halfway round, I hadn't seen another rider in front of me and I grew confident that a podium finish of some level was on the cards. By three-quarters round, I still hadn't seen anyone ahead of me, but had noticed that I hadn't seen any riders behind me either. I was either set for a high finish – or had got the number of laps wrong.

Unfortunately, I soon had my answer. When I reached the intersection, now for the fourth time, the tables had been packed up, yellow-vested volunteers evaporated, the refreshments and water gone. The small arrows of different colours that had been stapled to trees had all been taken down. Tyre tracks went in every possible direction, as a result of the people doing different routes, and the thorough volunteers had removed all the signs for how to get home. I'd been leading, which felt good, but in a seventy-six-kilometre version of the race which no-one else had signed up for, as it wasn't an option. That felt less good.

I headed out of the forest. The light was fading fast, I was getting cold and wished I'd stopped to get some water earlier. I could see a road, on the other side of a small stream. I carried my bike across, knee deep in the flow, lifted it over a fence, and onto the road. All the rivers here flow towards the Loire, so I rode parallel and with the flow, as I was sure once I got to the Loire I'd find signposts to Bourgueil. I rode at a middling pace, not sure if I was the event's last surviving competitor or its biggest loser, fast enough for warmth but no heart to really push it.

When I finally arrived back in Bourgueil, the town centre was ringing with music, the *halle* glowing with colourful lights, strings of bulbs stretching out into the trees. The crowd from that morning was now more jolly, happy to be surrounded by their families, and refuelled by the complimentary local wine that had just run out. I found a plastic cup that was close to full and had been put down by someone else. I found another nearby, a delicious replacement for the water that had also run out, and wandered into the throng. I was hungry too, but while I wasn't above taking another half-empty cup, I drew the line at half-eaten bread and cheese snacks.

Presentations were occurring, and people were getting ribbons, small children a token for riding. Category winners received a basket of the local wine for their achievements. There would be no prizes given for the winner of the seventy-six kilometre, no points for riding more than the allotted distance – just a lesson in the benefits of knowing more about what you're doing before you take it on.

I loaded the car, headed home and thought about how to talk to the girls about this lesson. When I arrived, I did the first thing that came to mind: I told them I'd won.

Elsa cheered and gave me a hug. Angelique understood the emotion if not the words and gave me a big kiss on the cheek.

'What did you get?' Madison asked.

'It's not the prize that is important, Madi, it's about competing,' I said, or something equally sensible sounding – parent wisdom that is best imparted shortly before leaving the room. I headed upstairs to shower, until I was clean, warm and ready to tell them the truth over dinner.

XXIV

Our Visitor and the Importance of Fraternity

My brother came, so I took him to see a dog.

My brother was on the way to see us, and the girls were so
excited they were close to bursting. I was even more excited
than they were, so it was a good thing I had better bladder
control. We hadn't had what the girls called a 'real' visitor, and
it looked like he would be our only one this year.

Paul had been seventeen when our father died and was the
only family member not to be in the house that night. He grew
up, almost overnight. I used to find it odd that he wore the
same shoes as my father: hand-made English brogues, worn with
suits like my dad's, often double-breasted. He grew his businesses very quietly, yet makes some of the finest wine grown
in the southern hemisphere and raises a large number of cattle in
northern Australia. A successful entrepreneur and business
manager, he's also a fine repairman of Land Rovers and very
good at camping. An iconoclast if I have ever met one, warm to
kids, fun with his friends and the best dog owner I've ever met.

He's had a series of dogs, all of typically rambunctious breeds, but they've always acted as if he had them on a string. Yet I'm not sure he's ever owned a leash.

The year just finished had been a tough one in business – his *annus horribilis*, he said – and having made it through, he'd given himself and his backpack a ten-day holiday in Europe. I considered myself fortunate to have him as a brother and it an honour that he'd allotted thirty per cent of his vacation to me.

Time spent photographing a local winemaking family had given me a new perspective on my brother. The best wine, I learned from the Marchassau brothers, is not grown on the most fertile soil, and the best years are not the ones in which the rain fell regularly and the sun shone conveniently. The best vines often sit in the rockiest of soils, and it is how they are grown that provides them with a special depth of character. These vines are grown not from a seed planted in the soil. Instead, a cutting of a young vine is inserted into the rootstock of an established plant. The piece is called a scion and starts its new life with the ability to draw upon the root system of the great vine that stood before. The only explanation for my brother's wisdom is that he is drawing from the depths of those who came before him.

On the morning he arrived, I dropped the girls off and they made me 'pinkie-promise' to bring them Paul at the end of school. His train to Tours would be leaving Paris about now, I told the girls. It was scheduled to cover the 250 kilometres from Paris in fifty-seven minutes and I knew that if I drove fast I'd make the forty kilometres to the station in just about the same amount of time. The TGV is famously punctual. Even if today I hoped it wouldn't be.

Tours was the capital of France for twenty years in the fifteenth century and also for about three days in 1940 when Paris fell to the invading Germans. Today it's a mid-sized provincial centre and university town, divided through the middle by the sprawling sandy wash of the Loire River. Four bridges do their best to connect the north and south sides of the city, made more of a challenge by an ambitious development of a light-rail network that was in the process of digging up most of the town centre and two of its bridges.

It was just before nine when I came out of the forests and sprouting fields to the north of Tours. As I got closer to the city, the temperature of the other drivers made it apparent that I'd joined the impatient end of morning rush hour. Land Rovers do bumper-to-bumper traffic poorly; one moment mine was threatening to drive over the small car in front of it, the next it was not moving fast enough for those beeping behind me. I felt like an imposter, like I was getting in the way of people who had places to go, important things to do.

With impeccable timing, my car began to have troubles. Perhaps it was finding the return to commuting as difficult as I was. More likely, it knew that Paul was coming and, if it spoke up now, it had a chance of getting fixed. I texted my brother to tell him that I'd pulled over and that I might be a few minutes late. In my message I explained that the problem was in the transmission, without really knowing what that black box does precisely. I am aware that it's important, but I'm not sure if a car can operate without one. Is it like a lung, a heart or an appendix?

I switched off the engine and consulted the operator's manual. I searched the index, looking for what to do if you hear a noise like bone grinding coming from under your seat. I found nothing helpful, but the five minutes spent cursing at the booklet seemed to do the job as, when I started the engine again, the sound had gone away. I was surprised that I was able to arrive at the station on time, but not surprised that his train had arrived exactly per the schedule.

Paul had flown from Western Australia to Singapore, to London, to Paris, before getting the TGV to Saint-Pierre-des-Corps, the train station for Tours. His last two sleeps had been on a plane but, true to form, he stepped off the train as bright as the sky that had opened to a cloudless blue for his arrival.

I'd decided to drive him to a restaurant for an early lunch. We were forced to pull over on the way to diagnose the grisly acts that had recommenced below our seats. He has driven his Land Rover (and dogs) across thousands of kilometres of the outback and he talks diesel mechanics with the same deep, calming authority with which he talks agricultural economics or diagnoses the problems with the Australian rugby team. He doesn't change cadence when helping you understand the fermentation techniques used in his wine business or the challenges of raising cattle in far-northern Australia. Paul confirmed my suspicion (truthfully, my guess) that the problem was in the transmission. Better still, he actually knew what was happening and what I should do. I made a mental note to do what he said.

I brought him to the Café de la Loire and impressed him with my ability to act like a local. I greeted everyone as I walked in, handshake and *bonjour*, and we took a table *dans l'extérieur*. The restaurant dog is a pointy-nosed black streak named Gringo. He's as tall as the ponies the girls had been riding, race-grade slender with an oil-sleek coat. From behind he proudly waves his testicles like he had just won them, and from his front protrudes a snout that barely conceals a length of teeth that would make a Kakadu croc proud.

Sitting outside, scarves and gloves on, the sun was warm on our faces as we smiled at each other. The cafe looked down over grass-lined banks to the Loire. Brown water flowed smoothly from left to right, wooden boats pulled gently at their bow ropes, while half a dozen ducks got busy in the rushes. The only mark on the otherwise spotless blue sky was a giant plume of white steam that rose from the cooling towers of the region's largest business, the Chinon nuclear power plant. When Paul noticed their unnaturally uniform shape and colour, it would give me an opportunity to discuss the country's carbon footprint with him, but first I'd let him enjoy the scenery.

Today the wooden boats work the river only for the tourist trade, which has grown into the region's second largest business.

Even during the hot summer months nobody swims in the river, as folklore holds that it flows with a hidden danger. When I pushed for some evidence of this, I was simply told that people die in it every year. In truth it's a calm river with gentle banks. It's hardly the river's fault that it must deal with bridge-jumping students and a generally low level of aquatic competence amongst those who live on its banks.

During the French Revolution, the river did claim thousands of lives. When the country was gripped with the excesses of the Reign of Terror, the jails of Nantes and Tours needed frequent emptying to make room for new arrivals. The incarcerated were loaded onto precisely the same style barges that take today's camera-toting tourists for a trip up the river. Once aboard, the guards pushed the boats into the centre of the river and they were scuttled by the cannons of the young Republic, a new regime that was teaching people Liberty but not swimming. Again, it's hard to blame the river for these fatalities.

From our seats outside the café, much of the operations of the *centrale nucléaire* were obscured by the trees, all of which, in the relief of early spring, appeared to be celebrating their recently-returned greenery. It could be easy to forget that the steam trail rising to our right was a by-product of a million degrees of nuclear fission, and see it as a majestic flourish above a historic town, a white feather rising from its helmet. I had a lot of explaining to do – and he had lots of questions. How I felt about leaving Australia so quickly, what had happened to the plans to write a snappy business book, why I needed to buy a new bike, what games did I play with seven-year old girls, and whether *Toy Story 2* gets better after a dozen views. (Spoiler alert: it doesn't.)

Paul's lessons in re-learning what he knew about France had begun by riding on the pride of the French transportation system. Cail and his associates started the French rail industry and they made it the most rail-roaded country in the world by the end of the nineteenth century. On the same paths that

Cail opened, and across the gorges that Eiffel once built the bridges for, the TGV had travelled a distance the equivalent of four times to the sun and back, without a single fatal accident. Cheap and plentiful coal had powered Cail's locomotives and produced France's first century of electricity. By the middle of the Industrial Revolution, France was probably the world's largest polluter, above its British neighbour which, while a bit richer, had only half the population. Today, France is arguably the lowest carbon-emitting developed nation, thanks, almost entirely, to the reactors like the one across from our lunch spot.

The reason that the country switched to a low-carbon power source in the 1960s wasn't either the high regard they hold for engineers, or an early embrace of an environmental movement: they simply had used up all their coal. France, I had learned, used to be a really big country. When it had its revolution, it had a population of 30 million; when America had its own, its people numbered just over three million. When Cail was possibly the richest self-made man in France, the country's one per centers were the world's wealthiest elite class.

Across the river, in an area about half the size of Cail's agglomeration at La Briche, the four reactors were silently generating about six per cent of the electricity that France needs to power all its television screens, drive its trains, refill its mobile phones and light the side of the Eiffel Tower each evening with its 11,000 sixty-watt bulbs. Chinon alone generates enough power to meet the entire needs of any of the world's 100 smallest nations. If you had a long enough extension cord, this plant could light up all of the Congo, Nepal, Gaza, Tonga, Chad, Gibraltar, Greenland, Liechtenstein and Rwanda, a combined area four times the size of Western Europe. It's a challenge to my thinking to imagine that if all the developing nations had the same emissions level as France, there would be no such thing as climate change, no issues of global warming.

With what I had learned, if I had to give one of the world's biggest civilian nuclear programs to any country, I'd give it to the French. While the hardest university to get into in the US is a school for those who want to start a business (I know, because I failed to get accepted by Stanford Business School), and in the UK it's one that specialises in helping students sound incredibly smart (I should know, because I went to Oxford), in France the most elite university is actually an engineering school.

My lecturing wasn't limited to my kids, and I pressed on with today's overseas student, still groggy from his trip. Paul was a natural sceptic, and, like many, a hardened Euro-sceptic. I moved on to cover the origins of the otherwise unexplainable European Union. After the Second World War, it had been agreed that power distribution could be done more efficiently by linking the continent's electrical grid, as opposed to the previous system of periodically invading the neighbour to plunder their resources. A treaty was created by an organisation called the European Coal and Steel Community. It was such a success that its ambit grew until it changed its name to the European Economic Community, which changed its name again into the thing we know today as the European Union.

Despised by many, but if evaluated against its original intent – which was to save the world having to send their young men to perish on beachfronts and battlefields – it has been an unqualified success. Before the different European Unions, two years out of every three in the preceding thousand had seen Europe's energy spent on internal battles. Since the creation of the EU, the number has been zero. With all this spare time, the countries have developed innovative ways to regulate each other, and battles are now principally staged on the football field and with incomprehensible song competitions.

Over our lunch I noticed that I was being enthusiastic, and it felt good.

'How good's that bread? . . . I love this beer; do you want to share one . . . And this is just the starter . . . Moutarde? . . . And there's cheese after this . . .'

I outlined the plans I'd made for Paul's visit, including a visit to CYFAC, lunch at the Bouff'tard, and having him join me on a school excursion with the girls' class. Tomorrow's school trip took a bit of explaining. A month earlier, Aimée had called a meeting for all parents to explain the outing she'd planned for the class. Sometimes my comprehension was hurt when I missed a key word at the start of a conversation, and then I'd incorrectly frame the rest of the information. I thought I had heard Aimée say '*Louvre*', the famous Paris museum, and then when she mentioned stone work and construction and something about a church, I assumed she was talking about Notre Dame. It sounded like she was planning a visit to Paris, and when she asked if anyone would like to join, I threw up my hand.

After the meeting I approached her, as there were bits I didn't quite understand; like how we were going to fit it all in in half a day. It turned out Aimée had said '*lavoir*', referring to the ancient outdoor bathrooms and clothes-washing stations that remain well preserved in some villages. After visiting one of those, we were going to an abbey to learn about the building materials used in the area. I would still have volunteered for a trip with her, but it wasn't quite the day out I had imagined.

Aimée had understood at least part of my embarrassment, laughed politely, and then leaned in to tell me something personal. She too had moved to this region, and had also fallen for it, but felt that it wasn't being appreciated by those who lived here. Most locals, she said, saw no outside validation of the benefits of the region, bombarded as they were by television images and movies set in Paris, as well as images of the lifestyle in Los Angeles and elsewhere. Her goal, thanks to the modest excursion budget of the *mairie*, was to expose the kids to some of the history of the area, hoping to build a foundation for them to value where they lived.

Paul and I stayed and talked until we had to leave for school pick-up. When we got there, the girls ran out and exploded in English all over him. I'd promised in advance to take them to our favourite playground, a fortress-style tree house that sits behind a fortress-style château near here. It would also allow me to give Paul a quick lesson on the châteaux and castles that make this region famous. Almost a thousand of them dot the region, thirty or forty of which are the focus of tourists, and they would apparently bustle during the summer months. In our time here so far, my brother had been the only tourist we'd seen.

When we got home, Paul was barely awake. The girls had so many things to show him, and more than enough energy to do it. When Paul said he had to sit down, they continued their show-and-tell by climbing all over him. Tall and well built, he was perfect play equipment. He was an ideal uncle for my daughters, except that he lived 15,000 kilometres away and had his hands full with his own brood. The girls adored him, which I imagined was because he was a slightly more smiley version of their father. We had lots more talking to do, but I sent everyone upstairs to bed early, as the girls had the school trip the next day and Paul hadn't seen a bed in two days.

The next morning, as we followed the girls in the school bus on their excursion, my brother would get his lesson in country branding. The French take being French very seriously. Through each town I would point out the red, white and blue flags, the national flag that has stayed unchanged for longer than any other country that flies the *tricolore* combination. At least one flag would hang from the *mairie* of each small town, engraved with a reminder for citizens and tourists of the motto since revolution: *Liberté, Égalité, Fraternité*.

I was in full lecturing mode, and set about explaining the French *ménage* of the three that is the key to understanding Frenchness. Liberty, the starting point, is understandable, given that the revolution's primary goal was seeking freedom from an inherited ruling class. Equality, which initially meant equality for all males, wasn't about reducing Piketty's type of economic inequality, but simply that all people were equal under the law. Fraternity is harder to define, trickier to actually do. It's a kind of brotherly love on a national scale, valuing the happiness of the whole, the role of community, and moderating the unfettered pursuit of individual liberty. The founders of a young America flirted with the idea of adding Fraternity to its ideals, but they chose not to, deciding that Liberty was enough of an organising principle. The result is a nation where the protection of basic freedoms – of speech, religion, assembly and the right to own a machine-gun – trump the considerations of the impact on the community of any of these.

In addition to an opportunity to advertise the theory behind the Republic, the *mairies* serve to point out just how over-governed the French are by the standards of us Anglo-Saxons. With six layers of government, this tiny, inefficient local apparatus looks far from sensible by our economically rational standards. The result, another genius move of the Republicans, was that in creating the Nation, they let people keep control of their village.

In one town, two white bedsheets hung over a railing and read *Sans École, Sans Vie dans les villages*. Apparently, school closures were threatening the small one we'd driven through, and the sign suggested that without a school, there would be no life in the village. I translated for Paul, and said I agreed with the sentiment; however, both of us have economic degrees that have taught us that this didn't matter. What we count, what our economic measuring tools measure, is progress in terms of growth of gross national product, and these tools don't measure things like the value of diverse rural communities, kids walking home to have lunch with their parents, or the protection of obscure cheeses made only in one location.

At the *lavoir*, the children were introduced to the ancient ritual of drawing water from the well, washing in the stream and the social connection that had once been formed by the women of the village gathering daily under a small slate roof. At the abbey, the children were introduced to the soft stone of the region that is used to build the houses, the hard shale that is the area's main roofing material, and the local wood that frames the houses. The children were encouraged to scrape the different stone with nails, hit things with hammers, pour vinegar onto stone to make it corrode. Then they all got to make small houses out of clay. Mud huts, I guessed, was the comparison being made. My brother had flown a European-made Airbus to Paris, then ridden a high-speed train to Tours, but at times it appeared I had driven him back into the eighteenth century. As much as I was being enthusiastic, I could tell that my attempts to impress him with this system weren't about to send him back to Australia to start a revolution.

I still felt I had my best cards up my sleeve. The next day, I intended to play them all: I'd open his eyes with a trip to the bicycle factory, soften him up with a Bouff'tard lunch, and finish by spending the afternoon with the owners of a number of small wineries. I knew the last stop represented my greatest challenge in the promotion of all things French. Paul is no great fan of regulations, yet despite the French wine system being the most regulated in the world, it consistently produces what everyone acknowledges (even if reluctantly) are the best wines in the world.

Entering the CYFAC factory we were met by Aymeric, who had said he was keen to meet the 'better Peter', as I'd described my brother. He bounced out, commenting that if he saw me, he knew that he must be at work. Recently I'd been spending more time in the factory than him, as he frequently had to travel to trade shows or to meet suppliers somewhere around the country.

At the 10 am coffee break, a joke had developed that I was the new boss. A boss who didn't speak the language, or know anything about bicycles, but seemed nice enough. They'd be able to do whatever they wanted under my rule, or so the joke ran.

Paul appreciated the ritual, if not the coffee, and then I got permission to give him a factory tour, proudly showing off things I had known nothing about months ago. I shared my amazement at the strength of materials I'd only just learned about, showed him examples of the precision with which things were done, and hoped he would marvel at the remarkable transformation that befalls the tubes.

I finished the tour at the noticeboard. Next to the official statements and announcements, taped to the walls either side, amongst countless photos of completed bicycles, were pages cut from magazines about the company, and one large-font quote from the firm's founder, Francis Quillon. I drew Paul towards it, and showed off by translating it:

Tous les boulangers commencent avec la même farine, certains finissent avec un meilleur pain. Every baker starts with the same flour, some finish with better bread.

'More elbow grease, clearly,' Paul added, suggesting he got it precisely.

At lunch, I helped him appreciate the diversity of the Bouff'tard's clientele. It was only the bank manager from the closest large village who seemed to be doing business over lunch – the rest were farmers and workers of different professions, enjoying the break.

The meal was working, and while Paul said he wasn't sure if it was the best he'd ever had, he said he was certain it was the best he'd had for anything less than three times twelve euros. The cheese course, which consisted of examples of three perfectly different regional varieties, came with a diatribe from me on the benefits of the French system of *appellation contrôlée*, the method by which France protects its regional products, its wines and its cheeses. At its core, it's a system of rigid regulation and de facto protectionism.

Twenty years ago, when France began to fight for the names of its products, I had been quick to mock. For a time, wearing my cattleman's hat, I had even worked against it. I remember the early days of the battle, when French producers argued that only they could produce the cheeses known by their regional names. I knew Brie as something I ate and, more recently, as the name of some American girls – not as a town or region for whom the cheese was almost its *raison d'être*.

How could a place control the use of a word for a product? Could not a cheese be made just as well in Wisconsin? After all, they had ample milk there, experience in making cheese, and an ability to let it go mouldy. The battle to control the product of your region was not a fight over the product, but a fight for a people, a way of life, a set of values that were manifested in a type of pungent cheese, or a variety of trustworthy wine. But in the world I'd lived in, regulations found few friends, and protectionism didn't fit anywhere in globalisation. Deregulation and free trade had been the assumption on which our growth and progress had been built. Regulation was surely only needed by the mediocre, and anyone fighting for protectionism must have been doing it because by definition they were weak, or possibly an enemy of the system.

The wine we had for lunch was from the region we were driving towards, the *appellation contrôlée du Bourgueil*. I'd met a grower there, Vincent Marchesseu. Educated in Paris and well-travelled, he spoke good English and made great wine. He'd agreed to meet the Australian who made wine. Few people know the region's wine by its variety – it's Cabernet Franc – but when people say 'a glass of the red' at an authentic French bar, it's the type you get served. For the bar owner to feel secure in buying from any of the regions' 500 wineries, there needs to be a system to ensure every producer in the region is producing at, or above, some level. Without this control, it's the tragedy of the commons, the destruction of the whole thanks to the unbridled pursuit of an individual producer's liberty.

To ensure the reputation of the region is maintained, Vincent described to us how every part of the process is strictly regulated, and then how his process is closely watched by a local quality-control committee. They begin shortly after the first crush, tasting what is still grape juice. They return when it's nearly ready, and then again when it's done. At each juncture their approval is required. If the committee doesn't like the way it is maturing, they'll request changes to the mix, or even relegate it to a lower grade of wine. They have the power to determine your vintage is only 'table wine', which can be sold, but the packaging must never reveal its origins. For the worst cases, they send it to its death at the hands of the distiller; where it is boiled to ensure the evidence is never traceable.

As a wine grower, Paul got this lesson quickly. He'd heard enough and wanted to ask a question.

'If all the variables are controlled, if regulations restrict everything that you can and can't do, what makes any of the wine better than the rest?'

'The difference,' Vincent said, 'is only the work.'

Neither Cail nor Quillon could have said it better.

In detail, Vincent described the work that the hardest-working vintners do to lift the quality. In the mid-winter, when the vines are most dormant, he and his siblings and a small group of labourers cut back every vine. The more the vine is cut back, the less it will produce, but the better will be the grapes. When the grapes are harvested, the more inspection and more rejections, the better the juice. At each part of the process a decision can be made to increase quality, reduce production, and in each case it takes more work to do it.

'But why do all that work? Why do people here go the extra mile?' I asked, because I wanted him to make my point for me.

Vincent looked back blankly. He is one of three siblings who run the family operations, and he's a proud member of a long line of winemakers. He is educated, makes some of the best wines in the region, but didn't understand how that was even a question.

We thanked Vincent – he didn't know how much it meant to me – and bought a few bottles from his cellar door.

The sun had remained out for Paul's third day, which I chose to believe was another gift from our antipodean visitor.

I wanted him to know it wasn't always this pleasant, and that the girls and I had to get through the tough, short, cold days. I was proud he noticed that I was doing a good job learning the trade of a single dad. I was well organised at home: the girls had hair that was well-conditioned and no longer dreadlocked, there was French toast every morning, and I got them to school on time. To my brother, I was being as close to me as I could be. I didn't really have to define myself here. Happy in what I was doing now, but clearly not sure what I would do next.

Before sunset Paul asked me carefully about my writing, remembering my well-announced plan to write a book of business wisdom and keys to success (and how to bounce back from the opposite) in the world of big business, celebrities and stock exchanges. I had to admit that I'd been derailed, my attention now drawn to ideas that called into question many of my base assumptions.

I'd visited factories and caves, farms and fields, photographed the mushroom grower, beekeeper, stonemason, builder of amplifiers, the distiller, butcher, baker and the sausage maker. I'd made a hundred visits to the bike factory and visited the same wineries half a dozen times, seeing the cuttings, from which came the first buds, that I now recognised as small leaves. I'd ridden every road in a fifty-minute radius, driven around every town within a short drive. I'd studied every part of Cail's grand plan, picked over its ruins, ridden over the memories of its rail system. I'd lived with the ghost of a self-made man and industrialist, France's prototype for the businessmen who would come after him, those who followed him up to and including into an early grave. In the process, what I'd seen, and how I'd felt, had challenged every assumption I held about how to live and how to work.

Paul listened to my stories and pushed me on. 'Keep going, brother,' he said. I realised suddenly, by his tone, that he'd come here to check in on me. To see if I was alright. There was no greater gift he could have given me than his time; a true bromance, where bro is short for real brother.

The next morning he had to leave and the girls and I took him back to the train station. We stood together on the platform, at precisely the place where it was indicated his carriage would stop, across the platform from exactly where he'd stepped out three days before. When the train arrived, the doors opened, and out poured people, some walking off with bags, others leaping out for a quick smoke. Paul put his backpack just inside the door, and then jumped out and pretended to light a cigarette, mimicking the lunge of the smokers.

The train stood at the station for about half a cigarette. Paul gave us a last laugh. We all hugged again, and he leaped back on. Given that the girls were there, I decided not to give my final lesson: 'Paul!' I was tempted to shout. 'Even though the French smoke a lot and eat the type of fatty foods we're warned against, yet they live longer than us!'

The doors slid closed and the train slid from the station. He'd gone from the same spot he had materialised in, a well-tanned vision from another world, departing in a cloud of smoke like a magic trick played on us. I waved towards the train but at nobody in particular. As my brother effortlessly slipped back into the twenty-first century, I hoped one day I'd be able to re-enter that world as easily.

XXV

Learning to Ride: My Second Cycling Victory

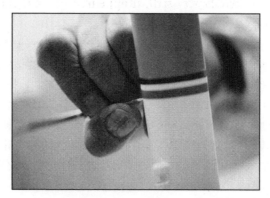

There were good reasons why my bicycle
build was going slowly.

The girls and I continued to rely on the small notices posted
beside the road to alert us to activities we could turn into our
weekend adventures. We knew we might not understand the
subtleties, and despite our early setbacks went along anyway,
the unknown now adding to the excitement. Our favourite
were the signs that introduced us to the frequent *bricolages*, a
sort of all-town jumble sale where families would try to sell an
extraordinarily wide range of items. The girls and I had got some
well-priced items we actually needed, and some baffling bargains.

I was doing my best to help the girls learn about the value
of things discarded, the theory of one person's junk being
another's treasure. Madison had become determined to find
roller blades, even though there was nowhere to skate around
here but dirt tracks. We found a pair, which I bought for her
for twenty-three euros, half the price we'd seen them for new
in the Super U. Lesson taught. Then, when at the same sale,

Elsa found another pair, exactly the same colour and size but in slightly better condition, for two euros, my lesson was lost in all the excitement.

One recent notice had easily caught my eye: *Le Festival du Bicyclette*, an entire carnival of cycling. It was to be held in Anjou, about an hour to the south, a particularly picturesque town on the Loire. Better still, it appeared to have races of five, thirty and 100-kilometre lengths.

The fine print showed that bicycles for the longest race must be antique, which apparently is the class that includes any bicycles made before 1983. Frits confirmed his bike qualified, and proudly told me that the racing bike I'd been training on was of the same type as one that had won a stage of the Tour de France that year. 'Antique bike race' sounded like a bit of an oxymoron, but I wouldn't have cared if it was on penny farthings, or against senior citizens – I needed race experience and I immediately registered online.

The race started very early on a Saturday morning, meaning we'd have to drive down the night before. I found a hotel nearby and the manager said she knew a university student who, for a modest fee, would be delighted to look after the girls while I was at the race.

After dinner, while the girls watched some TV cartoons in English, a rare treat, I got ready for the next day's early departure. The fastest growing thing here at this time of year is still my leg-hairs, and I lay in the bath to shave down. I didn't care if their real impact in terms of friction was minimal, the freshness of your legs against the wind felt fantastic, even if getting there still came at the cost of some small cuts. I was nearly finished when Madison told me the babysitter was at the door. She'd come tonight to introduce herself as we'd agreed I'd be leaving when the girls were still going to be sound asleep. I rushed out of the bath, dabbing off most of the blood. The hotel was of the standard where they had to provide dressing-gowns, which were always short on me. This one significantly so.

I knew part of France's job was to test me. Test me as a man, as a father, and as a cyclist. Could I, as a man who saw himself as a man of business, live another way? Could I live without company, or the constant uplifting of a supportive team? Could I write for long stretches with little reward, battle inconvenient truths about myself, and stick to the task? Tonight's test would be: could I look composed at my hotel door in only a too-small dressing gown, with a watery stream of blood flowing down to my feet?

I should have guessed it, but of course the 'would be delighted' local college student was a striking young lady, who had arrived at the door, backlit by the golden rays of the evening's last light, standing in a cotton dress alongside what appeared to be her almost-copy in every way.

'I brought my sister, hope that's okay,' she said in perfect English.

'*Bien sûr*' – of course – I replied, looking down at my feet and trying to wipe some of the red that had gathered on the top of my toes.

If Angela was thrown by my appearance she didn't show it, and we easily made a plan for the morning. I'd head off just before 6 am and they would come around seven, take the girls to breakfast, and then spend the morning playing around the hotel and with the pens and paper I had brought. She was a twin, she said, hence her excitement to bring her sister. With everything organised, I went back to finish the shaving job, which I chose to do in the shower. It's one thing to draw a hot bath and begin shaving, it's another to get back into what has become a tepid pond, on which float soapy clumps of man fur like little hair islands.

The next morning, I left the hotel feeling frankly ridiculous, dressed the best I could as a cyclist from the early part of the last century. I understood that the dress was meant to be 'period' and prizes would also be given for the authenticity of the costumes. I was soon joined by another rider, a young man in an impressive period costume that featured a tweed waistcoat and silk pocket handkerchief, riding a well-worn vintage bike. As we passed each intersection, other costumed cyclists joined in.

The ride in was about ten kilometres, and as I rode it began to feel like the cycling version of the gang gathering of *West Side Story*. At each junction or roundabout, cyclists were coming from every direction. Soon we were riding in a large pack, our collective empowered because our attire now set the style. It would grow, I was told by the hotel manager, to over 4000 cyclists by the time we reached the start.

It felt good to be part of a gang, although as I looked around I wasn't sure we'd be winning any scuffles with the Sharks. There was a spattering of strapping young men, riding what looked like pretty recent machines. I made a note of them. One older gentleman was riding in a pressed shirt and bowtie, his wool knit pants buttoned at his knees, his moustache neatly twirled at each end. The bikes, too, were of all shapes and sizes. There were some that even I could tell were not authentically antique, but new, single-speed machines that had been styled to look retro. The closer we got to the start, the more 'family' it became. One contraption had two tyres, three seats, mum, dad and infant, all pedalling. If I'd done an honest inventory of our battalion, it was about fifty per cent boys and girls under thirteen, riding things that looked like they were made last Tuesday.

As we began to slow down and form a single mass behind the starting line, I could see that the shortest distance races were only for kids and were designed to take place while the thirty and 100-kilometre races were underway. It would have been perfect for Madison and Elsa, but their father hadn't understood the poster well enough.

The racers for the longer versions were corralled towards the starting line, and it was clear that only a few hundred of the few thousand of us were taking on the longer routes. Each of the authentic bikes showed their year on a small plaque and their ages stretching back to 1908. Amongst them slipped the remakes, the recently released bikes that had all the styling but none of the rusty gears (and much less of the weight) of the real old frames. Standing together, the theatrical mood got more business-like; fresh deodorant smells, masculine vibes and competitive tension rippling through the pack.

Like most forms of competitive sport, cycling starts with being all about what you look like. While this was some sort of cycling costume party, the competition was just as intense, only with the different variety of materials: more cotton and wool than lycra, tools carried for both practical and aesthetic reasons, inner tubes slung over the neck for repairs and huge credibility, metal water bottles with cork tops, goggles of all types, lots of leather seats with copper rivets. There were even lights on the oldest bikes that had been lit with a match. Some riders wore the old-style leather helmets, but as most wouldn't dare ruin their attempt at period costume with the addition of a plastic helmet, they rode with the limited cranium protection provided by a cotton cycling cap. I'd found one of these amongst Frits' tools and I didn't tell him I was borrowing it in case he told Mum and she worked out I'd be racing without a helmet.

The costumes probably helped the mood, as it was as jovial as competitors can be at that time of the morning. It was a social race, after all, but it didn't stop the slow creep towards the front that men seem to need to do. Then the flag dropped. Instantly the programming that runs inside most of the males on the planet kicked into gear. In less than a dozen rotations of the pedals, the elite riders exposed themselves, transforming from carefree hipsters to ruthless competitors. Some of the most impressive were much older riders, the proudest of whom were a small group of men who were riding the bikes that they'd ridden when these bikes were state of the art, and they'd stayed true to their ride. Age ensured they weren't the quickest riders, but experience gave them the smoothest cadence, and the wisdom not to start as fast as I'd taken off.

After the mistakes of my first race, I was determined to ride today's correctly. This one even had sponsors – a brand of dried meats, as well as a number of the larger local wineries – and a well-printed map with instructions in both English and French. I had studied this map carefully. The 100-kilometre race would cross over the Loire twice, had refuelling stations at two wineries, and was in three stages, with one leg of ten, the next twenty, before a final out-and-back loop of about seventy kilometres. Given this was my first road race, I'd asked Aymeric for advice on a strategy. He suggested I try starting as fast as I could, ride the middle section as fast as I could, and then towards the finish, speed up. I took him seriously, and intended to follow his advice.

The first ten kilometres

Some of the riders were clearly a class ahead of the herd, and within half a kilometre they'd broken fifty metres ahead. I pushed my way to the front of the trailing group and indicated to my fellow riders that we should see if we could catch them. There were no takers for pursuit at this point. Everyone was happily riding at that pace, and the guys ahead were, according to the consensus, *les idiots*.

The first ten kilometres passed like this, me leading the chasing group that was not chasing, and the breakaways, about a dozen, making steady progress away from us. I made a few more attempts to motivate the group to see if we could chase them down. One method is to get a short break on the group, maybe five metres ahead, and, while keeping that distance, look back with eager eyes and see who'll join you. It's a 'Who's going to storm the barricades with me?' type of call, done while showing people your butt and looking over your shoulder.

Some sports, such as cricket or basketball, look like team sports, but they've been shown to really be a series of individual performances, with very little impact of one person's performance on the others. Cycling, on the other hand, looks like an individual sport, but is very much a team sport. It's true whether you're in an official team, riding with the same jerseys and the same sponsors, or a weekend rider in a social pack.

Whenever you're on a bike, wind resistance is the shared opponent. Riders alternate riding at the front of the pack, taking the wind for some time, then pulling out, easing off the pedals and drifting to the back of the line, until their turn comes up again. Groups riding like this can be ten to twenty per cent faster than a solo rider, usually making it a pointless exercise to try to catch the lead group alone. Practising rare prudence, I yielded to the laws of physics, and after a minute or so of riding ahead by myself, with nobody joining me, I simply slowed down and slipped back into the group.

Just as I was about to try to rally the troops once again, signs pointed us to a sharp left, off the road and onto the loose stones of a parking lot. Before I could work out what was going on, the other riders had pulled to a stop and were off their bikes. I followed them into what was clearly a winery, the name of which I recognised from amongst the sponsors listed on the numbers we all wore on our chests. The winery was set into a rock face, looking down on the Loire, and the path led us into the mouth of a cave, a narrow white-sided canyon that was mostly open to the sky, with other darker caves heading down and off to each side. I would have been interested to show this to the girls – if it weren't in the middle of my race – and it was no novelty; it was a working winery and I had to jump out of the way of a forklift bringing a pallet of wine from out of the caves.

I wasn't able to catch up with the leading group while on my bike, but I'd caught them here. Half a dozen or so of the muscular leaders, including two with the not-quite-authentic bikes, were all standing at a table covered in a red and white checked tablecloth, talking and laughing and drinking wine. Of course, I mean it was about 8 am on a Saturday, we were standing in a cave, one-tenth of the way through a bicycle race: why not stop for one or two plastic cups of local wine? Still,

I could drink wine well – in relative terms, probably better than I could race a bike – so perhaps I'd be well suited to this particular event.

I got a cup of wine and stood alone, watching the lead group finish their second and start to gather their leather gloves, pull on short-peaked cotton caps, and adjust the bandanas they'd tied loosely around their necks. The bloody French had done it again: thrown me another challenge, where you not only had to look great but show prowess in both the local custom (drinking wine) and some other, normally-unrelated task (racing an old bike).

As they started to move out, I looked to slip in behind them, making up what I couldn't on the road here in the valleys of the winery. Just as I was leaving, the group I'd been riding with assumed I was confused and welcomed me heartily to stand by their table. The joke at my expense was always '*Vite! Vite!*' – 'Fast, fast' – and then, showing a more chilled pose, someone said, '*Lentement, lentement*' – or 'Slowly, slowly' – and in English, 'There are ninety ks to come.' They kindly got me another small plastic cup of wine and let me into their circle to stand and talk and laugh, as if I understood all they were saying. Out of the corner of my eye, I could see the leading group were now on their bikes and would soon be riding off. As I tried to leave for the second time, I was prevented by another example of French generosity, being introduced to the cut sausages of the lead sponsor, as well as being thrust a third small cup of wine.

The second twenty kilometres

It turns out that quaffing a couple of glasses of red wine is a much better pick me up than a bottle of Gatorade. As soon as I was on my bike I felt the warm power coming from my stomach, the sugar in my veins and enough alcohol to blur my judgement. With that, and disregarding what I knew about team riding, I decided to take off to see if I could run down the faster kids on their cooler rides. As we rolled over hills, I could see this would be unlikely. I might be able to stay within sight but there was no way I was going to catch them by myself. I had too much pride to slide back to my group, so I kept going solo, the long wasteful purgatory of a rider stuck between the two worlds.

The route included the only steep hills I'd seen in the region, very short, very sharp climbs and then perilous downhills with a ninety-degree turn at the bottom. This unnatural geography owes its heritage not to the gentle carving of the river, but the mining of these hills for their building stone. We were essentially riding up and down the sides of ancient stone pits.

At the bottom of one, a sign indicated a sharp right into a winery. I'd been following carefully the signposts of distance covered, and knew it couldn't be another wine break yet as this leg's twenty kilometres hadn't passed. A man was positioned to force me to immediately take another right turn, into what looked like a warehouse abutting the stone walls of the riverbank.

Once inside, amongst pallets holding tens of thousands of empty wine bottles, I was directed to take another sharp right turn and head down a ramp. As I looked quizzically at the race steward, he pointed straight, shook his arm, and said, 'Four kilometres.' Much to my surprise, I'd be trying to catch the leading group, with a belly full of wine, through a network of underground cellars that stretched for four kilometres, all at the constant fourteen degrees Celsius of the caves here. When I emerged, happy for the lights and warmth, I found I had arrived at the second rest stop, and half of the leading group enjoying another glass of wine.

The final seventy

With none of the original group to hold me back, I was able to leave this rest stop with the half of the leading group that had not already taken off. It meant I only got one plastic cup of wine and a handful of the tiny individually packaged sausages, two of which I unwrapped and stuffed in my mouth, the rest I put in the pocket on my back.

This group was far from friendly, but much closer to competitive. The ones with the fake antique bikes were in this group, and they let me know that two of their group had broken further ahead. I had correctly identified those two before the start of the race as the most dangerous of my competition: one younger man with tanned muscular legs, each one the size of my chest, and a slightly older man with long wiry legs, thin arms that showed their thick veins, and a sharp jaw that naturally cut a determined profile. I wished I'd been able to leave with them, but I was happy to join this unsmiling handful, as they announced with bravado that they were going to try to catch the breakaways.

I slipped into the foursome, taking my turn to lead, before slipping back to the rear, resting, working my way up to the front, and then taking the wind for the team again. The key, I learned quickly, was that when you get to the front, your job is just to keep the same pace. My adrenalin tends to run a bit high, and the first times I took the lead role, I'd look back after my minute or so and find that I was five to ten metres ahead, having unhelpfully left them to battle the wind themselves. I was admonished a couple of times, but when I got the rhythm I was thanked by the group and finally given a warm welcome.

We continued this for maybe thirty kilometres, but it became clear that we weren't going to be catching the lead pair who remained a stubborn distance, maybe a kilometre, ahead of us. For me, the temptation was too great. It was my first race on a road bike, the conditions were perfect, the sun soft, the roads smooth, so with some red still in my belly, and a back pocket of small sausages, I decided to take off after the leading duo alone. My group said goodbye in the way I'd learned was the custom. *Idiot!* I flipped up the brim of my cycling cap, put my head down and took off.

I began to shorten the distance, and with every indication I was making up ground, I went faster. When I was only a few hundred metres away, they noticed me, and picked up their pace. So did I. When I finally caught them, sweat was dripping through my cotton top and my lungs were burning. I'd achieved more than I'd ever expected to achieve in the race, and I considered answering my heart's request that we pull over here and call it a good day.

The younger and more athletic of the duo asked me in English if I had ridden with anyone to catch them. 'Just me,' I panted, and he responded with the nicest thing a man can say to another man. *Impressive*. He organised for me to ride behind him and the other man, each of them sharing the front riding, giving me a complete break that I welcomed for ten kilometres – even though it felt a little like I was being carried in a stretcher between them. The group behind us were not making any progress, so it was going to be just the three of us as we passed the sign to say we were within the final twenty kilometres.

The older rider then invited me to take my turn to help with the wind, and I joined the rotation. As we picked up the tempo, he said a polite *au revoir* and wished us the best, which felt much nicer than being called an idiot. That left just the two of us. In the moment we found ourselves the race leaders, we immediately formed a tight team, rotating in a smooth circle. My companion made it clear that, as I'd ridden solo for longer, he'd do more than his fair share. He egged me on when I started to flag, helped me come in close behind him to get the full benefit of the aerodynamic envelope he'd created, and passed me his water when I couldn't remove the cork that I'd pushed into the aluminium canister that was given at registration.

The route had taken us out and back, and the last ten kilometres was alongside the Loire, on a road that had been recently paved and made into a magnificent straight towards the finish. With my partner's pushing, and riding like a loosely connected tandem, we were flying as fast as I'd ever ridden. The closer we got to the finish line, the busier the road was getting as we began to meet the riders who had been on the shorter routes. We were dodging and weaving, enjoying the rush that you get when you're passing other people, your speed feeling even faster. With five kilometres to go, as I was taking another turn at the front, he gave me the word in both French and English: 'Bon, go!'

I'd been helped to this point by a stranger, a guy I had caught, and he'd automatically switched to a support role, becoming my domestique. Now, he was releasing me, to sprint on behalf of our makeshift team to the finish. With the determination of someone riding for his teammates, his sponsors and perhaps his adoring fans back home, I sped off. When I turned to wave thanks, he was already twenty metres behind, sitting up in his seat drinking from his water bottle. I put my head down and rode hard for my new team.

Riders were flying backwards to my left and my right. Admittedly about half of them were children. Some were even riding the other way, having already finished the short route. It didn't matter. I had less than five kilometres to go, and legs that had found another gear, lungs that were cooperating, and a head that believed this was the final stage of the Tour de France. In the last kilometre, I alternated between sitting and standing up to sprint, rushing inappropriately close to bewildered amateurs and their wobbly children until I lunged my bike across the finishing line, the outright winner of the 100-kilometre race.

Not that anyone noticed.

Around the finishing line there were a selection of stalls offering local delicacies – free for riders – retro cycling attire, and lots of cheese. I collapsed on the ground next to a line of people waiting for free samples of local wine and sucked in as much air as I could. I guess I was also swallowing some pride.

I know it hadn't seemed like a race when we lined up at the start, but it certainly had when the flag fell. When we stopped for wine, I guess I could have seen then it wasn't a race:

certainly, the subterranean leg and the second stop for wine should have given it away. But the final half, surely that made it a race? Perhaps whizzing past pre-teens and mothers with child seats on their bikes should have been the clincher.

My newfound teammate rolled in, and I thanked him, assuring him I'd done the best I could with the position he'd given me. I got a big hug, a congratulations, and then he took me by the arm to meet the organisers. The event's officials were under the Loire River Tourism tent and they were very happy to meet me. They gave me a small medal on a red, white and blue ribbon. Then they gave a similar one to my teammate, one each to a woman and her behelmeted son, and then two to a man behind me, so he could give one to the infant who had sat on the back of his bike and was more interested in his bottle than a medal. I was looking for something more substantial to show off, while my new partner was there just because he was proud of what he'd done to get me there.

The organisers were not enormously enthused with the news that I'd finished first, but were ecstatic to find out I was from Sydney. There were some other riders in the race who had driven all the way from Paris, they said, but everyone else came from the surrounding area. Proud that they had attracted a competitor from Sydney, they took to the microphone to introduce this.

I then added, 'Je m'appelle Peter. Je suis Australien.'

They loved my introduction and were impressed by my accent. Australia, though, was the highlight, and I got a hearty round of applause for how far I had come. But nothing, it seemed, for how fast I had ridden.

I thanked my new racing partner and rode back to the hotel to see the girls, and their babysitters, legs stiffened from the half hour off the bike. I'd won again, I announced, and this time I had a medal to prove it. I must have looked better than when the two older girls had first met me – I could tell they liked my outfit and were impressed by my athletic prowess. At least that is what I told myself they were thinking.

'Congratulations,' the older girls chimed.

'Well done, Dad,' Elsa said, as she jumped up and gave me a tight hug.

Always hugging, always loving.

Madison joined the hug and surveyed the front and back of my medal.

'*Participant*,' she read. 'Did everyone get one?'

Always helpful, always perceptive. Even when I wanted her not to be.

XXVI

Aimée Proposes a Meeting

Spring had, in all its glory, sprung.

Each day when the girls returned from school, the first thing I'd do was go through their bags to look for notes from Aimée. Into their notebooks she would write details of any homework the girls would have to do. She spared the girls most of the latter, telling me that the days at school were hard enough, and when they got home they should just play outside, release the words they had held in all day, and have some fun.

The other notes were for announcements of upcoming school events and those weekend activities in the area that often became the theme of our week, the encouragement that I'd use to get us through any emotional dips. I had learned to translate the notes on my computer after I made an early mistake where I thought that the upcoming 'teste' at the school was something the girls should study for. It was for everyone – *toute école* – and something cerebral, as it said *tête*, or head. At the time we'd been there only a few weeks and I was worried for the girls. I asked Aimée how to prepare for this sort of exam, only to learn it was a schoolwide inspection for head lice.

Today was different, however, as Aimée had handwritten a note in one of the girls' books addressed to me. I didn't need Google Translate to tell me that she was asking to meet me tomorrow, after dinner, at the school.

I'd come to terms with the fact that in the story of my time here, Aimée would only be in the role of school *maîtresse*. Frits was to blame for starting the irresponsible idea that there might be something else. Early in my stay he'd egged me on before I had even met her, asking me teasing questions in front of my mother. It was the perfect romance for Frits, one in which he was not involved, nor pay for the consequences, but he could enjoy from the outside. Nothing would happen – I'd admonished him and reassured my mother – but it didn't stop me enjoying the cliché that the male character in my story had arrived in a small country town and the woman entrusted with the care of his girls was cast as a lady of unusual beauty. Even in the Hollywood version it wouldn't be believable that she had a professional athlete as a husband.

Aimée had lived up to Frits' descriptions, not that I was the least bit objective. Each day at school she appeared statuesque, in part because she was normally found towering above tiny children. I found her eyes mesmerising, in part because they were the ones that looked upon my girls with a warmth that I only hoped to match.

Her care for the girls had been comprehensive – always soft, always warm. I loved the compassion she gave them, and the girls were besotted with her for the same reason. I began to think she liked me too, although it was probably in the same way Elsa said she loved the bird that we had rescued after it flew into our kitchen window: something that needs a stroke on the head, or to be put out of its misery.

The night of our meeting, I arranged for Angelique to stay late. As I drove off to the school, there was still some light left in the sky. The evenings now had as much light as midday had in the depth of winter. It was now late May, spring was in full swing, and everywhere there were hints of the magic ahead. The greens were almost iridescent, the light a soft wash that gave everything a photogenic blush. The smells of the forest blossoming were now beating out the smells of agriculture, and small flowers broke out beside the road. Like the tourists, the birds that had flown off in the winter were back, holidaying in happy pairs. All these elements might be helpful for the movie version, but I kept focused on what was a straightforward parent-teacher meeting.

It wasn't just the season that was helping me consider staying here. I was writing in a good rhythm, I had what I felt was a small community of friends, a disconnected gang that had started with Phillippe and extended through the bicycle factory to the people I'd met through their work in the surrounding villages. At times I could even understand full conversations. I'd begun to enjoy the isolation from the rest of the world, loved that my phone never rang, never beeped or sent me an alert. They were nearly finished with my bicycle build, and I was approaching my race weight. I had learned how to shave around my knees without a single cut and could negotiate the more delicate bits as well. I had competed in two races and could tell myself I'd won both. In short: things were trending well for me.

For the girls, I knew things were harder. The language was the greatest challenge. Perhaps I could put them in a French course for the summer and return in the autumn into Grade Two at a passable level. I knew that more of the language was seeping in than they let on. If I was talking to someone and I paused a sentence in an extended *errrr*, one of them might fill in the word I was looking for. They'd now sing along to lines of songs on the radio and ask me for a translation of words they weren't getting.

I'd kept my plans to myself, as I knew the girls would think a summer of French intensive would only be inflicted by a wicked parent. It was unlikely to fly with their mother, whose road trip was bringing her closer to her Germanic roots, something that came with a rigorous pursuit of academic progression and a dislike of all things French.

Aimée had become the symbol of France to me, replacing 'Marianne' from Delacroix's painting *Liberty Leading the People*. When Delacroix painted Marianne as the symbol of the fight for freedom, she was shown with a flag in one hand, storming the barricades in Paris, one breast exposed. When she was given a third dimension, expanded twenty-fold, and given better chest coverage, she became the model for the Statue of Liberty.

The torch-carrying Lady Liberty was an idealistic, visionary French idea that couldn't be built using traditional methods of construction. It was Gustave Eiffel who invented the technique that made her possible, utilising an internal core of steel on which the outer shell was draped. His system would become the standard by which all future skyscrapers were built. Cities of short, squat, stone buildings were replaced by metropolises of tall, slim buildings, thanks to Eiffel's search for how to build the world's tallest woman. Aimée is not made from the soft rock of the Loire; she's got more of the height, strength and principles of the French lady in New York Harbour.

When I arrived at the school, all lights were off except for the one I knew to be Aimée's classroom. The outer door of the school was ajar, and I quietly let myself in, closing it behind me. Aimée was seated, writing on a piece of paper that she'd placed on the only rectangle of actual desk on her desk. Around her rose precarious paper towers, one of reading books, countless piles of exercise books, and a heavy slab of official-looking papers. She was in her spring uniform, a long cotton dress with riding boots, shoulders covered for the evening chill.

I knocked and entered her room, and, as I'd done on numerous occasions at drop-off, caught my foot on the leg of a small chair, inadvertently swinging it round until it noisily hit my shin. We both laughed at the familiarity of the scene, and I rubbed my shin, making more of it than it really was.

Our conversation was always a mix of English and French, both of us making mistakes, correcting the other. We were both practising the other's tongue, both making the same type of mistakes; getting the big words correct, but often the small words completely wrong.

One of the benefits of approaching French as an English speaker is that there are lots of what are called 'true friends', words that are pretty close to the same sound and meaning in both languages. I use a disproportionate number of these words. *Problème* is problem, *adore* is adore, *possible* is possible, and so on. All you have to do to have reasonable French pronunciation is say the English word like you're making fun of it.

The danger of relying on 'true friends' to speak the language is the large number of so-called 'false friends', words that sound the same but have very different meanings. The word for paradise, *paradis*, is pronounced just like parody.

When I made a small mistake, which was often, she'd quickly catch it, and gently correct me, both of us enjoying the humour of my mistake. When I did tonight she leaned in, laughed, and with a casual touch of my arm, apologised for correcting me.

I smiled inside and imagined how this scene might play out in the movie version. After this soft piece of forearm patting, the lead actors would collide in a physical bonding that the audience had been willing on for the first hour of the film. Passion would bring their lips together, movie magic ensuring no teeth would ever clash in the process, two actors locked together by the mouths, freed from the requirement to breathe that burdens regular humans. I knew how to do the next part: with a bold sweep, the desk would be cleared, paper, pens and clothes flying across the room.

But that's the movie version, not real life, and it would not be playing today. Probably a good thing too, as I am not sure it is something either the girls or their mother would have appreciated. Not to mention Aimée's large and handsome husband. And besides, there really were a lot of papers on her desk and cleaning up would have been a big task.

My attention had clearly wandered, and Aimée got me back by saying there was a *problème*. Madison had had *un jour difficile*, a difficult day. Apparently, in the playground, a boy called Simon had told her he loved her. Aimée said she'd tried to explain to Madison that in France that was considered a nice thing. I replied that in our own culture it was also considered a nice thing. I promised Aimée that when I got home I'd help Madison to understand this and would comfort her.

With the *problème* quickly sorted I could tell her a story from recent days, another discovery on a bike ride, another tiny business I'd found producing something rare. She'd heard me share stories of this type, and had enjoyed them, suggesting other discoveries I could make. I would seek to do so, knowing it would also show how far I could ride in the ninety minutes before pick-up. Aimée could tell I was beginning to enjoy myself here, however her expression changed and I got the message this wasn't the time for my cultural observations or showing off my cycling progress.

'The girls are not advancing,' she said.

In cycling terms, I was now going over the handlebars.

She explained that her attempts to teach them French were not going well. She understood how hard the girls were trying, and she was proud of their progress. She also knew that on some days it was just too much. She'd taught her family English so she could practise often, and the school gave her permission to add an English lesson for the class twice a week. It had seemed like a great idea, even better as the girls would be sharing the teaching, standing at the front of the class pointing to the blackboard with a long pointer. It had unexpectedly backfired, as the kids, particularly the boys trying to get their attention, would follow both girls around the school, repeating over and over again the word of the day. The girls had described how, for an entire lunchtime, Simon had chased Madison, repeating, 'Chair, chair, chair.'

Language was proving a problem for all of us. I was trying, but not making much progress. The girls, on the other hand were naturals, but weren't trying. I suspected they were actively resisting. Small, soft and loveable the girls were, but inside they were as tough as nails with a subversive streak. *You can tear us out of Australia, Dad,* I imagined them to be saying, *but we're not going to speak this language, even if we already know it better than you.*

Aimée had done everything and had exhausted her ideas. She had got a classroom assistant so she could give them more attention, and even got the *mairie* to agree to pay for the swimming, a rare opportunity for my girls to show what they were made of. Everyone had tried, but the girls were still not learning the language. Aimée then went up another notch:

'They will have to leave at the end of the term,' she said. 'You will have to find another school.'

There was nothing she'd said that I didn't know, but it felt like she was breaking up with us.

I agreed, hoping to show how much I wished it had worked out for us. I promised we'd find the girls a good solution for the start of the next school year. We smiled and sealed the agreement with a handshake, a warm and confident single shake, the formality of which helped remove my lingering awkwardness.

Then she changed to a distinctly softer demeanour, dropped her eyes slightly, and told me that before I left there was one thing she wanted me to do.

Caught between the movie and real life, I think my heart stopped. Like really.

Turns out what Aimée really wanted was for me to do a presentation to share my experience of living here for the people from the town, the parents of the children, the team at the factory.

'Like the one you gave in the classroom,' she said, motioning to the small table in the centre of the room.

Earlier in the year, Aimée had invited me to give a presentation to the kids in her class to help them understand the girls' former life in Sydney. I'd taken my laptop in, sat on one of the tiny chairs, and given a PowerPoint presentation to a room of five to seven-year-olds.

'Just like that one,' she repeated, 'with more pictures. And in French.'

I could rent the local hall, she said, and if the request came from her, they might even give it to me for free. She suggested I do it at the end of term, when the weather was nice, when evening light extended until almost 9 pm. She'd help me advertise it on the local message boards and send notices home to all parents in every student's bag.

I agreed on the spot, which was probably because I would have agreed to anything she asked of me. I mightn't have had a trade that I could ply in this region, but I'd shown her I was handy with PowerPoint, and with my laptop and camera I had all the tools I needed to make the presentation. Aimée promised to talk to the *mairie* to get a list of the available dates.

I thanked her one more time for caring so much about the girls and said goodnight. I let myself out of the school, into an empty parking lot swept clean of the last of that evening's soft light. That I didn't have a cigarette ready was a further reminder that this wasn't the Hollywood version.

XXVII

Learning to Ride: My First Cycling Test

Finished, or rather just the beginning.

My bike was finally ready, and I decided to walk to the factory to pick it up. Aymeric was fond of saying that he'd never sold a bike to a person who lived within walking distance, so I thought I should actually do it.

The day before, I'd left my camera bag and cycling shoes in his office and, after lunch, I set off to walk to the factory. Out of La Petite Briche I turned right and passed Cail's ruins that were benefiting from the reinforcement brought by another season's growth of blackberries and moss, then the Château la Briche, its windows flung open and rugs thrust out like tongues of a resting hound. Inside, the activity suggested it was being cleaned in anticipation of the summer residency of its Texas-based owners. The surrounding fields were greening rapidly – everything was enjoying the early summer months. Growth was coming quickly, the ground was warm again, moisture levels still high, and hours of sunlight long. I cut through to the

Plan d'Eau. The water across the old quarries was smooth now, with enough shine across its surface to suggest it might soon be enticing. After one final cut through a farmer's field, I arrived at the back door of the factory.

It had taken nearly four months to make my bicycle frame and, as Aymeric frequently complained, I had been the reason for the delay. From the very first day to the 120th. I was either taking other photographs in the factory or not available when work was scheduled. It was now ready, and hopefully I was too.

As the frame was being built, it had moved smoothly between perhaps a dozen pairs of hands, the responsibility effortlessly passing from one person to another, like a melody moving between members of a tight jazz band. Each player used a different instrument, before passing to the next person, at each stage moving closer to the resolution of all the threads. For the *assemblage*, the stage that brought it all together, the crescendo of a three-month set came down to a solo for the youngest of the CYFAC family.

Hugo works with a series of specific tools and measuring devices, opening boxes and attaching pieces. He starts by positioning the frame, unwraps the part, finds the particular tool for its fastening, attaches it, tests it, checks against the specs and measures it. Then he repositions, tests, measures and checks again with the specs, then repeats. When the repositionings are imperceptible, he moves on to the next part. He flows between his tools, the box-fresh parts, the measuring devices, exuding the type of cool that comes only to those who are unaware of their coolness.

While my decision to get my bike made out of steel, the cheapest option, had disappointed Aymeric, it hadn't stopped him trying to upsell me some of the components. He'd been successful, and the boxes Hugo was opening were marked with the exotic ingredients of carbon-fibre, Kevlar and titanium. The final step was to set the seat for the desired height, and then he simply said '*Fini*', and stepped back to regard. No smashing of cymbals, no final pounding of the drum, just a gentle lowering of the bike to the ground. He rolled it towards the back wall and leant it next to his. He finished with the same grace with which he had performed and, as he turned to clean up his work space, he suggested I take a test ride.

I pushed it out of the side door of the factory, and towards the road. When I attempted to mount, my habit of stepping over Frits' bike clearly wouldn't do, and it took me two attempts to be able to get my leg over. When I did get up on the seat, I had to check that I had sat in the proper orientation. The saddle on Frits' bike felt like a pair of helpful hands, cushioning my backside; this one felt like it was affronting me.

When I started to ride, the bike was so light that I wondered if I'd left some of it behind. It certainly didn't feel like a thing made of steel. Part of each rod had been left unpainted, to show the brushed steel. But the rest we'd painted white, and it felt as if it had been made from feathers. The wheels were so thin they looked like they'd slice into – rather than roll over – the road when it was softened under a summer sun.

The handlebars provided my second 'You're kidding' moment. They were so far forward that I feared I'd picked up a bicycle cut for a basketball player. The resulting posture certainly felt race-worthy, but it would test my flexibility. I was also going to have to ask Aymeric where I should put my testicles, because this rack had made them the point of contact with the leading edge of my seat.

The next difference, when I actually started to push firmly on the pedals, was direct transfer of energy from my legs to the wheels. It was like the difference between driving an electric car with the rush of the immediate torque, versus the spongy acceleration of a diesel truck. The bike let me know it was up for whatever I pushed its way. I took it easy as I imagined that at any moment, like a horse just let out of its stall, it might gallop off. This was a wise call, because I was still at trotting pace when I tested the brakes. The brakes on Frits' ride worked like a signal to the bike that I'd quite like it to slow down sometime soon. These ones were designed to indicate the precise spot at which you wished to stop, and if I squeezed them hard enough, they would no doubt comply. Even if it would send me over the Kevlar-covered handlebars.

Bike tested, heart racing, I returned to the factory and confirmed that I thought it was working well. Like asking a learner driver to check out a Ferrari, I said with confidence that it was all good and I was ready to ride it home. Hugo didn't know what to do with that, as it had never happened here before, so he went in search of Aymeric to get approval.

Aymeric came out grinning to give the bike a quick check. With a flourish, he bestowed his approval on our union. I hadn't made the final payment, he reminded me. 'But I know where you live,' he joked.

With that, it was done. No ceremony, no passing-out parade, just the end of a day's work. CYFAC makes bikes to be ridden, not stared at, and the process is completed when you're cycling on it, not when it's leaning against a wall. As I was about to ride out, Hugo said he'd come with me as he was heading home. We rolled out of the factory together and I turned left, Hugo right. With a fist tap and a smile, we rode off in different directions, the fine machine between my legs feeling like it was still more his than mine. I'd recently learned he had applied to apprentice under Bernard and would take over his metalworking when the master retired in a few years. How many connections like this he'd create, only time would tell.

I rode home and parked the bike in the kitchen, leaning it on the dinner table to make sure the girls would see it when they got home from school. I didn't get quite the reaction I'd hoped for, both girls noting that they'd seen it before, or at least its photo, 'many, many times'. Still, for that first night it joined us at dinner, taking the head of the table opposite its proud new owner.

My first proper ride was the next day. Aymeric had suggested that I pick him up after work, and he'd ride with me to his house, about thirty kilometres away. He'd try to teach me all he could in an hour riding together and then leave me to ride home.

When I arrived, Aymeric was ready to go, dressed like a pro, but joking again that his top was a little tight around the belly. Since coming to France, my body had been reshaped by cycling. I'd managed to lose nearly all of my ten-kilogram target, most of which came from my upper body, and an undefined amount from the loss of all hair below the waist. I'd bought a cycling outfit that matched my bike. It is one thing to shave your legs for a machine, but admittedly it gets weird when cyclists dress themselves to match their rides.

We headed out of CYFAC together and turned south towards the Loire. Aymeric immediately complimented my posture, which I appreciated, until he smiled and said that it meant he had fitted the bicycle to me well.

He rode like he was one with his cycle, and appeared to be holding the bike in his legs. I felt like I was using mine to hold me up. His elbows tucked in easily, which I copied; his back was a smooth curve, which I tried to copy. His legs moved up and down with an even exertion on both parts of the stroke, pulling up as well as pushing down. I tried to copy that too. He sat up to give me pointers, touching the bike here and there, explaining the reasons for the things he was teaching. I tried to sit up too, but quickly grasped the handlebars.

Aymeric and I started fast and kept a solid pace. I was pleasantly surprised that I was making him pant. With half our distance covered, the master's lessons were over, and as the apprentice I was keen to show him that what I lacked in finesse I could make up in fitness. We reduced the talk and did what men do best: compete. Rule number one of this manly pursuit is never look like you're competing. Tricks include being the first to point out a picturesque field, and asking a question that sounds like you're not really that focused on breathing. You must always be willing to accept a sprint up a hill, answering with an 'Of course', rather than an 'If we have to'.

It was a friendly ride, and we covered the distance to his house in good time, he said. Work had kept him very busy, he added by way of excuse, and observed that it had taken me getting a bike to get him out on his. We made light banter, but we both knew there were more serious matters afoot. For all the jolly that Aymeric put into his work demeanour, he was serious about what he produced and wanted to see his bikes put to good use. They were not sold as collectibles for the few who could afford them – they were to be ridden hard, not hung on walls.

I, on the other hand, wanted his blessing. I wanted to be up to the bike, and for our union to be blessed. I felt I got that from him: not because he said much, but because he couldn't say much, still out of breath. An ancient ritual had been completed, no less heartfelt just because we were talking bicycle and wearing lycra. I said goodbye, turned right and right again, and headed back to La Briche on a parallel route to the one we had raced.

As I rode around the corner I stopped pretending and slowed down to a grind.

'Oh fuck, that was hard,' I said to nobody but the trees.

The pace, the posture, the pretending. But I'd done it, and for at least an hour I'd made it look like I knew what I was doing. There were still two weeks to go before my race, although Aymeric had advised that, with one week to go, I should taper down to very little, if any, riding. Fine by me. I'd relish the break and, besides, I'd developed a rash between my thighs from too much training.

I headed north, happy that I'd achieved one of the three goals I'd set myself here – to make myself a cyclist. I'd written down these three objectives early in my stay, because goals and milestones were what I knew how to throw in the face of any challenge. Goal two was to be a great father to the girls, and there was no way to test that. As for making myself into a writer, goal three, I had certainly failed. My 'how-to' book of business success would not be written. Trying to understand a world that confounded me had become more important than propagating something I could no longer say I believed in.

The news that we had to leave the school had actually come as a relief. I'd been repressing the concern I had for the girls' little hearts. I knew school was tough and they deserved more playmates, and to understand more of what was being taught. We'd all done our best to normalise our experience here, but the best thing for them was certainly more family.

Aimée's request that I give a presentation had given me another challenge to put my energy towards, another diversion with a point. It was the type of thing I was used to doing: a task that I wasn't obviously qualified for, something to which I could bring an outsider's perspective. Besides, it was a PowerPoint presentation, a milieu I knew well. It looked like I could get it down to about forty-five minutes long, and Marie-Françoise was confident I could memorise it all in French.

Spring was merging into summer and the light was with us deep into the evening. I picked up the pace a little. I was warm and happy. Happy that we'd done our best with our time here, pretty sure the future couldn't be worse, and happy on my new bike. Until I suddenly flew over the handlebars.

Deep in thought, I hadn't seen a raised ridge that ran across the road. To my right I hadn't noticed a factory that made cement, and, as its trucks had left the facility, they'd dropped a thin trail of now hardened concrete across the road. My front tyre hit the accidental curve and turned sharply right, then folded under, sending me flying over the handlebars. Because we were clipped together at the pedals, the rear of the bike followed me over. Instinctively, I twisted so that my back would hit the road first and I landed, as I did in that cold lake, on my bum. Unlike the soft, wet landing of the lake, the road was hard and hot, and after my backside hit, my shoulders followed, whiplashing the back of my head toward the surface. The last thing I remember was the sight of my bike soaring over me, in all its brand-new, factory-polished glory. My shoes had now come unclipped, and it was flying horizontally over me, its two wheels still spinning like a flat Chinook helicopter. Then there was a sharp crack as my helmet hit the road.

When I woke, I wasn't sure how long I'd been napping. I lay still. Even though I could tell I was in the middle of the road, I took the time to do an inventory of myself. 'What's the chance a car comes?' I thought. My hands were tingling, my elbows bleeding, but all was attached. One knee was hurting more than the other, but again, all working. What about the crack at the back of my head? As I began to gingerly move, it was clear it was the helmet that had cracked, not my skull.

I couldn't have been out for long, but there was a lot I can't remember about what happened next. The roads were usually quiet around here, and as it was about dinner time, they were deserted. When I got up, still nobody had come by and nobody had seen me spread-eagled while my bike lay nearly ten metres away. It too was in one piece, but it had landed on a concrete road divider, denting the top tube right in the part that had been left as exposed steel.

I never found out how I got home. It felt like a big night out gone wrong. I had to ask everyone. Aymeric, did you drive me home last night? Merit'oh, did I call you and ask in slurred words to be picked up? Perhaps I hitched a ride. Like a blacked-out drunk, by the next morning I had no idea how I even got to my bed. What I do know, from the stories of the girls, is that I came home, and they thought I was a little grumpy. I'd said I was going straight to bed and didn't want any dinner. They took this in their stride, microwaved their own dinner, put their plates in the dishwasher, and got themselves off to bed. The next morning, they woke themselves and got dressed for school, before coming in to wake their hungover dad.

XXVIII

Girls, You Can Do Anything

The girls running, over and through the potholes.

I decided to take the girls to their favourite play spot, the play-ground behind the Langeais château, to have our discussion about leaving. As with all break-ups, it was important to get the location right. I stopped on the way to get Madison a plain baguette, Elsa a lemon tart. Over the last few months, Divonne and I had exchanged emails about a compromise for the family if it didn't work here. She'd voted for the US, me for Australia, and we both thought the girls would vote for anywhere but France. We'd found an English-speaking school in Switzerland, which appeared to be another example of the benefits of the alpine nation's neutrality.

I started by telling the girls about the conversation I'd had with Aimée, letting them know I appreciated how hard school could be. I gave Madison a hug over the story of the boy who'd said he loved her. I reminded them of the high points of our stay and thanked them for their amazing attitude and also their support of me. But we were going to have to leave and find a school where they taught in English.

'But you love it here, Dad,' Madison responded.

'I like Simon, Madison. He wasn't being mean,' Elsa said, demonstrating her capacity to be on a different wavelength from others.

'But okay,' they joined together to say.

And with that, the conversation was over. The girls said they understood and looked forward to our next adventure. Newly fuelled, Elsa took the lead in their game in the nearby treehouse, unperturbed by the larger themes of family realignment, moving schools, moving countries.

'LoveyouDad,' they chorused, giving their standard sign-off before taking off.

Throughout our stay the one constant had been their insatiable desire for play. As long as there was something in their stomachs, they could occupy themselves in any environment with a smile on their faces, their bodies in motion. Give them a slope and they'd practise the different ways to roll down it. With a bit of flat ground, they could whizz around until one or both fell over. A medium-sized tree would be climbed, a large tree would be a trunk to hide behind. We came with no toys, made plenty, and when there was nothing obvious, the girls might repurpose sticks, using their imagination to transform a straight one into a bow, a bent one into a violin. Then together they'd invite me to sit down to listen to a silent symphony they had composed for the occasion.

They could last eight hours in a car with only some pencils and paper for entertainment, and there was never a single 'Are we there yet?' Not once had we thought that life would be improved by some rechargeable digital devices; hand-sized boxes that enable you to escape any boring moment by watching a video or contacting a friend. It seemed as if adding things like that would be a stupid idea, even if they are called smartphones.

Aimée was right – the girls weren't progressing at school in areas that were likely to be helpful for their future learning. Education is at its best when it serves to switch on the minds of children. They were not a vessel to be filled, but a fire to be ignited. My girls had been taught resilience, toy building, game invention, bike repair and teepee construction. They had learned about delayed gratification, and the long wait for things being carefully built. They only missed one day of school due to someone's high temperature, but they were otherwise never late for school. They brushed their teeth twice a day and ate like horses most nights. They didn't do much homework, they ran outside without shoes when it was warm enough, and peed in the bushes behind the house.

Their curiosity was running wild. They constantly asked questions, regardless of whether I was driving, cooking a meal or on the toilet. Our deal was that I would record the question, write it down if paper was handy, and give them a full answer as they lay in bed at night.

> *Why do humans have round heads and animals mostly long*
> *heads?*
> *When were bricks invented?*
> *How come you make square photographs out of a circle lens?*
> *What do banks do with the money overnight?*
> *Why do only women make themselves pretty?*
> *Can motorbikes go backwards?*
> *Why don't grown-ups laugh much?*

Some questions were easier than others, but I've never been one to use one word when two will do, give a short answer when a story can be told. As they lay in bed each night, the first and only time they would have stopped moving that day, I'd unfurl an answer to an earlier question. They might have asked a simple thing about the functionality of motorcycles, but if they were still awake after twenty minutes I would have given a complete history of two-wheel transport, of the invention of the bicycle, the story of the first person to screw a small motor to a bicycle frame, and how they kept expanding the engine until the combination became more a motor on wheels than a bicycle with an engine.

'Yes,' Elsa would be the one most likely to get me back on track, 'but do they go backward?'

I was far from a perfect dad, was slow to respond to minor medical issues, and their hair was a disaster for a month. I hadn't kept their mother around, either, which was possibly the thing they missed the most. I had failed at dinners, probably been too emotional at times, and was many times away in my thoughts. I'd been fortunate to achieve some business success early, because I've found that the quicker a person finds success the sooner they can start asking if it was worth it. Men like Cail, men like my father, never got that chance, as they both died with their heads in the business building stage. I had escaped a world I knew well, landed here, and in the disconcerting quiet, began to just sit and watch. Sometimes it was in a cafe as the water went by, sometimes as the cars spun through a roundabout, but mostly it was in a small factory, on a reinforced IKEA stool, as bicycle frames circulated around me, the objects that enabled an observation of a complex dance of work, the pursuit of excellence in the way people worked.

I'd seen that same pursuit of excellence in a wide variety of professions, in work with steel and stone, in Phillippe's agricultural struggle. In places where I didn't expect to find it, it was the excellence in the work, the pride in the production, which was creating fulfilling work. I'd been trained to think that happiness only came at the top of a hierarchy of professions, rather than within each and every job a person could take on. It had become my guide as I set the evening table with increased precision, and I saw it in the way the girls left their room immaculate or adjusted the pretend TV on the wall to get it to hang straight. They too had taught me not just to do it, but do it really, really well.

I hadn't felt it at the beginning, but I had been fortunate to be stranded here. The girls were right that I did like it, and I knew we could have made it work if we needed to. The girls and I had bonded into three little coils of optimism ready to spring on every test and make it a positive. I'd thrown myself into the challenge of their parenting, but hadn't expected how much benefit would come back in my direction. Most of all it had been my heart that they'd switched on. I felt the trees now, noticed the light, and looked into their eyes more. I loved these girls more than I could helpfully express.

As we drove home, the girls remained in a jolly mood. A favourite activity in the car was to sing a riff they'd developed out of something I had once said.

> *Toilet jokes are not appropriate at the dinner table,*
> *Not appropriate at the dinner table, the dinner table.*

They could sing this song for entire car rides, the only variations being the volume and how much they'd laugh as they sung it. Sometimes one would take over, giving the other a break, then they'd swap responsibility to keep it going, and finally join back together to reach a crescendo timed with turning onto the road that led up to La Petite Briche. Never has such a gnawing jingle filled anyone with as much joy as it did me.

As we approached the bumpiest part of the road, the girls asked to get out, preferring to run ahead of the car rather than bounce around inside it. I let them out and slowly followed behind them, navigating the rough track that we'd silently crept over on our approach that initial cold January night. Both girls ran ahead, shouting to each other. I took a photograph out the side window and it shows them swinging their arms wildly as they leap over the familiar potholes.

Nearby, a solitary farmer, the one who kept the two dinosaur-sized dogs, looked towards us from the back of his plot. 'What a horrible father,' I imagined him to be thinking, 'forcing his girls to run home while he sits in the comfort of his English car.'

XXIX

Giving in Gizeux: Un Australien dans les Touraine

Opening the door, racing to hold
a community together.

The public hall in Gizeux stands out from the rest of the village's uniformly agreeable buildings as the only one constructed in the last one hundred years. The indiscriminate use of concrete, uninspiring roofline and narrow windows means even a novice in French architecture (like me) can tell it was not built in any ambitious decade of the last ten. I'd been able to secure its rental free of charge, thanks to some lobbying by Aimée. It came empty, and was to be returned, broom cleaned. I rented a projector, screen and microphone, but I could use the benches which would seat about a hundred. I was confident at least a tenth of that would turn up.

For what I presume is the benefit of the town's tourism promotion, the much-used facility is set back from the road, and largely hidden by half a dozen plane trees. The girth of all six suggest they pre-dated the arrival of the hall by at least half a century. On one side sit the administration offices of the *Maire*, and on the other side, a large gravel parking area that waits patiently for the *camping-cars* that visit in the summer months.

When not used by the trickle of self-driving tourists, it is only inhabited by the town's recycling bins. I parked in the still-empty lot and took out my bike and our recycling. The girls, their mother and their brothers were at home packing up and my other job tonight was taking out the garbage on the way to the hall. The three large bins stick out of the surface like the heads of three Cyclops, all with a mouth where the eye would be. On my way in, I'd fed all three, each one surviving on its own peculiar diet: one eats paper; another, nothing but plastic; and the third is a strict glassarian.

I'd called the presentation '*Ici*', or Here, '*Un Australien dans les Touraine*' – An Australian in the region of the Touraine. I was not above using my outsider status if it would sell tickets. Even if the price of admission was *gratis*. I'd designed a poster on my laptop and got fifty copies printed from a shop next to the Super U. The system of posting on community noticeboards had worked to get us to all sorts of events – so I hoped the same would work for my talk. People might not understand what was being advertised, as I hadn't always with theirs, but I hoped they would take the risk, just as I had with theirs.

It showed the time as 8.30 pm, as well as the location, and I added that there would be wine and *degustations*, further copying the local style. I pinned the poster onto a dozen or so local boards, taped it up at the Super U and stapled it on the CYFAC noticeboard. I got permission to stick it inside the door of local shops. I wrote a letter of invitation that Aimée made sure was sent home to all parents of the school. Finally, over the previous month, riding on my bike, I'd hand-delivered a copy of the letter to the shops, houses, factories and farms of every person I'd met here. I made the most improbable of bike messengers, and I never stayed long enough to know what they thought of me as a lycra-clad letter deliverer. Nor what they thought about an invitation to hear me tell them about here.

Angelique offered to make the *hors d'oeuvres*. I did as I always did with her offers: accepted thankfully and asked no questions. She always delivered, even if I never knew precisely what. She had arrived right on time, with a mightily ambitious quantity of sliced baguette topped with a pâté made from unknown animal. She immediately busied herself with their garnishing. Vincent, the wine maker who'd given my brother his masterclass, had offered some wine at a price that could not have covered the costs of the bottles. His father had driven up from Bourgueil to drop off a few cases and, as he was staying for the talk, joined the garnishing crew.

I arranged all the benches, but thought better about unstacking the four columns of blue plastic chairs, as that might be considered tempting fate. The rented screen came with its own three legs and a tall spine, and I pulled up its rectangular sail. I tethered the projector to my laptop, both laptop and projector to the power, and tested everything was working. To be thorough, I quickly ran through each slide of the presentation. I was all set to go, one-third of the two hundred *hors d'oeuvres* were topped, and it was all of 7.15 pm.

I'd made more presentations before 8.30 in the morning than I had at the corresponding hour in the evening. Aimée had advised that I must start late enough so that even the parents in the towns furthest away could finish dinner and still make it. I'd given myself an hour-and-a-half of just-in-case-something-goes-wrong-time, rather uncharacteristically, and nothing had, also uncharacteristically. Never one to waste an opportunity, I'd brought the trouble myself. Into the silence of the empty hall, I began to fill it with my demons. The first arrival was the anxious version of myself that I hadn't seen since arriving here. Like a Ghost of Presentations Past, a light-chested and weak-bladdered version of me crept into my shoes. Gradually, pang of uncertainty by twitch of dubiety, each pew of the hall filled with a different messenger of misgiving. I knew them all well. I hadn't seen them for ages, and not missed them either.

I slipped outside, in search of a place to pee, and a tree to hide behind, but my doubts followed me. I had a printout of my presentation and intended to talk it through and show all the uninvited visitors that there was no place for them here.

Of greatest concern was the fact that I was giving the talk in French, or, more accurately, words I'd memorised that were French. I began walking in circles, stomping heavily on the key words which I'd typed phonetically in all CAPS. *Mes filles courageuses* – 'CO RA GERS'. CYFAC *qui fabrique des vélos de classe internationale* – 'AN TEAR NA SION NAL'. *Aymeric très persuasif* – PER SWA ZIF. Then, over and over, I practised the word that formed my conclusion: épanouissant, a tongue-challenger that means 'fulfilling'. Marie-Françoise had helped me learn it as 'EPAN OUWI SUNT'.

At important points I would gesture, my hand-cutting scythe-like. With each swing, I rounded up another group of uninvited guests, and with each staccato-delivered phrase, sent a volley of self-assurance into them. I ran through it all at double speed. I knew it word-for-word, syllable-by-syllable, absurd-pronunciation-by-absurd-pronunciation. After three times rapidly through it, I thought I would be alone. I should have known better: the self-doubting spirits were multiplying. Like the walking dead of movies, my insecurities thrive on what I fire at them. Cut them in half and they grow to be two – worrywarts that are emboldened by the attention I give them; their only fear that I'll stop believing in them.

By about 8.25, there was still nobody there.

The sun was losing its grip on the day, evidenced only by a few thin streaks of pink that marked like fingernail trails across an otherwise perfectly clear sky. The conceit of what I had attempted to do was becoming clearer to me. '*Ici?*' I'd only been here for two-and-a-bit seasons, and my interpretation of the region was largely done without the aid of language. I had taken French lessons, but my sessions with Marie-Françoise were quickly distracted by long discussions on what I'd seen on my bicycle orbits through the local area.

My study of French history had been mostly taken as an online course at the University of Wikipedia. Of the two-and-a-half books I had read here on the subject, only one was written by a Frenchman. Victor Hugo's retail-based love story had taught me more about the origins of consumerism than I had wanted to know. The reliability of the other two was always going to be in question as they were written by Englishmen. The first was a quick read, Graham Robb's observations about France from the seat of a bicycle, but I was still getting through Charles Dickens' *Tale of Two Cities*, his improbable love story set amongst the violent excesses of the French Revolution. When I first started writing here his book had set my word target for my book, but I was now firmly bogged. I was up to my axles in the mud and blood of revolutionary Paris, lumbering under the weight of his adjectives, spinning in the contradictions of that age, confounded by the similarities with today.

With less than a freshman class of theory, I had done the rest of my study outside the classroom, a series of field trips to observe the relationship between people and their work. My concentration had been a four-month, 12,000-photo lesson in a bicycle factory. There had been no practical experience; I had not lifted a single hammer, torn into one field, or practised the husbandry of any animals. All my learnings had come through the window of my own eyes, the bias of where I pointed my camera, watching from a safe distance before writing them down in English, often under the influence of the Bouff'tard's coffee.

My understanding of La Briche was mostly thanks to the small pamphlet in French prepared for the 1867 Expo. When Mum had left me a copy as a gift on her departure, I had thought it as useful as giving a telescope to someone about to go scuba diving. In the 150 years since Cail had it printed, it was showing its age. Its pages had spotted like the skin of those who have seen too much sun, but its memory for the time remained crisp. The numbers of all livestock, the paths of railway, amount of coal burned and sugar produced, and the numbers of souls reformed, were all detailed down to the last calf, metre, tonne and young man. The vision it presented in its finely detailed maps and drawings was as sharp as the best of my photographic images. Very little else exists about the life of Cail – what's left is preserved by a small society for the appreciation of the man, in the town in which he was born.

I'd contacted the society before the speech and nobody spoke English. A few email exchanges had pointed me back to the same sources, one of which was a digital copy of the 1867 pamphlet I'd brought with me tonight. I had it safely in a plastic envelope, less for show and tell, more to bolster my own authority.

What I knew about road cycling had been crammed into six months of desperate training on the surrounding flat roads, mapping the region in a series of ninety-minute darts, out-and-back extensions that stretched spoke-like from the school parking lot. My two racing victories were really not victories at all, but helpful lessons delivered on misfitting bike seats. As for actually riding a real, properly-proportioned, astonishingly-light and dangerously-fast CYFAC bicycle, I hadn't had long on one, and had come close to snapping it in half on my first proper ride. The factory had surveyed the damage, and despite the superficial wound, Bernard deemed it strong enough to avoid having to put it back under the knife, saw or welder.

I had done what I could to understand what was happening in the world, not easily achieved when sitting in Europe reading English language websites. I took to rescuing lonely newspapers – French ones I'd find sitting in cafés, looking like they had nothing to say to the empty coffee cups. Some of the best papers here came with lots of cartoons, particularly the two with the oddest names: *Le Canard Enchaîné*, or 'The Duck in Chains', and another called *Charlie Hebdo*. Politically to the left of Marx, with a satire that was often as dirty as an old man, both featured illustrations in the style of cartoon best described as 'Artist Was Drunk'. Through these unreliable goggles I watched the themes of the second decade of the twenty-first century as they began to coalesce.

I had covered plenty of the region in my car. To me, my Land Rover felt like a square-sided, utilitarian box on wheels. I hadn't thought that it might look to the French very upper class or, even worse, British. It didn't help that my steering wheel was on the wrong side. Mostly I had been seen riding a bicycle in the middle of the afternoon. I really didn't know what impression I had given. More than once someone had misinterpreted my introduction to mean that I lived at the Château La Briche, leaving me to emphasise, '*La Petite, La Petite Briche.*'

I had seen myself as being gainfully employed, working to learn the trade of writing, working to become a better father for my girls, and working to be ready for my race. My riding had been done with a sense of purpose. I rode because I had to! I was training for something serious – I wasn't out there for the fun of it. It had never occurred to me that I might have been perceived by people here as a man of leisure, of a class to be avoided where possible.

At school, I thought I'd established myself as just another parent, a single one to boot, juggling priorities while working in a new role. I know I was often the only man at pick-ups and meetings, but I did my best to fit in. I had been at school every day, volunteered for everything, and made the best small talk I could when I bumped into the school mums in the supermarket.

If anyone needed any proof that I had tried hard in the parenting department, earlier that day I'd won the school raffle. The prize had been donated by the Super U, a basket of things in tins, a cache of cleaning products, and a dozen items of baking basics. It was a competition based on guessing the basket's total retail price, which I got to within twenty euro cents. I had beaten a competitive field of seasoned shoppers, all of whom were at school on the last day to see me leave. I'd said goodbye to everyone, leaving with two smiling girls by my side. In one arm a wide stack of their paintings, collages and drawings and, in the other, a ribbon-topped, cellophane-wrapped trophy to my parenting prowess. If it had been a little gold Oscar presented by the Academy, I wouldn't have valued it more.

It was now precisely 8.30, and there was still precisely nobody there.

The reason I had decided to do this presentation – actually promised to do it – had been Aimée's belief that my sharing my experience would help others see what was around them; the natural and man-built beauty, the careful way people went about their work, true artisanal production and locally-sourced food, the abundant nature, and its clean air. Above all, time with family: the type of thing that developed societies are trying to reintroduce. She saw the benefits here for families, how some took the quality of life for granted, while others no longer saw the value in it. She wanted my help to get others to appreciate it, hoping they'd follow her lead and fight to maintain it.

Right now, the army I'd raised looked pretty small; just the two team members chatting away while they dropped olive slices onto the pâtéd bread.

Will anyone fight for this to remain? History says the French once knew how to fight. Their revolution is still the gold standard for people-powered change. But the fastest growing movement here appears to be the rush towards the low-cost retailers along the Loire. Today the enemy of community is carried by all, in their own hands, hung on their walls. These small, infinitely rechargeable hand grenades seem effective on all forms of human-to-human connection. Anywhere the screens go, the casualties on citizenry are heavy.

Already there were signs the war was being lost in the region. When the satellite TV goes up on the wall of the pub, conversations stop. A local café had added a betting terminal that now held the dominant position in the room. When children hold devices centimetres from their eyes, curiosity vanishes. When a single TV plays all day in the living-room, the silent bonds of family are cut, and its members begin an outwards drift until everyone is in their own room, each with their own screen. What is piped to each screen is never about the logic of local, the benefits of the small, the courage it takes to stay where you are.

Nobody runs advertisements for what you already have. Heroes rarely get the girl by slowing down. I doubt you can buy a video game where points are scored for every time you share a laugh with your family over lunch. Gold medals are never given out for 'first dad to purchase the right cream' in the 'daughter has a rash' race.

Nobody had turned up for my talk, and I turned my anger on us. We've asked our politicians for growth, and more growth. We've asked for our quality of life to be paved over, we've carried the seeds of our own distraction, and if nobody cares enough about what they have, then we'll be to blame for the loss of that as well. The widespread lack of interest for my talk, as evidenced by the continued lack of arrivals, did have the benefit of clearing the hall of my demons. They'd slipped away, terrified most of all by the collective apathy.

I was once again of full chest: I had done my bit here, and if nobody cared, well then, I could always make a late change to the presentation. 'Fuck the French!' I'd announce. I wouldn't need Marie-Françoise's help to translate that. 'Don't you appreciate how lucky you are? Universal healthcare and month-long-holidays lucky. Five hundred types of cheese lucky, cheap great wine lucky, summer evenings like this for free lucky, indulging in your ridiculous language lucky.'

I'd moderate my language, of course, if my girls ever turned up. Or maybe I'd just cancel the talk and drown my sorrows with Angelique and the wine-maker's father. We had more than enough wine to get properly drunk and I'd had worse dinners than a hundred pieces of now-garnished bread and pâté.

Just as I was about to start our three-person wake, I saw Aimée walking towards the hall. She was accompanied by her handsome husband and her, not surprisingly, beautiful children. I gave her a warm greeting and said thank you. Given the low turnout, I'm not sure I sounded sincere. Her husband introduced himself and said he had heard so much about me, but was more excited to meet the famous Madison and Elsa. They were running late, I explained, as we were packing up to leave in the morning. I made sure I told him at least once that it was because I was off tomorrow to ride a day of the Tour de France.

Aimée's husband still had the shape of a professional baseball player and I resisted a joke about the implausibility of baseball and France, knowing that the retort about Australians and cycling might set me back. I need not have feared. He was suitably impressed by my ride, and even knew the course well enough to warn me about the Telegraphe. It was the first of the three mountains I'd be riding over, and it was the killer, he said. Riders tended to get excited at the start and go too fast early on. Wow, he really did know me.

Next came my girls, characteristically running, along with a couple of children I knew from school. Behind them, George and Robert, together, smiling broadly underneath the largest heads of blond hair in the district. Divonne was walking in with some other mothers from the school I recognised. Many had brought the husbands I hadn't met. Marie-Françoise walked towards the hall, dressed as if tonight's performance was a ballet from Paris. Corrine arrived without her husband, as she'd told me she had kicked him out recently. 'Out with the old!' she had allowed herself to joke, in a rare use of English. Ian and Vicki had missed the winter months and returned for the summer. I used my best French to say that I was now the real Touraine-ian and welcomed them as *les touristes*. Ian enjoyed how far I had come with my French, corrected some of the pronunciation, and then, in the custom of Australian men greeting each other, said he was surprised they were not the only ones there. Now that I'd inconvenienced everyone, he added, I'd better not waste their time.

People were flowing now with the consistency of a group that had all just got off the one big bus, rather than arriving, as they had, in separate small cars. They came too quickly for me to greet everyone. Franc the bird man. Merit'oh and Catherine. Winemakers of two families. Lots of the CYFAC crew, led by Aymeric, up to and including the cleaning lady. The family from the Château du Gizeux had walked to the hall together. The hints of deference with which they were greeted by others suggested that the egalitarian levelling of the Republic had not ironed flat all of society.

Three generations of the Fontaine family came. Sadly for me, Phillippe couldn't make it. His wife Karine apologised: he had to care for a cow having a *problème*. There were many I didn't know, and they didn't seem to know me either, as they walked straight past me and into the hall. Some had dressed up; ties on people I'd only seen before in overalls. Ian was right in a way. I was being given something by each family, and up to now I'd been thinking only about myself, my fears. I'd been concerned I would look silly, not whether they would have a good time.

Within a few minutes of the arrival of Aimée and her family, the hall had filled to the point where Ian was now unstacking some of the plastic chairs to augment the benches. Angelique and the winemaker's father were doing a brisk trade in free appetisers and complimentary wine. It wasn't that people had been late – they were spot on time. It was just that 'the time' was the announced time, plus the socially agreed upon number of minutes that are polite to give one's host. It was now my turn to get the party started.

With one touch of my finger, I woke up my computer and it jolted the projector back to life. With another, I killed the lights, silencing the room. Well, mostly. Some kids had to be pointed to the side door, a release they welcomed. I launched into the presentation. I started with slides from the PowerPoint I'd prepared for Shanghai, the same one I'd modified for my presentation to a room full of first graders, and then extended it with the images and stories of my time here. It now stretched over 140 slides. Under normal conditions that would be enough to kill any audience; however, my talk would be short on words, big on images. It was a format I was confident would work, even on those with the shortest of attention spans.

I knew well my first dozen or so slides – the colours and faces of Sydney, its iconic opera house and Harbour Bridge – and trusted that what had worked in Shanghai, simultaneously translated into Mandarin, would work in my version of French. It was a great opener, as few can resist the contrasts of a beachside city, the incongruity of a sail-topped Opera House, and the imposing solidity of the bridge, its riveted iron proof that man can link even that which nature has worked so hard to separate. Many knew me as the man who had arrived with less than a pocketful of French words; now, from out of my button-down shirt, I was overflowing with them. I was probably speaking too fast, a little overconfidently, when I made my first pronunciation blunder. It had rendered a key part of the introduction impossible to understand. Instantly I could tell I had lost the audience.

Quel horreur! Ian shouted, correcting my mistake so quickly that I suspected he'd been waiting for such a chance. I had learned that even the smallest of mistakes can render deaf any of the French. The offences include the horror of pronouncing the consonant that is meant to be silent; the blunder-headed error of getting the gender of an inanimate object wrong; or the sin of pronouncing a vowel with an inflection it does not deserve.

For all its natural beauty, unintended sexiness and romantic indolence, French is actually a highly regulated language. Its users are meant to work from a rule book, updated annually by the Académie Française. To the French, English is loose and unprincipled, taking foreign words as soon as they step off the boat. The French have pride in a type of immigration control, an ancient body that works to ensure that the new arrivals are only allowed in if they won't be taking the job of an existing French word.

The attempt to centrally control the *langue française* has done little to prevent the various regional accents and dialects squabbling with all the vehemence of siblings. It is said here that the accent in the Touraine is the finest in France; something that is said more often here than elsewhere. This combination of national honour and regional pride made it even more delicious to the crowd that my first mistake was so emphatically corrected by none other than the mangle-mouthed Australian in the front row.

Ian made much of my mistake, I made much of being corrected by him, and we both repeated the correct version of the line in harmony. All this was of great joy to the crowd, creating a much-welcomed moment of levity. We couldn't have done better had we rehearsed the duet. Neither of us would ever pass as locals, but our respect for the language was what we were demonstrating, a linguistic genuflect that is a condition of entry to the hearts of any French crowd.

Back into the presentation, I returned to the icons of Sydney, subjugating them to Eiffel's tower. Flattering the French is frankly not that hard; worn like a rosette, it's easy to see where to press their pride button. An easy way is to praise their pointy, vertical span of bolted iron, and I gave it the title of the world's most recognised man-built thing. If I needed another tool to get them onside, it was the sucker punch that Cail provided: the man whose name is stamped on the side of the national treasure, and who'd chosen this region to build the world's most advanced farm. Once, admittedly a long time ago, this place was, like, famous.

I was working hard, but I needn't have ever worried. I might have been the one hosting tonight, but the girls had done all the real work to ensure there was a supportive majority in the hall. Every time I flipped over an image of one or both of them – knee deep in the Sydney surf, rugged up against frozen fields, or climbing over Cail's ruins – the sympathy of the audience was barely contained. To an extent I hadn't understood, my two girls had become local heroes. A schoolful of their classmates had gone home each day carrying stories of their perseverance. Well known were the tales of their bravery, prowess in the pool, and, according to some boys, their beauty. Every day, the two with no language would be dropped at school by the silent giant; all day they would look and listen and try to understand what was taught. At lunch they would look and listen and try to understand what was served. In the playground they would look and listen and try to understand what was played. At the end of each day they would run to the silent giant, who was often in tight shorts, drive off in their farmer's car and, without fail, return the next day.

On hearing the stories later that night, adults told me they thought they wouldn't have lasted a week. The girls were particularly famous for never shedding a tear, except for the unfortunate incident of the over-amorous Simon, a story that all messengers had ensured was delivered. Apparently, they could swim like dolphins, run like cheetahs, and grazed like a herd of two, ensuring that whatever was served at lunch was eaten by at least one. Everyone had a story about them, something they had dealt with, some small act of kindness, some mishap that they shrugged off. Madison, legend held, had heard the sirens of the village fire alarm, and, not understanding the announcements that it was a drill, had run terrified to the Mayor's office.

The *Maire*, Aimée and class all united to water down the embarrassment of running in fear of an *exercice*. Elsa, the same legend held, was never afraid of anything, so she hadn't budged even when she thought the school actually was on fire. The girls had grown an adoring community around them, families who had shared and expanded these stories, three small townsful of love for two girls with whom they couldn't communicate.

With the audience firmly on our side, I could risk saying that on arrival I thought I'd landed in *Centre de Nulle Part*, the middle of nowhere. If offence was to be taken, I let them know the phrase came from Aymeric. When I pointed him out, he was wearing a smile and standing, having given up his seat for a late arrival.

Nobody needed me to present photographic evidence of the challenges presented by this region's off-season. The images of darkened, unplucked sunflowers with a fresh face of winter frost, roads empty but for the passing fog, fields of silent earth, cropless in their winter dormancy, and Cail's ruins, suitably dark and forbidding, all elicited the type of solidarity that is only wrought through the mutual experience of the challenging parts of life. Nothing bonds communities like the hardships they've all endured, unifies religious groups like the persecution they've all felt, or unites sports fans like the refereeing injustices they've witnessed.

It was a cross-section of a community, a group pulled here tonight by my girls' bravery at school, the time I had spent sitting in a factory, plus the thread of my regional crisscrossing on a cycle. It is not often a person comes on holiday to your own town, spends six months in the off-season, photographs relentlessly until they've captured a full selection of its otherwise hidden charms, then rents a projector and a microphone to show it back to you. Aimée's gaze caught my eye and reminded me that I was here with a purpose. As Ian had said, don't waste their evening.

It's easier to sell an idea when the person can actually purchase it. I hadn't come with anything to sell, as what I was showing was what they already had. Selling is a transaction where we exchange, while highlighting is helping another see what they have, and the vendor doesn't need credibility as the work is done by the observer.

The advantage of advertising is that it draws us towards the unrelenting supply of new. It's easier to sell big ideas, easier to sell the future. The big idea is an Eiffel Tower, Cail's agricultural experiment, the broad sweeps of revolutions, dazzling inventions, promises of big new technology. But a long-lived life is a series of small things, a hundred thousand chances to sit down with those you love, those you work with, for a coffee break or a meal. If we were to greet with warmth each person we meet on our random travels, say *bonjour* to all those in the bar, with bright eyes say good morning to the kids at school, lovingly welcome your family at all times, pick up the phone and make a call, then over a long life we'd get close to a million chances to spread a moment of connection. These are the bits of life, rippling outward long after the large things are built and ruined, the companies started and closed, the awards won and collecting dust on the mantelpiece.

But I was leaving town, after all. Tomorrow, at dawn. I was leaving the plains to ride up tall mountains and I was at risk of being another cake-eater telling those without bread what to have for dinner. Who was I to be selling 'here'?

Once again, I need not have worried. As I shared each discovery, told another story of a surprising find, showed the photo of someone here, it became clear that there were more than enough local heroes in the crowd to carry this story. As families saw themselves, or someone they knew, approval rippled out. The little girl who'd directed me to her parents' farm to buy cheese elicited a roar of approval, Franc's raptors got a gasp, the Bouff'tard a cheer. Clearly it was fondly held, even by those who only visited once a year on special occasions.

Some faces got a cheer, others a laugh. The kids who'd been sent out to play were gradually drawn back to the doorway, and then made their way back into their family grouping. I tried with humour to introduce the school's bus driver. Her shock of red hair meant that everybody knew her, her driving fast each morning well known. My remarks of 'Vite, vite' – fast, fast – were universally understood. Before tonight, Aimée had given me the context for why she'd be appreciated so warmly. As other schools in the areas had closed, her services were increasingly in demand. Each time the school asked if she could pick up a new student on her morning route, she never shied. She began to start earlier, drove as fast as the law would allow, and made sure every kid who wanted to come to school could get there. By driving as she did – which in reality was only the speed limit; I'd been the slow one – she was able to sweep up more children, and deliver them to school and home again. She was racing against the forces of community disintegration and doing her heavy-footed best to keep ahead.

My only job here was to stop all movement with my camera, to turn to where most weren't looking, and to frame the everyday. Once I was into the part of the presentation inside the CYFAC factory, I showed each stage of the bicycle's construction, sometimes from closer than anyone would sensibly look. I knew that to show was better than to tell, and fortunately I had 12,000 images – from which I had to select half a per cent.

For the sceptical, I'd even brought the bike. It was the shining manifestation of each gram of the care, each brush-stroke of attention, the shape given by every hand that had passed over it. As close to technical perfection as is possible, it showed the foibles of its human owner, thanks to the dent across its top tube. If that wasn't enough, the boss, head of the syndicate (or union), workers of all stages – from tube connection through to painting to wheel fitting – office staff (of one) and factory cleaner were here as both witnesses and proof.

What started as an exercise in documenting bicycle con-struction had become a study of the men and women who'd worked to make it look as beautiful as a piece of art, with the functionality of a faultless machine. From the moment I'd been stretched and measured, the parameters were set by science, so the difference became only the work.

The effort to go from good to excellent may be great, but what does it say that the price uplift from this quality increase is small? Bikes like mine will ride perfectly and last longer than the rider; however, bikes that are not nearly as well made, but are stickered with a better-known brand, sell for far more. In a world dominated by the price makers, it is up to the individual to set the value internally. Our ability to put value into things is our greatest protection. We don't control the big levers, the big moves, but we all control how we see the small steps. It's not a battle with the outside, it's a battle within ourselves. And those are the ones we are uniquely capable of winning.

What I'd learned was not by any deliberate study, but through the unintentional process of being open to here. Almost exactly twelve months earlier I had been in China, diving boots and all into the manufactured froth of the Shanghai Expo, to promote a city I felt qualified to represent. In the theatrical smoke and lights of the world's biggest trade fair, I'd been quite sure that the Western, first-world, unbridled capitalist, free-trading, tall-building world was where one could find 'the best place to live *and* work'. Here, where the only smoke was when things needed to be burnt, where the light was mostly natural, always soft, and where the only froth I had seen was across a Bouff'tard beer, I'd reached the same conclusion. Only now I believed it.

Divonne and I had once been a very good team, and elements of it would no doubt remain into the future for the benefit of the kids. It was an effectiveness built on knowing well each other's weaknesses. One of my many foibles is getting distracted in my own thoughts. So when she could see I had made my point, she began to spin her hands, forefinger of each hand rotating over the other, a spinning wheel-like sign for 'Speed up'. When that failed, the advice escalated to waving an open palm in front of an open mouth below closed eyes, the suggestion that the audience would soon be preparing for bed if I didn't wrap it up.

All I had left to do was make sure I didn't stumble on my conclusion. I could see Ian remain at the ready. '*Ici*' – here – I said, it was possible to find the elements necessary for happiness: '*stabilité*', '*beauté*' and '*travail épanouissant*' – work that was fulfilling. For a week I had wandered around repeating the final tormenting line. The French word for work, *travail*, entered the language from the Latin for a type of torture. I knew its English friend well, travail, as in something hard to get through. Épanouissant was another gift from the Romans, meaning a way to describe the blossoming of a flower. The combination of the two, torture-like work and blossoming joy, recognised the type of deep fulfilment that only comes when we put an almost painful level of exertion into something.

Nearly an hour had evaporated, over a hundred images flashed and were replaced. What I had said must have been passably pronounced as Ian had remained cocked, but never fired. I thanked people for coming and hoped I hadn't wasted their time. Unlike my Shanghai presentation, when I had finished I wasn't looking for the elevator to dive into. Instead of leaving with pockets full of business cards, I collected plenty of hugs. A loose line formed, I got the jabs I expected from Aymeric, a hug I didn't from Ian, another from Aimée. There were greetings from people I hadn't met, goodbyes from those I had. Otherwise it was the blur of people who were going in different directions: an audience standing up, a speaker coming down. They were leaving to go home, I was staying to clean the hall.

When the hall had almost emptied, two of the last were a man from CYFAC who I'd seen before but never spoken to, and Marie-Françoise. He worked between the metal and carbon trades, looked powerful but kept to himself. He was holding her arm, leaning heavily on her as his linguistic crutch. She said he'd asked her for her assistance to say something but wanted to do it when everyone had left. In a combination of English, which she helped him with, and French, which she helped me with, he wanted to thank me. He'd moved here all the way across the country to take the job in the factory, and was shocked to find he'd landed in the '*centre de nulle part*'. We laughed because we all understood that. '*Mais*' – or but – he said, and then he began to tear up, 'I will be happy here now.'

I stayed until the very end, Divonne took the girls and boys home, and Angelique remained for a while to help. When she gave her apologies that she had to get home to her kids, it was just me. I had to fold up the screen, untangle it all, and then sweep the floor, put back the benches and stack the chairs. At this show I would be my own roadie, I thought, and I'd be a good one too. I made sure I left the hall in a state better than I'd found it. I locked up and walked next door to the *mairie*, lifted the brass flap over the mail slot and pushed the key in. The key bounced on the stone floor, scampering deep into the entrance hall. I hoped I had left things here better than when I'd found them; as they had me. Just as the key now lay out of reach, there was no going back – the direction I was heading in was determined.

I said goodbye to each of the slumbering green dumpsters and returned the parking lot to its usual untenanted state. On my way home, I said *au revoir* to a few cows that my lights lit by the side of the road. They'd watched me train for six months, and I hoped had noticed my progress. We would leave early the next morning, and in thirty-six hours I'd be racing through the Alps, up the sides of three mountains, and down the back of two; on the bike made just along the road to my left; wearing a new helmet I'd buy to replace the one I'd broken on the road to my right. I turned up the rough track towards La Petite Briche, welcomed its small bumps, thanked them for their role in helping me learn how to slow down.

XXX

How to Win the Tour de France

Riding, and happily so (image thanks to the
organisers of the *Étape du Tour*).

My first training ride had been about twenty kilometres, pedalling behind Frits on the spirit-level-flat roads of Hommes.
This morning, to get to the start of the race in the village of
Mondane, my ride was twenty-two kilometres and slightly
uphill. I left my three-person support crew, the girls and
Divonne, sound asleep, which seemed a very sensible thing to
be doing at 4.30 in the morning.

When I'd booked my ticket for the race it included local
accommodation, and we'd been allocated rooms in the dormi-
tory of a vocational college for the trades specific to working
the diamond-hard granites of the French Alps. I'd been told
that rooms were allocated based on your bib number, so as
I was riding today as number 7982 out of 8000, I understood
why we'd been put in the trade school way down the road.
It turned out to be far nicer than any similar institutions I'd
visited, and it seemed only right that we were staying where

they taught the skills that build the roads, bridges and tunnels that we'd be enjoying today. They also trained people here in alpine rescue, which I hoped to not need today.

I left early as I wanted to make sure that if I got a puncture, I'd still make it to the start on time. I'd ridden puncture-free since coming here, despite riding the equivalent of across and back the width of France twice, but suspected that if the cycling gods had a sense for the poetic, it might happen this morning.

I needn't have worried. The ride in went smoothly, a gradual uphill that actually served as a good warm-up. As I rode, the sky gradually brightened and the surrounding mountains debuted, looking larger than they had back in January, now with their white blankets removed.

Before I was even halfway there, I was surrounded by hundreds of other cyclists, all travelling with the type of collegiate and understated mood that competitors share before any race. When I reached the town of Mondane, it looked like it had been hit by a tsunami of lycra and graphite, every road and footpath flooded by cyclists and their bikes. Above the crowd a sign showed that I still had another 1.5 kilometres ride to get to my area.

Numbers were allotted based on your times in other officially sanctioned races, and none of my local 'victories' counted. As I rode past each of the tranches, to get to the very back of the queue I'd be getting a good view of my competition. The competitors were organised into sections of 1000, and each grouping had a slightly different character than the one before. I'd never seen so much bicycle hardware, so many fit men, a few women, so much tight clothing, so little smiling. From the front to the back, the amount of tension reduced gradually, but the nervousness quotient grew.

The first riders, who included the semi-professionals using this race to climb the rankings, were almost universally the same size, plucked from the same mould that produced five-feet, six-inch, intense-faced European men with big legs. Diversity of sizes and sexes didn't start until about the 4000s, and smiles weren't evident until the 6000s. When I finally got to my grouping, I was amongst the last to arrive, and my position was close to the barrier that marked the very back of the pack. In front of the barrier at the start, there had stood various support cars, medical motorbikes and camera crews. Behind the barrier at my back, kids were playing soccer, people were walking their dogs, coming up to have a sniff and then turning around.

We still had forty-five minutes before the start. Fortunately, everyone seemed to understand that a marathon worth of energy could be wasted in pre-race nerves, so it became a collective responsibility to keep the peace. The key was to act like you just happened to have parked your bike here, and would be surprised to learn there was a race about to start. You also needed a nonchalant visage that was only slightly more alert than of one asleep, and to keep movements to an absolute minimum. A superficial calm was held together, but as humans display their level of nervousness by the frequency with which they go to the bathroom, I could tell that people were terrified: there was one portable toilet with a long queue and other bushes that were at risk of being washed away.

Down this end of the pack, the variety of shapes and sizes, of riders and their rides, was the only consistent variable. We were mostly men and some women, with a wide age range. Some of the fittest were those on the older end. The German-speaking man behind me couldn't have been less than seven feet tall, and another man had only one real leg and a prosthetic one. Up close, the different cycling hardware was a truly impressive combination of the sleekest carbon-fibre bikes, perfectly-fitting cycling attire, aerodynamic helmets and electronic timing devices strapped to wrists, on wheels and displays on handlebars.

My bike stood out and got immediate attention. A man nearby asked simply: 'Steel?' As he'd asked in English, I replied in English and in the affirmative, that it was made by CYFAC. I loved that this got a ripple of approval from some of the older riders, one of whom explained to the group in French that CYFAC was a famous, very good, but very, very small producer.

'*Ils ont gagné le Tour une fois!*'

They've won the Tour once, he said, and I didn't correct him.

But the winning bike had been painted with the name of a big manufacturer, he went on to explain. Another said he'd never seen a real CYFAC before, referring to the days when CYFAC frames were rebranded and raced under another company's logo. I didn't want to correct him that they'd always been real CYFACs, only with fake Super Us, Raleighs or whatever logo had been painted over.

The second question was simply 'English?' I replied, '*Non, Australien,*' to show I knew enough French to understand most of what they were saying.

'Ah, Cadel!' The shout went out. No need to do my kangaroo impression here – they had me pegged.

'*Regarde, c'est Cadel!*' one man said – 'Look, it's Cadel!' – pointing at me. It was a mantle I was happy to take on, despite the fact I was a foot taller, a third heavier, and my chin was on the delicate side, while Cadel's was a perfect dimpled twin protrusion. Oh, and he was currently sitting fourth in the real Tour de France, and I was standing about 8000th in this one day of it.

'Do you know 'im?' someone asked. It was sort of a silly question, as there are more than twenty-four million people in Australia, but as I did, I answered yes. Again, the answer wasn't important, it had just been a conversation starter, a place where the cyclists knew they could begin an argument. 'I think he will win,' one said. Another disagreed, mentioning the name of a French cyclist, which got almost universal approval. With that, the men were off, talking with deep certainty about this year's Tour at a great pace that left me far behind.

Aymeric had taught me that Cadel was a cyclist's cyclist: known less for his big personality or loud voice and more for being a generous team rider, and a notoriously hard trainer.

If there was ever an opposite to Lance Armstrong, it was Cadel. The sport of road cycling that is broadcast is about race-day excellence, big-event excitement, crushing wins and surprising upsets. The reality of high achievement is more about relentless training, precise preparation and a bit of luck on race day. When insiders from different sports talk about the champions who have been successful, there are invariably the stories of how they trained harder than the rest. Michael Jordan, legend holds, threw more practice shots than any of his team-mates. Cadel, cyclists said, had put more miles in his legs, as cyclists call it, than anyone else on the Tour.

As a young boy I'd learned to morph into my sporting heroes in an attempt to channel their skills. When you do this, you're practising how they play, not how they've trained. As a child, when I ran around the backyard with a football, I was frequently alone, so I made a small team with my heroes, the Krakouer brothers, two Aboriginal Australian Rules football players. I might have been lanky, uncoordinated, all alone and very white, but it wasn't me out there, it was Jim or Phil Krakouer.

So when it came to pacing up and down the French countryside, I was well practised in the art of implausible transformations. I had easily turned myself into a member of Cadel's elite team. In real life, I had ridden by Cadel's side, albeit for thirty minutes in a charity race over the Harbour Bridge in Sydney. That hadn't mattered: because over the last six months, for ninety minutes every day, I'd been imagining I was out riding with him. When I told the group that I actually knew him, little did they know I imagined myself to be here as part of his team. In my dreams I was riding as the advance member, learning the route, sprinkling a little Aussie gold dust for Cadel to follow.

Spot on 7 am the horn sounded, and the race was off. Well, at least it was for the riders at the front – we had to wait until seven sections of 1000 riders each rolled across the starting line. While we could all see we'd have to wait our turn, the horn sent a stiffening ripple of tension through the group. A couple of people clipped the helmet straps that had been hanging loosely. Others stood up and swung a leg over their bikes. Mini bicycle computers were fiddled with, glasses were placed over eyes, completing the visual presentation of determination. Breathing changed, nobody spoke. Everyone waited.

Looking down the hill, over thousands of helmeted heads, we could see the elite semi-professional riders fly off, followed by the 000–999 riders who took off after them with a deluded pretence of pursuit. Despite their quick start, it still took nearly ten minutes for all of the first batch to cross the starting line. Numbers 1000–1999 were slightly faster as they had more room to roll up to the line, and I sensed the excitement building. The 2000s followed, a little bit quicker, a little more excitement around me.

Sadly, the 3000s had been stacked on a side road, out of sight. As they poured in, it gave the impression that 1000 other riders were pushing in, and the perceived injustice riled our group, giving our misfit tribe a common enemy to bring us together. It took nearly forty-five minutes for our group of 7000s to be released from our corral and start the careful roll – to cries of 'Lentement, lentement' – slowly, slowly. It had been over three hours since I'd woken and had got my first hit of adrenaline. Most sporting events are over in less time than this, and by the time we got to the start line I could have done with a sit down and a sandwich.

I knew the first part of the race well, as it was back down the same twenty-two kilometres I'd ridden in this morning, to a sharp turn that was just outside our accommodation. Few men can restrain themselves at the start of any race, and most on the road were men – and men of the overly-competitive type. Various attempts were made to slow the pace. There were more stern words of lentement, then prudent, which needs no translation, and sensible phrases in English like 'We have a long way to go'. When those failed, and the group kept picking up the pace, came the whiny complaint of 'Come on, guys'. All attempts failed. So instead of the group keeping a steady pace, even those complaining about the speed got faster and faster. The faster it got, the more people protested, but kept riding just as fast. It was a collective act of self-harm: we all knew it, and we were all doing it.

Humans – and I'm including the few women in the group who were as bad as the rest of us – are really poor at sacrificing when others are not prepared to. Why didn't we slow down when none of us wanted to ride that fast? Why did riders actually keep riding faster themselves, even while calling on the group to slow down? It's similar to the challenge of getting people to consider consuming less, buying less, eating less, while others are clearly not going to. Our nations won't stop polluting, mostly because some other nations don't intend to. We might be very unsure about the need to buy something, build something bigger, or send our kids to a certain school, but if others are doing it, it is an impossible draw. Fear of missing out appears to be a stronger force than the fear of getting what we don't really want.

After the long and uncomfortably-fast downhill, the signs all pointed to a sharp left. These were followed by large signs on both sides of the road, warning about the sharpness of the left. These were followed by race officials on both sides of the road shouting to slow down to take the sharp left. The challenge of riding in a large pack is you can't slow down too much, as you'll get hit from behind. I figured the race officials knew something we didn't, and I concentrated hard on taking the corner.

A few riders hadn't heeded the warning, not made the turn, and wrapped themselves into the barricades. Just as I was nearly through the bend, I was sure I could see – behind one of the barricades that wasn't holding a cyclist together – two girls who could have been Madison and Elsa. While making the corner was important, so was letting out a little smile and raising my right hand for a moment off the handlebar, in the hope that they saw that I'd seen them. When I straightened out of the turn, I was able to sit up and wave over a shoulder and hoped they wouldn't think I was trying to show off.

With another sharp left we were suddenly on the infamous Col du Télégraphe, named because it was a helpfully pointy peak for someone who once wanted to plant a radio telegraph station. The long downhill from the start had stretched out the pack, but the incline had a sudden foreshortening effect and riders were now jostling for space across the road. The road up was as steep as I had heard, about ten kilometres long, and rising almost one kilometre. When climbing like this, the pace isn't fast enough to make the friction from wind an issue. Riders focus on keeping their momentum and riding a steady pace, spreading out across the road rather than sneaking in behind each other.

The race was essentially three peaks: the first, Télégraphe, was particularly steep; the second, Galibier, belligerently long; and the third, Alpe d'Huez, when our legs were least prepared for it, the sadistic union of both steep and long. I had reduced my apprehension for the race by not doing any research beyond this. I knew I couldn't change anything. I got that it was 100-plus kilometres long, which didn't seem so far when some of it had to be downhill, but found it hard to imagine what the four kilometres of vertical gain would be like.

All of my designed ignorance seemed to have immediate benefit: I was already having much more fun than anyone else. For road cyclists, the enemy is the road, and as it is ever present, a smile is never part of the uniform. Even though we were on our first climb, riders were already pulling faces at the surface beneath them: some rode with a deadly serious gaze that suggested the road surface had done something bad to them; others bore a grimace that looked like they were having trouble chewing, rather than riding on, the road. Still others looked like they were having trouble passing it out the other end.

Having survived the first turn, and finding the first climb easier than expected, the faux-stoicism and projected pain of the other riders was a reminder of just how fortunate I was. The application for the race said it was only for 'experienced and highly trained riders', a box I'd ticked even though both were untrue. I'd come to France with no experience and no bike. I had fresh eyes and fresh legs. Far from pulling a face, I went to the other extreme and wore the smile of someone who could hardly contain how lucky they felt. Worse, I was going to show it to as many as possible.

I was travelling well up the Télégraphe and passing large groups with each short exertion. I'd peel out to the far left, stand up on my pedals for a dozen strokes, round a group and then swoop back to the inside, before taking off to pursue the next school of black-butted, dark-faced pedallers. Once I got to them, I'd repeat the path, swing out, pedal hard for a dozen strokes, and swing back in, swooping up another ten or twenty places.

Whether my serpentinian sprinting was sensible or not, I didn't care. What I was enjoying was that I was having so much more fun than anyone else. I'd come to France begrudgingly, thinking I was taking the worse of the only two options on the table. If my travelling-elsewhere wife was right about one thing, it was that living away from the pressure of any spotlight, particularly the largest one – the one I put on myself – would do me good. Now, where nobody knew me, and fewer cared, I was riding up the hill like a clown, and enjoying passing the crowds toiling away with their heads in the Télégraphe.

The first climb was steep; thankfully also short. I'd gone out hard and I was already well into those with numbers in the 6000s, seeing some that started with a 5. At the top I welcomed a break, changing character from upstart to casual competitor. The downhill was short, and because it was another form of fun, I found another gear and rode on hard. We were in nature, where man's careful trowel had paved a blissfully smooth surface on which to enjoy ourselves. To the sides, waterfalls dropped steeply, sometimes providing a sprinkle of water over the side of the road, a cooling shower that I hoped would be offered in a few hours.

All the roads had been closed to oncoming traffic, and we had both lanes to ourselves, able to choose the best line possible to slice through the chicanes. Dotting the route, families sat on camp chairs behind a cardboard sign or a bed sheet on which was written some encouragement for their family's representative. By the road, their youngest children worked as flag bearers, waving and shouting indiscriminately at riders.

As I rounded one corner, a group of young women, all with their t-shirts tied at the navel, were cheering us on, bouncing with enthusiasm. I kicked up a gear, adjusted my posture in case it had slipped, and, from my chin, wiped away some sweat as a masculine accent. I had sped up, but for the first time I hadn't gained on any of my competitors. Turns out that cheering girls had the same impact on all of the men with me. As soon as we were around the next corner, we carefully slowed back down, all pretending we didn't just do that.

Each of the three peaks served a specific purpose: the Télégraphe, was to wake us up, I knew Alpe d'Huez was there to finish us off, and the job of Galibier was surely to numb us. The route is an unrelenting twenty-nine kilometre ride, with a rise of nearly 1500 metres, and it is the thug of the trio.

I began it well among the 5000s. The supportive cries of the crowd were now less an expression of shared enjoyment and more likely to be earnest messages of advice. I still wore my happy face and welcomed the long grind to get lower in the numbers. Each group of a thousand would tempt me forward with a straggler or two – the first time I saw a number starting with a 4, it was like blood in the water, suggesting there were hundreds more where that one came from.

Galibier was the biggest mountain I'd ever ridden up. It was already feeling big when we broke above the tree line and its full bigness was exposed. Like someone had dropped our ant race onto the back of an elephant, the small black dots I could see in the distance were the only thing that provided some perspective. To make it over this pachyderm, the insects joined forces. At each flatter section we'd form small informal bands, sharing the lead duties, riding each other to the beginning of the next steep bit. It was a series of practical unions, teams that formed and reformed as riders helped each other keep up the pace. These effortless bonds of solidarity were broken at the beginning of each new steeper section. Self-interest was excused as each cyclist found their own rhythm for the next climb, each of us taking the climbing section alone, and then regrouping with whoever arrived at the next plateau at the same time.

Cooperation is essential for the thriving of so many species, not least the road cyclist. On the flatter parts, we took turns to take the wind for our new sub-clan, share a round of encouragement. The groups rode together to a pre-determined social compact, unspoken rules which benefited everyone: when it was your turn at the front you rode hard, just enough to keep the pace, but not so hard that you separated yourself from the group. When someone got a flat, someone we'd only just formed a team with, a couple of us would pull over to help change the tyre. Of course, like any microcosm of society, there were the more selfless ones and more selfish ones. And me, the clueless one. I still let the rush of leading the group distract me, and often I'd pull too far ahead. When I'd look back, and see that I'd once again broken the contract, I could either apologise like it was a mistake, or just keep going and make it seem like I was breaking away.

Approaching the top of Galibier, it was noticeably high; the air thinner, the view limitless. The sun, left alone by this morning's thin clouds, was ready to scorch any skin washed of its sunscreen by a couple of hours' persistent sweating. I pulled my arm warmers up for their sun protection, certainly not needing their warmth.

Reaching the peak signalled that the worst of the Galibier was over, and I got another invitation to the fun club: a thirty-five-kilometre downhill on a perfectly smooth road. It had been recently repaved for the professionals coming in four days, but it was us amateurs getting the first go. Cycling is fun at the best of times, the joy of the wheel, flying at a low altitude – and with only one climb to come, on a bike built for exactly this moment, this was as good as it had ever been for me.

What was even better is that downhill favours those with more mass. I was at the very heavy end of all competitors and on this downhill I appeared to be the fastest thing on the back of the mountain. Tucked on top of my bicycle I was catching the 4s, and eating the tail of the 3s. Aymeric said the downhills would see most travel at over fifty kilometres per hour, while some would reach seventy. I was speeding past riders so frequently that I must have been towards the upper end of Aymeric's speed estimations. The last time I'd flown past other cyclists like this was when I'd been on an antique bike and they were five-year-olds. I'd never travelled half this fast on a bike, and I was loving it. Nor had I ever gone this fast into a tunnel, which I was about to discover was the opposite of fun.

We hit the first tunnel at the end of a particularly long straight and I was at top speed when the lights went out. As I flew down the mountain it had been silent but for the rush of air, but as soon as I entered the tunnel it was a cacophony of shouting, the reverberating chaos of one hundred cyclists screaming 'Shit!' in nine different languages. The water curtain that fell over the entrance had not been welcome, as slippery was not the surface we wanted. Braking could only be done very, very carefully.

The screaming continued as people tried to slow down and move to the sides, hoping that ducking into the edges would protect them from large, fast-moving objects from Australia. I had my dark lenses on, and my eyes were adjusting slowly. I was too afraid to take a hand off the handlebars to remove my glasses. All I could make out in the pitch black was a small semi-circle at the other end of the dark tube. Otherwise I was riding almost completely blind at the fastest pace I had ever travelled on a bike. I pointed towards the light, applied the slightest hint of brakes, and called for the blessings of the cycling gods, the mountain fairies, and Cadel's manager that I'd make it through safely. The screams and crunching I heard from behind me evidenced collisions that I hoped were not my fault.

Then, almost as quickly as the lights had been switched off, I was spat out the tunnel, into the bright light. Still upright and, better still, I figured I had cut through perhaps thirty riders, my straight path protecting me. The trial by tunnel had been like a combination of falling under a farmer's combine harvester, sliding through a rugby scrum, and being locked in an industrial dishwasher, before popping out the other side and not understanding how you did so unscathed. It didn't make sense, and it didn't matter, as there was another long downhill to take, and another tunnel to prepare for.

Each successive tunnel would feature the same panicky blend of complete darkness, wet road, multilingual swearing, and vain attempts to slow riders before the entrance. In this situation, there actually is no point in slowing yourself down if others are not; better to take the risk of hitting someone from behind than be hit from behind. Besides, at greater speed you were out quicker.

This time I supported the logic of the maddening crowd and understood why nobody slowed down through the dozen or so death tubes that punctuated the long downhill. The exhilarating combination of rare speed with the chance of dying is the foundation of many popular spectator sports but, up until now, not something I'd enjoyed first-hand.

Arriving at the base of Alpe d'Huez is like arriving at the front door of a tall office building when you know you're late for a meeting on the top floor – and being told you'll have to take the stairs. I had immediately ignored the laconic warning of 'Don't look up' from another rider and marvelled at the challenge ahead of us. It was a stone-grey monolith, and the monster climbing it was a black serpent, our road, switching back and forth towards its peak. At the very top, instead of a spire, were a series of buildings. I recognised them as the apartment buildings that Corrine had told me about, but from the base they were tiny rectangles that looked like windows at the top of the Empire State Building.

I was well amongst the 4s and 3s now. I was far from alone in playing the numbers game, and overheard others using it to judge their progress, enjoying the double-take I got when people saw my number started with a 7, a marker that I was a member of a caste that people didn't want to be passed by. A few times, when I rode by someone, and they got to see my number, they'd break into a sprint to catch up to me, giving me another reason to ride faster.

I'd been accepted by my own tribe that morning, the misfits and disorganised 7000s, the pissing Frenchmen, the giant German, the one-legged guy, the quiet woman in pink. I was enjoying riding for the outsiders, for people like Cadel who had been discounted because of the assumptions others made of them. For Cadel it was because he'd started in the unfashionable discipline of mountain biking, and that he had the unlikely origin of Australia's Northern Territory.

In addition to riding for the 7000s and for Team Evans, I was also competing for the young me: the boy who'd been sent to boarding school, the skinny kid singled out to be bullied, the one who didn't make the top sports teams but who was often hit by those who did. I was riding Alpe d'Huez as I had thrown myself at many challenges in life: with everything I had, believing I was making up for past injustices, making sure people saw how much I was enjoying it.

This final climb was broken into twenty-one switchbacks, each shorter than the one before, each steeper than the one before. Between successive corners, more riders were taking a break, retiring or getting medical attention. On each one, the grind was slower, the expletives more frequent. Each one was another reminder that the challenge I'd taken on was entirely self-imposed, a competition that had been invented for people who had the luxury of excess energy, time and money.

Frits had once ridden this exact route. He'd done it on a weekday, by himself, taken the day and stopped for a nice lunch. I had made the biggest challenge in my year a race I'd signed up to do, whereas the challenges that the girls faced were entirely put on them; daily trials they overcame without all the swearing and grimacing, no handy gels of energising goop, no roadside cheerleaders.

Madison had asked why grown-ups don't smile as much as children. Elsa asked at what age they stopped. If they were here, they might wonder why thousands of adults pay to cycle in a race, and then look so comprehensively unhappy while doing it. I'd make sure that if the girls were to see me, they'd see that I was doing this with a smile. If not the smile of a child, then of a grown-up appreciating where they had got themselves to.

With about half a dozen bends to go – I kept losing count – the route took a decided turn for the serious. If you were going to make up any places, there was not much time to do it, and slow going made it hard to peg back those in front of you. Suddenly everyone was racing. I'd had the surreal experience of not being passed by anyone all day. I had ridden past, and at times nearly over, something like six thousand riders and I wasn't going to let this perfect record be ruined.

A few of the riders were helping me catch them by getting off their bikes, some lying down, others just leaning against a shady section of the rock face. The riders who kept going shouted words of encouragement, telling their resting comrades to get a drink and come back to the road.

To my right, a rider collapsed on his bike just as I was about to overtake him. He'd been riding in front of me for a while, and I'd worked hard to catch him. My first reaction was disappointment, as he'd robbed me of the chance to pass him. He'd collapsed suddenly, slumping forward like he'd fallen asleep in the seat, melting towards the road. I instinctively shouted for him to get a drink and come back to the road, which was the wrong thing to say to someone face down and motionless on it. Much of the solidarity that we'd developed in the middle of the race was gone now, and I kept going as the other riders did. When we looked back, the first spectators had rushed in to help.

The turns were tightening even further, forming twists that would trouble even my car. We were heading into the last stretch of mountain before the town that sat at the peak. The apartment buildings were now – true to Corrine's description – outsized for the location. Sensing the end was coming, I found a way to pick up the speed. The crowd started to get thicker, growing to one or two deep, when I saw an inflatable arch stretched over the road that read 'FIN', or finish. It had come up quicker than I had expected. There were only half a dozen riders between me and it, and I gave it my all. Using what little I had left in my legs, and singeing my lungs with the hot dry air, I caught them all easily – as if they weren't even trying – thrusting my bike over the line.

It immediately became clear I had, once again, misunderstood French race instructions. 'FIN' had just meant we'd reached the town in which the race finished. A number of spectators worked out my mistake, and called out for me to continue. One even ran up beside me to encourage me and let me know that there was still another kilometre to go.

Wanting to thank them, I noticed my smile was not coming – for the first time my clear sight and positive visage had deserted me. Riding slowly away from the inflatable arch, I was deflated. In sprinting too early, I'd blown up my legs and popped my confidence. My unbroken passing record fell, not once, but half a dozen times. If there is anything sillier than trying to win races that are not races, it's sprinting across finishing lines that are not finishing lines.

I assume that professionals don't make these mistakes. In the years Cadel Evans had come close to winning the Tour, he faced challenges greater than simply misreading the location of the finishing line. History shows that he was the only man to come second, twice. What history was likely to bury is that when one of the riders who beat Cadel into second was found to have tested positive for steroids, Cadel kept dignified; never complaining that he should be moved up a place in the history books. Even though commentators had already written him off as too old, he had quietly returned to race this year's Tour. He'd built a tight team around him, and those in the know were saying he was more than ready for the Alpe d'Huez. What is most said about any of us, what is eulogised and tapped into a tombstone, what sits in cyberspace forever on Wikipedia entries, tends to record the achievements that can be counted, compared, categorised. Less is recorded of the moments where the true character of the person was on display.

Around the next corner was another inflatable 'FIN', big enough to be the real finish, so I picked up the speed while trying to look like I wasn't, in case it was another false finish. I didn't catch the six who had got past me, but it was okay as it was just another trick for the inexperienced. This time I noticed small signs that indicated we were within the last 600 metres.

I managed to wear down all the riders who'd gone past me, with the exception of one, a fellow member of the 7000 tribe. The crowds were deep on either side, and the two of us began a duel to the real 'FIN', rising out of our seats for a sprint that also helped me look for the girls. My eyes were a sticky mess of dried sweat and fresh sweat, so I wasn't sure I'd be able to see them. I hoped they'd see me; I'd found my smile, and with the other cyclist we pushed each other on and rode together, once again lunging across the line, not sure, and now not caring, which of us crossed first.

We dismounted, shook hands, smiled deeply, laughed and thanked each other for the final piece of pain we'd ensured the other would feel. At a long series of tents we took our recovery mixtures and a computer-generated certificate that showed our finishing places. Mine, 1980, was both my placing and the year

I'd landed in that far-off boarding school. Randomness tricks you into thinking that understanding it might bring you something of value. The truth is the opposite: there is twice as much power in learning that that was then, this is now.

I thanked again my co-sprinter, and he me. We held up our thin pieces of paper between two fingers, and laughed again, as if to say, 'And this is it?' I didn't even look at his number, nor he at mine. As we shared no other language, we both headed in separate ways to find our respective support crews.

I looked around for the girls, waiting for that scene of them running towards me, each one rushing in to embrace a sweaty thigh. I took my phone out of the plastic bag that had stuck faithfully to my back as I rode. I called Divonne to let her know I was just behind the finish line, on the left of the barricades, at the last of the sponsors' tents.

The response was 'Already?' They were still at the hotel, about an hour's drive away. It meant the girls hadn't been at the finish at all, and while it could have felt like uncaring behaviour, I chose to take it as a compliment. Turns out they had done some secret calculus of my expected pace and thought I'd be going for some time longer.

I searched for somewhere to sit and found that the only place with the benefit of any shelter came with the disadvantage of being on the road. One of the tents was throwing a thin strip of shade, and I sat down, happy to be out of the sun. My bike stood next to me, propped up against the tent. It had taken praise at the start, remained puncture free, flown me downhill, lifted me up the three mountains, and guided me past nearly six thousand riders. Yet it showed no signs of fatigue and looked like it was ready to go again. I wondered, though, what it thought of me – the crumbling man with shaky hands, fumbling for comfort on the hard road. I wanted it to be proud of my performance.

I had ridden for Team Cadel, hopefully I'd made my girls proud, I believe I'd shown respect for my bike and for those who'd made it. I had ridden for me, with a smile over my face to prove it. But now it was all catching up with me. As the remaining adrenaline trickled away, reality filled its place, a full man-load of pains and rashes.

My body was coming to its senses, with an indignation verging on fury, like an old friend from whom you've borrowed a car, driven it recklessly and returned it smashed up. The perineum pain was acute, and as each successive muscle in my legs regained feelings they were not pleasant ones. I drank another bottle of water, but my lips only closed on the parts that were the most swollen from the sun and dry. Now my eyes were burning. My good sense began to fade; my legs to fail.

I took off my helmet and decided it might be best to lie down on the asphalt. I found my arm warmers, damp but with the familiar texture of cotton, and folded them into a small pillow. I crossed my arms over my chest, placed my helmet over my face, and closed my eyes. As I urged sleep towards me as quickly as it could bring its relief, I composed a short note to Cadel in my head.

Cadel, I did my best. I didn't get a good starting position, but I think I knocked off about six thousand of them.

Watch out for the first turn onto Télégraphe, Galibier is easier than they say, and then the twenty-one bends up to Alpe d'Huez are tough but doable.

Frankly it's not much of a village when you get here, rather over-built. But as they say, it's not about the destination, it's about the journey.

Enjoy the ride, it will be a big night in Katherine if you pull this off!

P

FIN
THE END

Four days later, the professional riders of the Tour de France set out on the same course from Mondane to Alpe d'Huez. Cadel started the race in third place, but on the first climb, as he rode up the Col de Télégraphe, mechanical problems forced him to pull over. After two more stops to try to fix it himself, he eventually had to dismount and wait for a support car to arrive with a new bike.

With his bicycle replaced, his team members wrapped him up and with a combination of dogged determination and seamless cooperation they worked to make up lost time. Astonishingly, when Cadel reached the top of Alpe d'Huez he had climbed into second place overall. The next day, in the 110 kilometre time trial, he rode himself into first place. He would go on to become the first Australian ever to win the Tour de France, the oldest champion in the post-war era, and possibly the nicest guy to ever triumph in cycling's top event.

When asked what went in to make his victory, he first thanked his team, then added, 'Twenty years of hard work.'

I'm told it was indeed a big night in Katherine that night.

ÉPILOGUE

Inside the Davos bubble, or to be more precise,
an inflatable tunnel used to dash between.

Almost exactly a year after I'd driven to the remote hamlet of La Petite Briche, I ploughed my way across an icy Europe; this time dissecting Switzerland. I'd been invited to the Annual Meeting of the World Economic Forum in the alpine village of Davos. This would be my first foray back into the world I once knew, only this time I had been invited here as a member of the media.

Known to its friends simply as Davos, it's one of the planet's highest-powered gatherings; a week-long talkfest for economists and bankers, politicians and journalists, executives and billionaires. The three thousand attendees assemble at an altitude of 1200 metres, protected by a security force of five thousand, and serviced by an army of drivers, cooks, personal assistants and room cleaners that number over three times that.

I was alone for that January trip, but for the characters from the audiobook of *Tale of Two Cities*, Dickens' gory telling of the origins of the French Revolution. I had chosen – as my preparation to write about the current state of capitalism, rising levels of inequality, and the challenges of globalisation – to listen to a fictionalised account of a 200-year-old populist uprising, fourteen hours of political reform and economic redistribution, mixed with undying love and lots and lots of blood. As I approached the destination, I was at the part where the reform-minded mobs of Paris were, with the help of the invention of Dr Guillotin, removing the heads of the original one per cent.

The town of Davos couldn't have looked more different from the depopulated triangle between Hommes, Rillé and Continvoir. That is, when I could see it. That winter's snowfall had been the deepest in forty, sixty or 100 years, depending on whose report you accepted, and the town's celebrated charms were largely hidden beneath two metres of snow. As a skier, I had always welcomed the fluffy white stuff, a case of the more the merrier. But for those who have to live in it, trudge to work through it, the more that falls the harder your life becomes. Even for the natural inhabitants. Somewhere in the surrounding forests I guessed there were bitter squirrels whingeing about the cold, deer grumbling about a lack of grass.

On the first morning of the conference, I rushed to attend the opening remarks of the event's convener, the frightfully stern Klaus Schwab. I arrived late to the TV studio – the shuttle bus service not quite as efficient as I needed it to be – just as they were closing the soundproof doors. I was ushered into one of the only remaining seats, right in the centre of the front row.

As Klaus strode onto the stage my position meant I was looking straight at his shoes. They were the most radiantly black objects to behold. I wondered what process of hide-removing, leather-tanning and artisanal-cobbling produced shoes this perfect. When the pair were finished, no doubt they had been slipped into a velvet bag and delivered to a shoe shop, where they'd been bought by, or for, Mr Schwab. Sometime earlier that day they would have been carefully unpacked for this event, possibly even given a quick polish with a taut cloth to burnish them to military-grade shine.

Standing rod straight and dressed in an equally crisp double-breasted suit, Klaus announced, 'Capitalism, in its current form, no longer fits the world around us.' We were told we had 'failed to learn the lessons from the financial crisis of 2008' and that a 'global transformation is urgently needed'. It wasn't what I expected to come from such a respectable pair of shoes.

The ensuing response from the leaders of the organisations that dominate economic development – the IMF, WTO, World Bank – was a joint press release, a collective 'Call to Action'. It turned out to be an urgent plea for the continuation of free trade, the extension of globalisation, and increased central bank control. Their stated goals were the 'strengthening of growth, employment and the quality of life in every part of the world'. I suspected that billions of those who didn't get an invite to come here would rather the order of those three be reversed. Sure, the uninterrupted growth of the last forty years had helped so many, but now it appears to be benefiting a smaller and smaller number of the already wealthy, at the cost, in relative terms, to the majority. And in absolute terms, to the planet.

Over the week, I attended small talks, plenary sessions, private briefings, and workshops with live whiteboard animations. I tête-a-têted with multiple heads of state and a couple of people who thought they soon would be. As the sole representative for an Australian media company, I attempted to cover the entire conference for an entire nation. I got up early to attend the brittle and focused sessions where people would say more because they assumed – mostly correctly – that journalists were still in bed. I stayed up late to finish dinners with those who said more after they had too much to drink.

I did write my five, admittedly rather thin, stories, which I produced at the slowest ratio of word-output-to-time-input of anyone in the bustling media centre. I also got lucky with the American news website Huffington Post. As I dashed between sessions, I bumped (literally) into the founder. She was about to go on air and I saw that a tag from the dry-cleaners was still on her shirt. I approached Ms Huffington, pointed out the problem, and I asked if she'd take one of my stories. She removed the tag and said yes.

On the last day, after I'd paper-cupped coffee through another twenty-one-hour marathon, the only thing left to do was drive back to the generosity of my friend's spare room. His apartment was a half-hour back down the mountain, outside the town of Klosters. The shuttle buses were still running, and I found one that would take me to the hotel where I had parked my car. I collapsed into my seat – I had run out of steam.

My head was straining under its cargo of facts and figures, of names and their faces; a yet-to-be-categorised mix that combined carefully worded statements read from behind podiums with off-hand remarks snatched from the mist of wine and bottled water. Business cards bulged in my pockets and I clung to the optimistic delusion that I'd process them one day. Like the cards themselves, I had taken it all in, unsure what I would do with any of it.

By the time the shuttle reached my car, it was close to 3 am, and at least ten below zero. I'd stayed in the parking space far longer than I had paid for, but enough fresh snow covered my windscreen to conceal my expired ticket.

I tried to reverse out of my parking space, but I'd been almost completely boxed in by a black Mercedes and the hotel bus that had pulled in behind me. I rolled back as far as I could, then turned my steering wheel hard to the left, and edged forward. Then right and backwards again. A few inches of progress at most. Each time I turned the steering wheel, my tyres swivelled over the dry snow, and it let out a muted squeal. I felt a little sorry for the flakes; they didn't stand a chance under a tonne-and-a-half of aluminium and steel.

I'd not met any butchers in Davos, nor any bakers, farmers, road-menders, steelworkers or bicycle-makers. The forum had brought together representatives from all nations, thought-leaders whose job was to speak on behalf of the people of the world. There were plenty of capitalists, a few socialists, but not as many communists as the organisers had hoped, as the event clashed with Chinese New Year. These days, it's impossible to tell which team a person was playing for just from their attire: no-one was wearing a Mao suit, the far-right avoided jackboots, billionaires appeared in open-necked polos, and the top journalists squeezed into Savile Row suits.

I made two dozen tiny trips back and forth and eventually wriggled my Land Rover out of the parking lot. I turned left onto the frozen road and headed home, warmed only slightly by Dickens' tale of a Paris on fire.

The first wave of globalisation had been powered by steam. Jean-François Cail had advocated free trade *pour tout le monde*, believing that the people of the poorest nations deserved the same chance the French people had to benefit from the advancements brought by science and progress. Besides, he assured his fellow industrialists, France's industry was strong enough to withstand competition from the undeveloped parts of the world. I'd walked through his Paris mansion and château at La Briche, and it was clear that open markets had been good for his business too.

By the middle of the twentieth century, even left-leaning economists had joined the free-trade chorus. The argument was that letting the agrarian peasants of Asia/Africa/Eastern Europe/South America sell their rice/corn/wheat/coffee beans to the developed world would allow them to participate in the same growth trajectory of the West. They would transition from agrarian nations to manufacturing economies and on to service-based societies; their people from grumpy farmers to happy consumers. I remember being captivated by this logic at university. The West had money and needed stuff done for them, and the developing nations had people who were happy to do that stuff if you paid them just a little.

What happened next is well documented: goods and services, ideas and capital sloshed across the surface of the planet, changing much of what we see. With it, the fabric of the global economy was radically changed. Foreigners (and the local olig-archs they befriended) went on to acquire the best assets of the developing world and built giant factories that dwarfed anything imagined by Cail during the Industrial Revolution. In devel-oped nations, the progress of the working class was thrown first into neutral, then reverse. By arbitraging the competition from workers in poor nations, employers have been able to hold down wages in the West for nearly forty years. The well-meaning intel-lectuals who joined the capitalists to argue for free-trade-for-all have delivered the benefits to a narrowing few, and gifted a generation of disappointment to the working class of the West.

The contradictions in my own practices were an indication of how tricky this issue continued to be. I was still wearing the handmade boots from the company of a man I'd once shared campfire tea with; I enjoyed buying milk for my girls from a farmer I knew. Yet I was driving a British-designed, Indian-made but American-powered car, and I was relieved that my Cupertino-designed but Chinese-made iPhone was being silently charged by the cigarette lighter.

I turned up the icy hill, and as long as I accelerated gently, my car was able to keep a firm grip on the road. Even for these parts, it was particularly cold and slippery. I veered to the right, around a snow bank that bore the perfect impression of the front grille of a VW. Twenty kilometres an hour was the maximum sensible speed.

Growth and even faster growth seemed to be about the only goal of the economic policies on display over the previous week. Few people were talking about limits to endless growth. Nowhere did I hear talk of *décroissance*, a French philosophy that asks us to consider long-term de-growth.

Most of the planet doesn't live in the lucky countries that developed early, and they have a quite different set of concerns:

their worries are not about debt-fuelled over-consumption, life-shortening stress and eating too much. Not yet. The great majority of humankind is still in the line for the buffet. While they are waiting for their turn, increasingly impatiently, they are hearing complaints of indigestion from those who ate earlier. We fortunate ones might feel that something about consumerism isn't working, but we're still being told the solution is to increase consumption. We might be stuffed, but apparently we have to eat our way out of this cake.

To either side of me, no houses or hotels were lit, the only lights a line of street lamps that dropped a chain of disconnected orange circles ahead of me. I may have been the only moving object in this valley. I passed a white-walled church on my left, almost windowless and architecturally uninspiring. I was caught by how small it was. Any more snow and its steeple would be needed as its periscope. From the high riding position of my driver's seat I looked down on the small church – figuratively and literally – and wondered whether maybe it wasn't that it was small, but it was me who was a member of an oversized tribe for this globe.

I slowed down as the road sloped out of the village of Klosters. On the stereo, the streets of revolutionary Paris ran with blood, something Dickens explained in more graphic detail than a modern horror movie. Just then, I crossed a small claret-red speed bump. It was the only remaining evidence of a collision that had occurred the previous morning between a car and a deer. Her blood had flowed across the road, blended with the snow, and frozen solid.

A fresh patina of white powder covered the road ahead. Those who drove snowploughs had been busy that winter but had retired for the night. They'd made countless passes along this route in large trucks pushing enormous concave blades. Like giant trowels they'd scraped the road and, with each pass, added some of the icy mix into the vertical sides, tossing the surplus over the lip. The snow walls that ran on either side of the road were over two metres high, plumb straight, and would have made a master stonemason proud.

By now my windscreen had fully defrosted. The clouds had lifted, and the night sky became a clear matt for a dreamy overlay of stars – I must have sighted the giant stag a long time before I realised what I was looking at. He was trotting towards me, moving into the middle of one of the orange islands of light. With every other stride, he looked to his left or to his right, searching for a break in the corridor wall. I slowed down, and so did he. I coasted, until it became clear he wasn't going to find an exit and we both came to a standstill about five metres apart.

He stood tall and strong, theatrically accented by my head-lights, silhouetted against the dark, framed by the snowy escarpments on either side. His antlers were as fine a crown as nature has ever provided: an inverted ivory-tipped chandelier that he held above his powerful eyes and proud jaw. His body, however, showed the ravages of a season in which heavy snows had buried most food. His legs were twigs, unworthy of support-ing his majesty; his backside hollow, ribs apparent.

I dimmed my lights, and he considered what to do. He stood statue still. I turned off my headlights completely and cut the engine. The glow of the lights inside my car, and the street lamp at his back, meant he would now be able to see me.

I wondered: what does the deer think of the man lit by the dashboard lights? A fragile specimen? What does he think of my red eyes? What colour are my knuckles against the black of the steering wheel?

The deer straightened himself further, pulled his chest up and forward, and with a subtle movement of his head posi-tioned his antlers to make the greatest visual impact. He was contemplating his options and looking great while doing it. I'd blocked the road in front of him and it hadn't occurred to me to reverse up the hill. Most animals only turned their back on a threat as a last resort. Besides, retreat would be undignified. The options to his left and right were blocked by icy embankments that rose well above his head.

If he was looking at me for suggestions, I was equally perplexed.

We both took a few deep breaths.

Suddenly, he did his best 'this is all going okay' jump into the snow bank to my right. It was an impressive leap. From a standing start, he shot up, embedded his chest into the top edge of the bank, and reached forward with his front hooves. One of his back legs remained on the ground. With the other hoof he scratched at the wall in search of a hold. His front legs paddled on the surface. He managed to get both back feet into the wall and extended his front legs up and forward. Drawing on whatever reserves of energy the winter had left him with, he strained to pull himself up and over.

He didn't make any progress.

He was unable to find any purchase in the soft snow of the plateau. For a moment he paused, muscles quivering, in the most undignified position for a king. More squirrel than stag, left clinging to the icy wall. He then began his slide down. His bony behind hit the road first, followed by his ribcage, shoulders, front legs, neck and head. It was as if an IKEA table had been tossed out an apartment window. Thin legs extended in every direction and his antlers looked as if the last thing thrown out the window had been a box of wooden coat-hangers.

Seemingly undeterred, he rolled his front legs to one side, thrust them out towards me, and attempted to steady himself. His bum was still on the pavement, and for a moment he was in control. He fixed me sternly in his gaze and began to rise slowly. Just before he got up, though, one leg slipped behind the other, crossing his front legs, rolling him onto one shoulder, once again a jumble sale twisting around on the road. Somehow, he was able to roll over, untangle his legs and, with a grace that seemed to surprise him as much as me, ended on his feet.

He steadied himself on the icy road until all four legs stopped shaking, never taking his eyes off me. With his pride somewhat restored, he set about adjusting himself. He squared his shoulders, discreetly hid his wasted rump, and again pushed his chest forward. To add the final touch, he turned his head a few degrees, returning his antlers to their maximum majesty.

He looked at me, I looked at him, and time stopped.

Neither of us was at our strongest – that much was easy to see. Just the two of us, frozen in this silent valley, seen only by the stars of the universe, our eyes united in the same question.

Where are we going from here?

ACKNOWLEDGEMENTS

'A good writer possesses not only his own spirit
but also the spirit of his friends.'
– Hear, hear, Mr Friedrich Nietzsche

'All writers are vain, selfish and lazy and one would never
undertake [a book] if one were not driven by some demon
whom one can neither resist nor understand.'
– Why thanks, George Orwell

When I had my first draft of this book, I got an offer from a prestigious publisher in New York. They rarely signed first-timers, never antipodean nobodies, and it happened after the first meeting I'd ever taken with a publisher.

This book is not from that publisher.

I also got asked to audition for the world-famous TED conference.

With the contract signed, I fell back into old habits. I worried that I would never live up to the hype. I decided that I had to write a book better than anything Hemingway had ever typed. I read half a dozen of his books and seriously set off in pursuit. I kept going until I had written three times the longest length the publishers had asked for.

As for the TED audition, I couldn't sleep the night before, drank too much out of nervousness, and performed looking like I'd woken from a three-day bender.

Around that time, we also got hit by a train, which was a terrible, terrible tragedy for everyone. Most deeply for the family of our friend who was killed in the accident. Somewhere in there, I lost my way a bit.

The TEDsters never called back, and I got dropped by that prestigious New York publishing house. I am indebted to both to this day. Their interest gave me the confidence to believe I had something to say, and dropping me was the kick that I needed. This is a book about falling on and off a bicycle, so it is no surprise that I had to learn to pick myself up and keep going. These acknowledgements are really a thank you to the great support team I had around me.

The girls and I left France and moved to Switzerland. We found a small school at which all four kids were reunited – living in a rotation between the boarding house, their mother's house and my apartment. Their mother and I divorced sensibly, and Divonne deserves huge credit for all she has done to help them grow into wonderful young people. The girls continue to thrive in a bilingual French/English school. I continued to toil to become a writer, worked hard to learn the trade of journalism, and researched more than was helpful in an attempt to understand our times. I got remarried to the most amazing artist and humanitarian I've ever met and followed her to live in Africa. From a base in Nairobi, I finally finished this book.

Cycling can sound like a solo pursuit, but at times I was just the typist for a few hundred of the smartest, kindest, most warm-hearted people I have ever met. There are those who read parts of this in depth, others who sent back a simple emoji to encourage me, and still others who made an off-hand comment that they would be unlikely to remember, but it changed my direction. I am indebted to the people who offered me a spare couch or room to stay, the ones who fed me dinner, poured me coffee, including one young woman in a café who snuck me free refills, and, when reading over my shoulder, told me to drink more water and tighten up the opening chapter. I did both.

I kept a pretty good list, hoping one day to thank everyone, but I am sure I have forgotten some. My best recollection of the big team follows after a few specific mentions I want to make.

Jason Donald, more than for writing help, coaching, keeping me going, also for all the ideas I stole. Your Write Time Retreat was excellent too. Your role in creating the Hemingway Appreciation Society of Saanenland brought me the invaluable readers of Diana Oerli, Kara Mcintosh and Maria Macaya Rhodes.

If good writers borrow, and great writers steal, then arrest me and throw away the key. Witnesses for the prosecution will no doubt include Roman Krznaric and Kate Raworth, two Oxford-based deep-thinkers from whose house of wisdom I took much. Follow both of them to imagine a brighter world, and Kate's Donut Economics for concrete ideas that are better than any I have.

I snuck into the World Economic Forum and grabbed every chance I could get my hands on. Thank you Adrian Monck for not reporting me to security. Thank you to the staff at the Landhaus, Saanenland's gathering place for those who really do the work, thank you for holding the little corner in which I felt safe.

For those who did a very deep read of a mistake-ridden manuscript, Katharine MacMahon, Michael Hanley, Amy Galland, Jo Ely, Mary Lu Everett, Wes Wooten, and my sister, Catherine, I can't say thank you enough for pushing through my poor grammar.

Someone once wrote that when a writer is born, a family dies, but there is no chance of that with my family's legendary vitality. Deepest thanks to my mum, who understood my father better than anyone, and knows that legacy is not what you are left, but what work is left to finish, and my siblings, Catherine, Simon and sometimes-coach Paul. Other Holmes à Courts include James, Simon and Katrina, William and Jane, Zara, and the big-hearted boys of George and Robert. Alissa Everett and my girls, Madison and Elsa, you ladies deserve co-writing credit. Alissa, you suffered more than you deserved through my various falls, picked me up more times than I can remember. When you got to use your full skills, both I and the book got better for it.

Jason Gissing, my old friend, sorry for everything.

Amanda Siggie, you are an inspiring lady, who has known hard luck, and remains sharp as a tack. England would be a better place if they kept folks like you closer to the throne.

Book folks: to my agents, Fiona Inglis in Sydney and Markus Hoffman in New York, thanks for sticking with me; the team at Penguin Random House in Sydney, Meredith Curnow and Patrick Mangan, thanks for not dropping me; and Anne Godoff and Scott Moyers in New York, thanks *for* dropping me.

Photography was greatly helped by the fact I married Alissa, one of the world's best, and post-production was done in Kenya by Rich Allela. All focus issues are entirely mine.

A collection of academics helped me with writing and economics, correcting and encouraging me, but they deserve no blame if you disagree. They include Kent Anderson of the Australian National University, Michael Claudon, John Isham and Jay Parini of Middlebury College, Diana Kelly at University of Wollongong, Jay McCardell at Yale, Ross Millburn and Roy Green at the University of Technology Sydney, independent scholar William Nuttle, Terri-Ann White and Keith Punch of the University of Western Australia, and economist Richard Samans of the World Economic Forum.

I rode this race with the lyrics of great artists pushing me on, some Millow, Five for Fighting, lots of Mr Mumford and his sons, too much Coldplay, plenty of Passenger, Zaz and a bit of Russell Crowe and Alan Doyle. I wrote to soppy ballads, but edited to EDM: thank you, Alex Cruz and Seth Schwartz.

In rural France I experienced an unbroken pattern of hospitality from the residents of the tiny hamlet of La Petite Briche, and the triangle made by the towns of Hommes, Continvoir and Rille. Ian Chapman and Vicki Parish, their son Bryn, Nathan

Waks and Candice Williams, Sam Waks, Vince Neoplan, Jeremy and Sonia Taylor, Corinne Berthelot, Thierry Commencais and Nathalie Begue, Laurence and Patrick Fabris, the former owners of the Bouff'tard, Collette, Dominic and Sandrine, Lucette and her husband, the parents and students of the Hommes École (apologies to the amorous Simon), Eric, Phillippe and the Fontaine family, Marie-Françoise Adam, Vincent and the Marchesseau family, and finally Angelique, to this day I have no idea of anything you said to me, but never was I unsure of your passion and care for my girls.

Celine Jacq, you are an example of the type of teachers that quietly go about making the world a better place.

The team at CYFAC, all of you, were so kind to continue your focused work while this man and his big camera sat on a stool beside one of you every few days for four months. It started at the front desk with Katia Blanchet and included Stéphane Goutard, John Brochard, Yves Babault, Francette Babault, Bernard Berthelot, Jacqueline Berthelot, Delphine Godefroy, Aymeric Le Brun and Karin (including your translation services) and Fabien Deweerdt.

If you ever get the crazy idea to ride une *Étape du Tour*, do yourself a favour and contact the folks who got me in: Tim Marsh of VeloNomad.com or Bruno Toutain from Cyclomundo. com. And do the training they recommend, not mine.

Then there was the enormous peloton that rode with me for different stages, which is such a big list because I really needed your help. It includes, with all the randomness of alphabetical ordering: John Adgemis, Tim Allerton, Chris G. Andersen, Chris Anderson and Kelly Stoetzel of TED, Rasmus Ankersen, Ben Ball, Lyssandra Barbieri, Layne Beachley, Claudia Becker, Anthony Bell, Lisa Bernhart, Michael Bodey, Michaela Boland, Peggy Boulos-Clark, Gwendolyn Bounds, Cortney Brown, Peter Buffett, Sharon Burrows, Luke Carra, Zach Carson, Angela Clark and Mel Jago, Shirley Claudon, Chris Corrigan, Diane Coyle, Russell Crowe, Sue Cunningham, Lyndon Da Cruz,

Mak Daguchi, Jamie Daves, John Duryea, Ed Eglin, Geoff Elliott, Tom Elliott, Peter Empter, Michael Epis, Janie and Ken Everett, Niall Ferguson, Richard Fidler, Jono Fisher, Peter FitzSimons, Julia Foote la Stage, Jonathan Foreman, Nick Fraser, George Frazis, Wilder Fulford, Alex Gansch, Ian Gardiner, Sylvester Gates, David Gilham, Remo and Melanie Giuffre, Teddy Grant and Brigitte Pirrie, Chris and Sara Green, Sippy Halsted, Maggie Handbury, David Hanley, Johnathan Harvey, Patrick Hazlewood, Jeremy Heimans, Doug Hepworth, Jody Hotchkiss, Arianna Huffington, Hamish Hume, John and Sam Hunt, Sue Huntingdon, Kirk Hurford, Eddie Izzard, of the Jarecki family there was help from Divonne, Andrew, Carol, Eugene, Gloria, Henry, John, and Nick, Dare Jennings, Diana Kelly, Linus Kerley, Brad Kessler, Dara Khosroshahi, Liz Koops, Antje Kunstmann, Noel Lanigan and William Voisone, Barbie Latza Nadeau, David Leser, Johnny Lewis, Nicole Long, Kristin Lozeau, Michael Lythcott, Tim Marsh, Rob Mather, Damien Mander, Ted Matsuda, David Maubaum, Duff McDonald, John McGrath, Lauren Miller, Lynda Monique, Simon Mordant, Dan Mori, Nanette Moulton, Nina Munk, Damien and Jo O'Brien, Suzie Owens, Nick Pappas, Sasha Patpatia, Ben Patrick, Hugo and Helene Pietrini, Albert Poland, Mark E. Pollack, Maria Popov, Carter Pottash, Jon Prescott, Oliver Preston, Madame Provost, Peter Remta, Shane Richardson, Justin Robinson, David Rockwell, Ferguson Rogoff, Kenneth Rogoff, Nat Rothschild, Marc Routh, Kevin Rudd, Nick Ryan, Eric Sakalowsky, Klaus Schwab, Cathy Schulman and Tim Allyn, Marco Scuriatti, Peter Seidler, Kate Sekules, Rob Skiff, Judith Sloan, Adam Spencer, David Sproule, Andrew Suckling, Marco Sucharitkul, Isabelle Taillebourg, Helle Thorning-Schmidt, Paul Torday, Keith Tuffley, Natalie Waters, Robyn Williams, Peter J. Wilson, Anthony Winetraub, and Helen Wood.

Finally, out of deep respect and with some tears, I mention those who have passed away since I started writing this book. They include Frits Steenhauser and Richard Jarecki, both of whom have important roles in the story. Big Tim Fischer leaves a big hole. I miss Pat Dempsey, who taught me much of what I know about the meat trade, and Tom Louderback, who taught me much of what I know about friendship. Patrick Green, man, you were a great soul.

For those I have forgotten, I'll make up for it with a profuse apology at www.peterhac.com/grateful.

Further reading:
In lieu of a long bibliography – that was looking suspiciously like a place to show off all the reading I have done – I have listed those that have inspired me, and those who take these ideas to the next level, on my website at www.peterhac.com/furtherreading.

The full pamphlet describing Cail's experiment at La Briche that he printed for the Exposition Universelle de 1867 can be found at www.peterhac.com/LaBriche.